The Catholic Biblical Quarterly
Monograph Series
32

Imagery and Imagination in Biblical Literature

Essays in Honor of
Aloysius Fitzgerald, F.S.C.

EDITED BY

Lawrence Boadt and Mark S. Smith

The Catholic Biblical Quarterly
Monograph Series
32

©2001 The Catholic Biblical Association of America,
Washington, DC 20064

Produced in the United States of America

Library of Congress Cataloging-in-Publication Data

Imagery and imagination in Biblical literature : essays in honor of
Aloysius Fitzgerald, F.S.C. / edited by Lawrence Boadt and Mark S.
Smith.
      p.   cm.—(The Catholic Biblical quarterly. Monograph series ;
32)
  Includes bibliographical references and index.
  ISBN 0-915170-31-0
  1. Bible. O.T.—Criticism, interpretation, etc. 2.
Imagination—Religious aspects. 3. Hebrew language—Figures of
speech. I. Boadt, Lawrence. II. Smith, Mark S., 1955– . III.
Fitzgerald, Aloysius. IV. Series.
BS1171.3 .I43 2001
221.6—dc21
                                   2001003305

Contents

Introduction

Some of the externals of the career of Brother Aloysius Fitzgerald, F.S.C., are easily told. He received the S.T.L. from the Catholic University of America (1961) and the S. S.L. from the Pontifical Biblical Institute (1963). His solid scholarship in Akkadian was acquired under two great scholars, Patrick W. Skehan at Catholic University and Wolfram von Soden (during his time in Europe). After a two-year stint at Manhattan College (1967–69), he began teaching Old Testament and Semitics at Catholic University in 1969, where he continued until 1996. From 1971 to 1983 he was chair of the Department of Egyptian and Semitic Languages. He was associate editor of the *Catholic Biblical Quarterly* from 1974 to 1977 and from 1980 to 1987. He was treasurer of the Catholic Biblical Association from 1981 through 1996 and held other positions mentioned below.

When we appraise people it is often in terms of their productivity. And when we appraise scholars it is often in terms of their publications. But when I think of Bro. Aloysius ("Aly" to his friends), what comes to my mind is the story about St. Lawrence. As deacon of the church at Rome he was responsible for the treasures of that church. Having been apprised shortly before his martyrdom in 258 that the Roman authorities were coming to the church to confiscate its treasures, he gave everything away to the poor. When the Romans arrived and demanded the assets, he waved his arm toward the crowd of the poor and said, in effect, "There they are"—irrecoverable for Lawrence and the Roman officials, but useful and precious to so many others. The stories about St. Lawrence are somewhat legendary, but the point I would like to make is still valid. A perusal of the Fitzgerald bibliography demonstrates the depth of scholarship in his chosen field, but far beyond the many riches Aloysius has contribute to the biblical movement that are easily visible and recoverable, that is, in the form of publication, are those that are cached away in the minds and hearts of the many whose development he has contributed to and encouraged in a manner hidden from the eyes of most.

The impetus for this Festschrift came from the Old Testament Colloquium that Aloysius founded in 1985. The first organizational meeting was held during the CBA meeting at the University of San Francisco; the first meeting was held early the following year. The eight tapped for this group were younger scholars who, on average, had received their doctorates just over two years earlier. If, as one asumes, the purpose of the colloquium was to encourage them to become productive contributors to biblical studies, it certainly has succeeded. From this group of modest size there have been several associate editors of the *CBQ,* a *CBQ* publishing editor, an *Old Testament Abstracts* general editor, a general editor of the CBQ Monograph Series, a CBA president, a CBA treasurer (two, if Aloysius is included), two members of the NAB Old Testament Revision Committee, plus a couple of revisers for that project—all in addition to their scholarly publishing and academic positions.

The same sort of zeal can be seen in the extraordinary care Aloysius has bestowed on the countless students who remember him with gratitude. On the wall by his desk was a poster featuring a stern-faced bald eagle and bearing the legend "I am smiling." It aptly characterized both the exigence and the humor with which he dealt with everything that came under his care, but most especially how he labored with doctoral candidates on their dissertations, selflessly expending time many others would have dedicated to their own advancement. One needs to have seen it to properly appreciate it. All of the contributors to this Festschrift are either members of the Old Testament Colloquium or former students of his or both.

And so many examples of the same sort of dedication to what needed to be done, without concern for self-advancement, could be given. During the time given to the revision of the Psalter of the New American Bible (roughly 1988–1991), the members of the editorial board for that project met one weekend each month to go over proposed revisions. No one contributed more to these meetings than Aloysius, nor could any of us who served with him doubt the truth of his claim that he spent two hundred hours of preparation for each meeting. Although listed only as an associate editor of *Old Testament Abstracts,* he was largely responsible for the Semitic words index from its inception in 1978 until he moved from the Washington, D.C., area in 1996.

The analogy from Saint Lawrence introduced above could have a more material application. Although as treasurer of the CBA Aloysius was concerned to safeguard and increase its resources, in this office he again manifested his concern for young scholars, for it was he who urged the CBA to institute the Memorial Stipends, an arrangement whereby doctoral students in biblical studies programs receive a subsidium to help meet living expenses, and later the Archaeology Research Stipends, by which CBA members receive funds to help make it possible for them to engage in a dig. During his tenure CBA finances were not such that the association could award scholarships; the fact that it does now is owing in part to the example and priorities he set for us.

JOSEPH JENSEN, O.S.B.
Catholic University of America
CBA Executive Secretary

CHAPTER 1

Vengeance and Forgiveness: The Two Faces of Psalm 79

LESLIE J. HOPPE, O.F.M.

Introduction

Psalm 79 has not attracted much attention from students of the Hebrew Bible, perhaps because much of its content occurs also in Psalm 74 and because much of its phraseology is found elsewhere in the Bible. Interpreters find that they have little more to say about the content of Psalm 79 than what they may have already said about that of Psalm 74. What has been described as the psalm's "anthological" character complicates the attempt to find a setting in life for this psalm. Indeed, interpreters have suggested dates ranging from the eighth to the second centuries B.C. for this psalm.

One of the principal concerns of this article is to deal with the matter of dating the psalm. The article proposes that there was a preexilic form of Psalm 79 which was used in ceremonies for rededicating the Temple after desecration by the presence of non-Israelites or by non-Yahwistic liturgical accouterments (see 2 Chronicles 29). In the exilic period, the psalm was reworked to incorporate the Deuteronomic perspectives regarding the fall of Jerusalem. The paper will deal with a question related to the dating issue: the circles responsible for the psalm in its final form. Also, some attention will be directed to form critical issues and the canonical setting of the psalm. The article will conclude with reflections on the theological dimensions of Psalm 79.

I. The Unity and Coherence of Psalm 79

One feature of this psalm that is significant is the number of its expressions that are found elsewhere in the Hebrew Bible. These are addressed on a verse-by-verse basis.

Verse 1

1ab: Lam 1:10b echo the first two cola:

Ps 79:1ab אלהים באו גוים נחלתך טמאו את־היכל קדשך
Lam 1:10b: כי־ראתה גוים באו מקדשה

1b: טמאו Commentators point out that the text does not say that the Temple was destroyed but only defiled. The same verb is used to describe Josiah's action against the high places (2 Kgs 23:8). This action likely meant the destruction of the high places.

1d: עיים. The plural form of עי appears in the construct as part of a place name [עיי העברים] in Num 21:11; 33:44, 45.

In Mic 1:6, the singular form appears in the same construction as in the psalm:

Ps 79:1c: שמו את־ירושלם לעיים
Mic 1:6a: ושמתי שמרון לעי

The singular form עי also appears in Job 30:24, but it is usually amended to read עני.[1] Both the NRSV and the NAB follow this emendation.

In Mic 3:12, the plural form appears as עיין but when this text is cited in Jer 26:18, the plural form is לעיים as it is in the psalm:

Mic 3:12c: וירושלם עיין תהיה
Jer 26:18d: וירושלים עיים תהיה
Ps 79:1c: שמו את־ירושלם לעיים

Verse 2

Similar formulaic expressions occur in Deut 28:26; Jer 7:33; 16:4; 19:7; 34:20. In 1 Sam 17:46, פגר appears in place of נבלה. The formula goes on

---

[1] E.g., Marvin H. Pope, *Job* (AB 15; Garden City, NY; Doubleday, 1965) 223.

to speak of human corpses as food for animals but the word that appears for animals is בהמה rather than the psalm's חייה:

Ps 79:2:

נתנו את־נבלת   עבדיך מאכל   לעוף השמים בשר חסידיך לחיתו־ארץ

Deut 28:26

והיתה נבלתך   למאכל לכל־עוף השמים   ולבהמת הארץ

Jer 7:33

והיתה נבלת העם הזה למאכל   לעוף השמים   ולבהמת הארץ

Jer 16:4

והיתה נבלתם   למאכל   לעוף השמים   ולבהמת הארץ

Jer 19:7

ונתתי את־נבלתם   למאכל   לעוף השמים   ולבהמת הארץ

Jer 34:20

והיתה בלתם   למאכל   לעוף השמים   ולבהמת הארץ

1 Sam 17:46

ונתתי פגר מחנה פלשתים היום הזה לעוף השמים   לחית הארץ

2a: נבלת: Dahood notes that the singular form of this word has a collective meaning and this usage conforms to Canaanite idiom in which "a simple stem of a noun may be used to indicate plurality or an indefinite number. . . ."[2] This word may refer to an animal's carcass or the corpse of a human being. In Leviticus (5:2; 7:24; 11:8 and *passim*) and Ezekiel (4:14; 44:31) it refers only to an animal carcass. These books use פגר to speak of the corpse of a human being (e.g., Lev 26:30; Ezek 6:5; 43:7, 9). This usage is also followed in Num 14:29, 32, 33; Isa 14:19; 34:3; 37:36; 66:24; Amos 8:3; Nah 3:3; and 2 Chr 20:24, 25. The use of נבלה for the corpse of a human being clusters in Deuteronomy and the Deuteronomistic tradition: Deut 21:23; 28:26; Josh 8:29; 1 Kgs 13:22; 2 Kgs 9:37 though Deuteronomy also uses this word to speak of an animal carcass twice: 14:8, 21. Jeremiah also uses נבלה to speak of a human corpse: 7:33; 9:21; 16:4; 19:7; 26:23; 34:20; 36:30. There are just two instances in Isaiah of such usage: 5:25 and 26:19.

Verse 3

3b: ואין קובר The same phase occurs in 2 Kgs 9:10 as a prophecy about Jezebel's death. Jeremiah uses the same formula but with a piel parti-

---

[2] See his *Psalms II* (AB 17; Garden City, NY: Doubleday, 1968) 250.

ciple: ואין מקבר (14:16). The prophet uses similar language as he threatens the people of Jerusalem:

ולא יקברו	לא יאספו	8:2
ולא יקברו	לא יספדו	16:4
לא יספדו לא יאספו ולא יקברו		25:33

1 Macc 7:17 cites the LXX Ps 78 (79):2–3 to explain the murder of the pious by Alcimus: Σάρκας ὁσίων σου καὶ αἷμα αὐτῶν ἐξέχεαν κύκλῳ Ιερουσαλημ, καὶ οὐκ ἦν αὐτοῖς ὁ θάπτων. While the citation is rather free, the formula κατὰ τὸν λόγον, ὃν ἔγραψεν αὐτόν (v. 16) makes it clear that the text was considered authoritative. This makes an early Maccabean period date for this psalm unlikely though some commentators do suggest a second-century date. Gunkel notes that this is the first citation of a psalm as "Scripture."[3]

Verse 4

Ps 79:4	היינו חרפה לשכנינו לעג וקלס לסביבותינו
Ps 44:14	תשימנו חרפה לשכנינו לעג וקלס לסביבותינו

Except for the initial verb, Ps 44:14 is a verbatim parallel of this verse. The verbs that begins Ps 44:14 is תשימנו ("You have made us"). Ps 31:12 reflects some of the language of v. 4a: . . . הייתי חרפה ולשכני . . . מאד. Jer 20:8 uses two words found in Ps 79:4 as a hendiadys (וקלס לחרפה) in a lament. All this may point to formulaic lament language.

Verse 5

Ps 79:5	עד־מה יהוה תאנף לנצח תבער כמו־אש קנאתך
Ps 89:47	עד־מה יהוה תסתר לנצח תבער כמו־אש חמתך

Ps 89:47 is almost a verbatim of v. 5. In both psalms, עד־מה serves to mark the transition from the lament to the petition for deliverance. According to D. Winton Thomas, לנצח has the force of a superlative.[4]

Verse 6
Jer 10:25 is almost a verbatim of vv. 6–7:

[3] Hermann Gunkel, *Introduction to Psalms: The Genres of the Religious Lyric of Israel* (trans. James D. Nogalski; Macon, GA: Mercer University, 1998) 336.

[4] "The Use of *netsach* as a Superlative in Hebrew," *JSS* 1 (1956) 106–9.

Ps 79:6

שפך חמתך אל־הגוים אשר לא־ידעוך על ממלכות אשר בשמך לא קראו

Jer 10:25ab

שפך חמת על־הגוים אשר לא־ידעוך על משפחת אשר בשמך לא קראו

6a: אל Several manuscripts of the LXX, the Syriac and the Targum suggest that the preposition in 79:6 was על as in Jer 10:25 rather than אל of the MT. Also, several MSS of the LXX, the Old Latin, and the Targum have "kingdoms" in Jer 10:25b as in Psalm 79.

Verse 7

Ps 79:7:   את־נוהו השמו   כי אכל את־יעקב

Jer 10:25c: כי־אכלו את־יעקב ואכלהו ויכלהו את־נוהו השמו

There is some MSS evidence for אכלו in Ps 79:7 as in Jer 10:25.

Verse 8

8a: The combination of זכר with עון also occurs in

Hos 8:13: עתה יזכר עונם
Hos 9:9: יזכר עונם
Jer 14:10: עתה יזכר עונם
Isa 64:8: ואל־לעד תזכר עון

Some translations render the expression עונת ראשנים as "the iniquities of (our) ancestors" (NRSV) or the like.[5] These translations obviously take ראשנים as a substantive meaning "ancestors," the meaning it has in Lev 26:45 and Deut 19:14. Still, it is more likely that ראשן should be taken as an adjective with its usual meaning of "former" or "past" as in Gen 25:25; Deut 10:1–4; 24:10; Hos 2:9; Hag 2:3, 9.[6] The sins in v. 9 are "(our) past sins" rather than those of "our ancestors." This accords with the clear sense of v. 8c. These verses assert that the present generation is responsible for the disaster. There is no pronominal suffix in the text, but the translation adds "our" for a smoother reading. The NAB does not insert "our" so the translation is ambiguous.

[5] See Dahood, *Psalms II*, 249, 252; and Hans-Joachim Kraus, *Psalms 60–150* (trans. H. C. Oswald; Minneapolis: Augsburg, 1989) 132.

[6] See NAB, Marvin E. Tate, *Psalms 51–100* (WBC 20; Dallas: Word, 1990) 297 and A. A. Anderson, *The Book of Psalms* (2 vols.; New Century Bible Commentary; Grand Rapids, MI: Eerdmans; London: Marshall, Morgan and Scott, 1981) 2.579.

8c uses a formulaic expression of lament found elsewhere in the psalms:

Ps 79:8: כי דלונו מאד
Ps 142:7: כי דלותי מאד
Ps 116:6: דלותי

Verse 9

9c: The LXX adds κύριε. The expression למען שמך appears in Ps 25:11; 31:4; 109:21; 143:11; 1 Kgs 8:41; 2 Ch 6:32; Isa 48:9; 66:5; Jer 14:7, 21. The expression or a variant appears more than thirty times in the Book of Ezekiel. It occurs with the 3mp pronominal suffix in Ps 106:8. R. J. Tournay observes that "beginning with the exile, the proclamation and invocation of the divine name occupies an eminent place in the hymns and prayers of Israel."[7]

Verse 10

10a is almost a verbatim of Ps 115:2 and Joel 2:17d:

Ps 79:10a: למה יאמרו הגוים   איה אלהיהם
Ps 115:2: למה יאמרו הגוים איה־נא אלהיהם
Joel 2:17d: למה יאמרו בעמים   איה אלהיהם

A few MSS of Vaticanus, Sinaiticus and the Coptic suggest that Ps 79:10 read, "Why do they say among the nations . . . ." Dahood suggests that למה should be rendered as "lest."[8]

10b: The phrase איה אלהיך occurs in Psalm 42:4, 11. Micah 7:10b has איו יהוה אלהיך

10d: דם־עבדיך: Deut 32:43 envisions God avenging דם־עבדיו. 2 Kgs 9:7 has Elisha commissioning Jehu to take vengeance on Jezebel דמי עבדי.

Verse 11

11a: The phrases תבוא לפניך and אנקת אסיר also occur in Ps 102:2, 21 respectively. The Syriac and the Targum read הותר as התר from נתר (set free). This reading does not effect the meaning of the verse.

11b: The phrase בני תמותה also occurs in Ps 102:21.

---

[7] See his *Seeing and Hearing God with the Psalms: The Prophetic Liturgy of the Second Temple in Jerusalem* (JSOTSup 118; Sheffield: Academic, 1991) 106.

[8] Dahood, *Psalms II*, 249, 252.

Verse 12

12a: The feminine dual form שבעתים is used for "sevenfold." This form is also found in Gen 4:15, 24; Isa 30:26; Ps 12:7; Prov 6:31. In Lev 26:18, 21, 24 and Ps 119:164 the feminine cardinal number שבע is used in the multiplicative sense.

12b: Ps 89:51–52 uses the nominal and verbal forms חרפה and חרף as this verse does, but in Psalm 89 the insults are directed at the people. In Psalm 79, the psalmist asks God to avenge insults directed at God.

Verse 13

The image of Israel as צאן מרעיתך is found here and Ps 74:1, 95:7, 100:3; Jer 23:1; and Ezek 34:31 though the formula is modified by the requirements of context. The image of Israel as God's צאן occurs in Isa 63:11; Ezek 35 *passim*; Ps 95:7; 100:3 and Zech 9:16; 10:3.

Especially significant for dating this psalm is the nearly verbatim citation of vv. 6–7 in Jer 10:25.[9] There is very little left of the psalm when the formulaic language and citations are stripped away. Still, it would be wrong to characterize Psalm 79 as a mere pastiche of traditional language and formulaic expressions than as a composition that reflects originality on the part of its author. There is an internal coherence to the psalm that gives evidence of a very careful and artful composition.

The psalm begins and ends with an attempt to identify Israel's plight with God's honor. Verse 1 describes the nations as invading "your," i.e., God's inheritance. Verse 13 promises that "your people," i.e., a liberated Israel, will thank and praise God. In v.1, the nations enter (באו) God's inheritance but v. 11 asks that the prisoner's prayer may come (תבוא) before God. Four references to "the nations" (גוים) serve to bind this lament psalm (vv. 1, 6, 10 twice). The psalm laments the shedding of the blood of God's servants (vv. 2–3) and then calls for that blood to be avenged (v. 10). In v. 4, Judah complains that its neighbors have mocked it and verse 12 prays that this mocking be returned to those neighbors seven times over. Verses 1–7 use seven verbs to describe what the nations have to to Israel and v. 12 prays that the nations receive what Israel received but seven times over. Psalm 79 displays a remark-

---

[9] The signficance of the similarity between Ps 79:6–7 and Jer 10:25 is discussed on pp. 4–5.

able rhetorical unity despite the obvious similarity of its language and expression to other biblical texts. This makes dating this psalm quite complicated.

But this rhetorical unity is not complete. For example, verse 6 implies that God's anger against Israel is misdirected. God should move against those nations that do not acknowledge God's sovereignty. Verses 8–9, however, suggests that God's anger against Israel is justified because of Israel's infidelity. Those who died when Jerusalem fell are characterized as "your (God's) servants (v. 2) while v.8 intimates that it was their sins that caused the city's disaster.

II. Dating the Psalm

The dating of of most biblical texts is usually a speculative and therefore a perilous task. While there is a consensus that the Book of Psalms in its present form emerged in the postexilic period, individual psalms may reflect much older theological ideas and may come from earlier life situations. Dates given for Psalm 79 range from the preexilic to the Maccabean periods with no consensus developing around this question. Rabbinic tradition connects this psalm with the destruction of Jerusalem by the Babylonians although there is nothing in the psalm itself that explicitly refers to that disaster.[10]

At least the *terminus ad quem* is clear enough. 1 Macc 7:17 cites the LXX version of Ps 79:2–3 (see LXX Ps 78:2–3) and 1 Macc 1:37 alludes to these verses. What is significant is the appearance of the appearance of the formula κατὰ τὸν λόγον, ὃν ἔγραψεν αὐτόν with which 1 Maccabees 7:16 introduces the citation. The formula makes it clear that by the middle of the second century B.C., the author of First Maccabees considered the Book of Psalms to be authoritative. This makes it unlikely that the psalm was written in the Maccabean period although there are those who associate the psalm's composition with the events that led up to the revolt against Antiochus IV.[11]

---

[10] Anderson, *The Book of Psalms*. 2:577. In the Orthodox tradition it is prayed on the 9th of Ab and on Friday afternoons at the Western Wall. See Tate, *Psalms 51–100*, 303. 4Q176 sees Psalm 79 as depicting the eschatological destruction of Jerusalem according to David C. Mitchell in his *The Message of the Psalter: An Eschatological Programme in the Book of Psalms* (JSOTSup 252; Sheffield: Sheffied Academic Press, 1997) 103.

[11] Kraus, *Psalms 60–150*, pp. 96–97 and 133–132. Marco Treves Marco has tried to

While the psalm may be pre-Maccabean, is its origin to be found in the preexilic period or the postexilic period? An important datum is the citation of Ps 79:6–7 in Jer 10:25. Unlike the citation of the psalm in 1 Maccabees, there is no formula that precedes the citation of the psalm in the Book of Jeremiah. Also, there are four minor differences between the text in Ps 79:6–7 and that in Jer 10:25. First, the MT of Ps 79:6a uses אל in the phrase אל־הגוים while Jer 10:25a has על. However, the LXX, Peshitta, and the Targum suggest that the Hebrew original also read על though the readings in the versions may reflect the attempt of copyists to reconcile the readings in the two texts (see above, p. 5). Second, the MT of Ps 79:6b has ממלכות while Jer 10:25b uses משפחות. Again, renderings in some manuscripts of the LXX, Old Latin, and the Targum of Jeremiah suggest that the Jeremiah text was in accord with Ps 79:6 (see above, p. 5).[12] Third, Jer 10:25c inserts ויכלחו ואכלהו following את־יעקב. Holladay regards the insertion as a conflation though Dahood does not.[13] Without the addition of the two verbs, Jer 10:25c shows a chiastic pattern of verb/object//object/ verb as does Ps 79:7. Finally, the verb אכל in Ps 79:7 is singular while in Jeremiah 10:25c is plural. Dahood vocalizes אכל as an infinitive absolute, noting the lack of agreement with השמו in the second colon of v. 7.[14]

What is the relationship between the two texts? The answer to this question is not easy to come by because of the complex compositional history of the book of Jeremiah. Both Bright and Carroll regard Jer 10:25 an an exilic addition the book.[15] While D. R. Jones considers Psalm 79 to be exilic, he suggests that the sixth century prophet may have been quoting a well known formula which was subsequently used in the psalm as well.[16] Holladay describes Jer 10:23–25 as the result of the prophet's adaptation of traditional cultic expressions shortly

---

show that virtually the entire psalter comes from the Maccabean period. See his *The Dates of the Psalms: History and Poetry in Ancient Israel* (Pisa: Giardini, 1988).

[12] William L. Holladay, *Jeremiah 1: A Commentary on the Book of Jeremiah, Chapters 1–25* (Hermeneia; Philadelphia: Fortress, 1986) 338 n. 25a.

[13] Holladay, *Jeremiah 1*, 339; Mitchell Dahood, "The Word-pair ʾākal//kālāh in Jeremiah xxx 15," *VT* 27 (1977) 482 n. 2.

[14] Dahood, *Psalms II*, 251.

[15] John Bright, *Jeremiah* (AB 21; Garden City, NY: Doubleday, 1965) 74; Robert P. Carroll, *Jeremiah: A Commentary* (OTL; Philadelphia: Westminster, 1986) 263–65.

[16] *Jeremiah* (NCB; Grand Rapids: Eerdmans, 1992) 180–81.

before the siege of Jerusalem in 598 B.C.[17] While differing with Holladay over the interpretation of Jer 10:23–25, Walter C. Bouzard agrees
that the prophet quoted Psalm 79 and that the psalm's composition
"sufficiently antedated Jeremiah's use of it so as to render its utterance
by the prophet meaningful to his auditors."[18] Bouzard concludes that
Psalm 79 was composed and almost certainly used in worship prior to
the destruction of 587 B.C.[19]

It is important to heed the advice of Antti Laato on methodological
issues related to the dating of the psalms. He notes that "a text which
can be dated to a late period may represent a reworking of an ancient
text."[20] This warning, together with the observations of Holladay
about the origins of Jer 10:23–25 and Bouzard's hypothesis about the
origins of communal laments in the psalter, underscores the difficulty
in dating Psalm 79. The vagueness of Ps 79:1–2 makes it unnecessary to
relate the psalm to a particular historical destruction of Jerusalem, and
the explicit citation of Ps 79:6–7 in Jer 10:25 supports the hypothesis
that the psalm is not dependent upon the destruction of the Temple for
its inspiration.

Another reason supporting a pre-exilic date for Psalm 79 is that is
does not describe the destruction of the Temple only its defilement—
unlike Ps 74:3–8.[21] But the failure to focus on the Temple with the
intensity of Psalm 74 may indicate that Psalm 79 came from circles for
whom Jerusalem—not the Temple—was of central importance. To sus-
tain the hypothesis of a preexilic date for Psalm 79 requires that one
explain the mass of formulaic language that appears in this text. The
preponderance of this evidence suggests an exilic or even postexilic

---

[17] Holladay, *Jeremiah 1*, 340, 343–44. Verse 23 is adapted from Prov 16:9 and 20:24.
Verse 24 is an expansion of Ps 6:2 while v. 25 quotes Ps 79:6–7.

[18] *We Have Heard with Our Ears, O God: Sources of the Communal Laments in
the Psalms* (SBLDS 159; Atlanta: Scholars, 1997) 184–85.

[19] A similar conclusion is offered by Michael D. Goulder, *The Psalms of Asaph and
the Pentateuch: Studies in the Psalter III* (JSOTSup 233; Sheffield: Academic, 1996) 135.
Apparently he also dates Psalm 74 to the preexilic period: "It seems very likely tht the
two psalms (74 and 79), both Asaph psalms, refer to the same occasion, and are composed by the same author," p. 132.

[20] "Psalm 132: A Case Study in Methodology," *CBQ* 61 (1999) 28.

[21] Bouzard, however, dates Psalm 74 to a time before the destruction of the Temple.
He shows that the language of vv. 3–8 reflects not historical detail but Mesopotamian
lament traditions. See his *We Have Heard*, 174–80.

date for Psalm 79 in its present form.[22] The problem with an exilic or postexilic date for Psalm 79 comes from what the psalm does not lament. There is no mention of a siege, war, the deposition of the king, the burning of the Temple, the scattering of its priesthood nor of the deportation of the Judahites. That is one reason some commentators favor the Maccabean period as the setting for this psalm. Still, it is a mistake to assume that this psalm has to provide the same detail as the narrative of 2 Kings 25.

It may be possible, however, that a form of Psalm 79 existed before the fall of Jerusalem and was used in rededication rituals such as those described in 2 Chronicles. The psalm would have been composed to accompany the rededication of a defiled temple rather than the restoration of a temple that had been destroyed. 2 Chr 29:20–36 describe such a ceremony following Hezekiah's cleansing of the Temple. During that ceremony the king "commanded the Levites to sing praises to the Lord with the words of David and of the seer Asaph" (2 Chr 29:30). 2 Chr 35:1–19 describe Josiah's restoration of the Passover during his "reform." During that ceremony, "the singers, the descendants of Asaph, were in their place" (2 Chr 35:15). While this evidence is not conclusive, it serves to strengthen the hypothesis of a preexilic version of Psalm 79.

The lack of consensus regarding a date for Psalm 79 reflects the usual concern to date the psalm as it now exists in one period or another. That interpreters are able to find evidence for a date from the preexilic to the Maccabean periods may suggest that the psalm may have existed in some form before the exile. It composition was occasioned by the rededication of the Temple during the reforms of Hezekiah or Josiah. This explains the citation in Jeremiah. The postexilic reformulation of the psalm reflects not so much the historical details of Jerusalem's fall and the Temple's destruction in 587 B.C. as much as a Deuteronomistic explanation for this tragedy, namely that the disaster came upon Jerusalem because of sin (Ps 79:8–9). None of the other Asaph lament psalms (74, 80, 83) has this feature.

---

[22] Among those who hold that the Asaphite collection as a whole depicts an exilic situation include E. Beauchamp, *Le Psautier* (2 vols.; Paris: Gabalda, 1979) 2.4; J. H. Eaton, *Kingship and the Psalms* (London: SCM, 1976) 76; K.-J. Illman, *Thema und Tradition in den Asaf-Psalmen* (Åbo: Åbo Akademi Foundation, 1976) 55–64; Mitchell, *The Message of the Psalter*, 105.

III. The Provenance of the Psalm

While there are serious problems with determining the setting of the communal laments in the Asaphite psalms, the presence of such laments in this collection suggests some connection between these laments and the circles responsible for the psalms of Asaph. On the basis of linguistic usage and presence of communal laments in Jer 14 and Hos 6:1–3, H. Nasuti identifies these circles as "Ephraimite."[23] While Nasuti does point out some of the problems with this hypothesis, he neglects to mention a most serious one: the viability of a theological tradition closely associated with the Kingdom of Israel some one hundred and fifty years after the demise of the northern Israelite state.

There are several words and phrases appearing in Psalm 79 that may help identify the circles responsible for it. The distinctive word עָ"ם (v. 1d) provides the first indication of the circles that produced this psalm. This words appears as part of a place name in Num 21:11; 33:44, 45. In Mic 1:6 the singular form of this word appears in a construction identical to that found in Ps 79:1d (see notes, p. 2). The plural form עִיִּין appears in Mic 3:11 in a prophecy about the destruction of Jerusalem, the subject of this psalm's lament. When Jer 26:18 cites the Micah text as a precedent for Jeremiah's prophecy about Jerusalem's destruction form appears as עִיִּים as in the psalm. The passage from Jeremiah is a textbook example of the tradition-historical process. It was the "elders of the land" (Jer 26:17) who took the two-hundred-year-old prophecy and applied it to a situation they were facing. The psalm describes the "actualization" of the prophecy of both Micah and Jeremiah.

A second indicator is the word נִבְלַת: (v. 2a). In Leviticus, Ezekiel, and other texts, this word is used to speak of an animal's carcass; however, Deuteronomy and Deuteronomistic texts use this word to speak of the corpse of a human being (see notes, p. 3). The description of corpses as "food for the birds of the heavens" appears in Deut 28:26, 1 Sam 17:46 and several passages from Jeremiah (see notes, p. 3).

Third, the phrase וְאֵין קוֹבֵר (v. 3) appears in 2 Kgs 9:10 while Jer 14:16 uses it in the piel (see notes, p. 3). The opprobrium connected with this image may reflect the law in Deut 21:23 that mandates burial on the day of death.

---

[23] Harry P. Nasuti, *Tradition History and the Psalms of Asaph* (SBLDS 88; Atlanta: Scholars Press, 1988) 125–26.

The similarity of v. 4 to Ps 44:14 and v. 5 to Ps 89:47 results from the use of the formulaic language typical of laments and, therefore, may not have tradition-historical significance.

The relation of vv. 6–7 to Jer 10:25 has been discussed above (see pp. 4–5). No matter how one dates this psalm, it is clear that the circles behind the Book of Jeremiah and those responsible for this psalm were in contact with each other and they were possibly related. The request made in v. 8 contains phraseology found elsewhere in the psalter and prophetic texts (see pp. 5–6), but the language appears to be formulaic without tradition-historical significance; however, the expression למען שמך (v. 9) likely bears such significance. This phrase appears several times in the psalter, in 1 Kgs 8:4 and its parallel in 2 Chr 6:32. It also appears twice in Jeremiah 14 (see notes, p. 6). It is important to note שם appears in six of the Asaph psalms (74, 75, 76, 79, 80, 83). The importance of "name theology" in the Deuteronomic tradition is well known.[24] R. J. Tournay asserts that the frequency with which "the name" occurs in the Asaphite collection suggests that the circles responsible for it were dependent on the Deuteronomistic tradition which see the name as "a sign and a substitute for the hidden God, really but invisibly present among the people."[25] He also notes that beginning with the Exile, the proclamation and invocation of the divine name occupies an preeminent place in the hymns and prayers of Israel: Ps 80:19; 99:6; 105:1; 116:4, 13, 17; Isa 41:25; 45:3; 1 Kgs 18:24–25; Joel 3:5; Zech 13:9.[26]

Verses 8–9 are crucial in identifying the circles responsible for the final form of Psalm 79. Israel's failure to listen to the prophets sent to it and to observe the Torah which God gave is the characteristic explanation found in the Deuteronomistic History for the tragedies that befell the two Israelites kingdoms (1 Kgs 8:46–53; 2 Kgs 17:7–20; 21:10–16). Unlike the other Asaphite lament psalms (74, 80, 83), this psalm associates sin with the disaster that befell Jerusalem and the Temple. The inclusion of vv. 8–9 in a communal lament psalm reflects the recognition that while the nations may have brought great suffer-

---

[24] Gerhard von Rad, "Deuteronomy's 'Name' Theology and the Priestly Document's 'Kabod' Theology" in his *Studies in Deuteronomy* (SBT 9; London: SCM, 1952) 45–59.

[25] *Seeing and Hearing God with the Psalms*, 110.

[26] *Ibid.*, 106.

ing upon Israel, the people of Israel themselves bear the primary responsibility for their fate. The petition for vengeance against the nations characteristic of communal laments that deal with historical disasters is supplemented with a confession of sin and prayer for forgiveness.

The question raised in v. 10a about God's presence is found almost verbatim in Ps 115:2 and Joel 2:17d. Similar expressions occur in Ps 42:4, 11 and Mic 7:10b (see notes, p. 6). Again, this usage may reflect form-critical usage and may not have tradition-historical significance. The expression דם־עבדיך (v. 10d) does appear to have Deuteronomic connections. Deut 32:43 envisions God avenging דם־עבדיו and 2 Kgs 9:7 has Elisha commissioning Jehu to take vengeance on Jezebel דמי עבדי.

The final expression that needs to be considered is צאן מרעיתך. A similar phrase occurs in Pss 74:1, 95:7; 100:3; Jer 23:1 and Ezek 34:31. The image of Israel as God's צאן occurs in Isa 63:11; Ezek 35 *passim*; Ps 95:7; 100:3 and in Zech 9:16; 10:3. This image then is common to a variety of sources and is difficult to isolate tradition-historically.

The above analysis shows that the phraseology and vocabulary that point to tradition-historical connections derive from the Deuteronomic tradition and literature such as the Book of Jeremiah that underwent a Deuteronomic redaction. It is likely then that the final form of psalm is a product of the circles familiar with and sympathetic to the Deuteronomic tradition. In fact, the psalm is, for the most part, collection of Deuteronomic phrases brought together to lament the destruction of Jerusalem.[27]

IV. The Form-Critical Question

While the question of the psalm's date and the identification of those responsible for its final form may be problematic, there is consensus around form critical questions. Psalm 79 is a communal lament. The two main components of this form are the lament proper, which describes the reason for the cry of distress, and petition, which asks for

---

[27] By dating the psalm to the preexilic period, Goulder has to deny any connection with the Deuteronomic movement. He asserts that at the time of the psalm's composition, "the Deuteronomists have still to develop a Name theology . . . ." See his *The Psalms of Asaph and the Pentateuch*, 135.

relief. In Psalm 79, vv. 1–4 are the cry of distress and vv. 5–12 comprise the petition for deliverance. Verse 13 is a promise to praise God for the deliverance. Other elements that sometimes appear in the form include an address to God, motives for hearing the lament, and words expressing the assurance of being heard. While Psalm 79 begins with an invocation of God (v. 1), it contains no expression of assurance as found in the other Asaphite laments. The use of the first person plural is often taken as an identifying mark of the communal lament. In Psalm 79, first person plural forms occur in vv. 4, 8, 9, 10, 12, and 13. In contrast to these forms are the fifteen occurrences of second person singular form with God as the referant. Second person singular pronoun forms appear in almost every verse. The frequent repetition of "your" in this psalm makes it clear that the community's cry of distress ought to be a matter of concern for God.

While there is some clarity about the formal structure of Psalm 79 as a communal lament, there is some problem about the setting of this lament–especially if one dates this psalm to the exilic or postexilic period. Gunkel suggests that the setting of this genre is in "a great complaint festival which the community tended to hold now and then in response to general calamities."[28] Nasuti proposes 2 Chronicles 20 as a narrative description of such a ceremony.[29] He distinguishes the "national lamentation ceremony" from the "generalized activity of the people." The former is a specific cultic act performed by the proper official. This official may be the king (2 Chronicles 20), a priest (Joel 1:9,13; 2:17), or a prophet (Jeremiah 14). Nasuti also claims that one element in this ceremony was a "divine response" mediated to the community by a prophet.[30] None of the Asaphite laments contains any hint of a divine response. This is noteworthy since in the passage from 2 Chronicles, an Asaphite delivers such a speech (2 Chr 20:14).[31]

If Psalms 74 and 79 are connected with the destruction of the Temple, the problem of a setting in a "complaint festival" has to be raised. Where and when would such a festival be held? Certainly, the

---

[28] *Introduction to Psalms*, 82. Kraus agrees. See *Psalmen I*, liii.

[29] *Tradition History and the Psalms of Asaph*, 120.

[30] *Ibid.*, 122.

[31] Nasuti notes that divine speech in prominent in Psalms 81 and 82, and he suggests that these psalms function as the divine response to laments in Psalms 79 and 80. *Ibid.*, 123.

Babylonian occupiers of Jerusalem would not allow any official ceremony in the city that decried their conquest of the city and destruction
of its temple. Similarly, it would be difficult to envision the likelihood
of such a ceremony taking place in Babylon. The irregular meter of the
psalm may suggest that it was not a hymn sung in any putative ritual
lamenting the fall of Jerusalem. There have been several attempts to
dissociate Psalms 74 and 79 from the Temple's destruction. Folker
Willesen suggested that "temple lamentations" offer an ancient Near
Eastern parallel to these two psalms.[32] These "temple lamentations"
were a component of the New Year's ritual or with ceremonies cele-
brating the restoration or purification of a temple. Bouzard advances
this argument in his dissertation comparing communal laments in
Mesopotamia and Israel.[33] The participation of "the sons of Asaph"
in the ritual of laying the new temple's foundation (Ezra 3:10) lends a
measure of plausibility to this hypothesis though the Ezra text
describes the singing at this ceremony as involving "praising and
giving thanks" (Ezra 3:11) rather than lamentation.

The original form of Psalm 79 was related to the ritual that accompanied the rededication of the Temple that had been desecrated by
non-Yahwistic accouterments of worship. It lamented the desecration
of the Temple and called for vengeance against the nations responsible
for it and the insult to God's honor that the desecration entailed. An
example of such a ritual occurs in 2 Chronicles 29. Later this psalm was
reworked to include the Deuteronomic explanation for the disaster
that came upon Jerusalem and the Temple: the people's sin (Ps 79:8–9).

V. Canonical Setting

Psalm 79 is one of the four communal laments among the Asaphite collection (Psalms 50, 73–83). The others are Psalms 74, 80, and 83. While
the fall of Jerusalem is the occasion of both Psalm 74 and 79, the latter
shows many more connections with Psalm 78. In fact, Robert Cole has
observed that the opening words of Psalm 79 are a direct response to
the final strophe of Psalm 78.[34] That psalm celebrates David and the

---

[32] "The Cultic Situation of Psalm LXXIV," *VT* 2 (1952) 290–306.

[33] *We Have Heard with Our Ears, O God*, especially 174–85.

[34] Robert Cole, *The Shape and Message of Book Three (Psalms 73–89)* (JSOTSup
307; Sheffield: Sheffield Academic Press, 2000) 80.

Temple (78:65–72), but Psalm 79 decries the fall of Jerusalem, the destruction of the Temple, and the slaughter of God's servants—the very opposite of what Psalm 78 celebrates. The latter characterizes Israel as God's people (עם) and inheritance (נחלה) (Ps 78:71). The same two words form an inclusio in Psalm 79: נחלתך (v. 1) and עמך (v. 13).

Psalm 79 laments the complete reversal of Israel's situation as described by Psalm 78. The former then asks how long this reversal will last (v. 5). It does not question God's anger directed toward Israel but complains about its intensity (vv. 2–3) and duration (v. 5) though v. 6 implies that God's anger against Israel is misdirected. It calls God to redirect that anger against "the nations that do not worship you (i.e., God)" (v. 6).

Psalm 79:5 and 10 show affinities with two other Asaphite laments: Psalms 74 and 80. Each of these psalms ask the same questions: למה (Pss 74:1, 12; 80:13) and עד־מה (Pss 74:9–10; 80:5). All three communal laments repeat questions that dominate Book III of the Psalter (Psalms 73–89): why and how long will Israel have to endure the consequences of Jerusalem's destruction. The Asaphite collection with its emphasis on the Exodus, guidance in the wilderness and conquest call for a new deliverance that will have the same effect as these ancient manifestations of God's power: Israel's peace and prosperity in the land of promise.

VI. Commentary

Verses 1–4: The Cry of Distress

The communal laments in the Asaphite collection deal with military and political disasters–not natural ones.[35] Psalm 80 (LXX 79) contains the ascription ψαλμὸς ὑπὲρ τοῦ Ἀσσυρίου (LXX Ps 79:1) that associates this psalms with Sennacherib's siege of Jerusalem (2 Kings 18–19 and Isa 36–37) while Psalm 83 begs for deliverance from a ten-nation alliance arrayed against Israel (Ps 83:7–9). Ps 79:1 has no heading in either the MT or the LXX that relates it to a specific event and, as is the case

---

[35] Mitchell identifies the Asaphite guild as prophet-musicians who lead a ritual of remembrance at times of invasion and siege. See his *The Message of the Psalter: An Eschatological Programme in the Book of Psalm*, 101.

with Psalm 80, a precise historical referent does not appear in the body of the psalm.

Verse 1, however, states the nature of the disaster as it addresses God: the nations have invaded *your* (God's) land and desecrated *your* (God's) temple. That the destruction of Jerusalem is the climax of the first tricolon implies the significant status that Jerusalem had among circles responsible for this psalm.[36] The implication here is that the fall of Jerusalem does not merely bring defeat and shame of Judah but, more significantly, it is an insult to God (see also v. 12).[37]

Though the psalm begins with the noting the desecration of the Temple, vv. 2–3 move to a description of consequences of the invasion for the city's populace and no more is said about the Temple. While v. 9 does see the fall of Jerusalem as a consequence of sin, v. 2 implies that many innocent people died along with the guilty. Fidelity to the covenant did not guarantee immunity from the power of evil. Still, it is important to remember that the psalm is addressing God when it says that *your* servants and *your* devoted ones were killed–their blood flowing through Jerusalem's streets and their unburied corpses left as carrion for vultures and jackals because the number of corpses in the city outnumbered the people who are able to provide them with a proper burial. Still, the description of the tragic circumstances surrounding the disaster that befell Jerusalem does not infallibly point to the events of 587 B.C. Neither 2 Kings 25 nor Jeremiah 39 speaks of a general slaughter that accompanied the fall of Jerusalem. After a two year siege, famine afflicted the city. Zedekiah and his army broke out of the siege. The text leaves the impression that Jerusalem was left undefended. The army abandoned Zedekiah who was captured at Jericho. The one bloodbath described in 2 Kings 25 took place at Riblah where Zedekiah's children were executed before his eyes (v. 7). It is 2 Chronicles 36 that implies that a general slaughter of Jerusalem's

---

[36] This makes Nasuti's suggestion of an "Ephraimite" origin for this psalm unlikely. Michael D. Goulder characterizes the third colon as marring the climax of this verse. See his *The Psalms of Asaph and the Pentateuch*, 133. On the contrary, the third colon speaks of the unique status of Jerusalem as mediating the divine presence in Judah. From this perspective, the destruction of Jerusalem would have been as much an outrage to God as were the invasion of God's land and the defilement of God's Temple.

[37] Gunkel suggests that this is to inflame God's anger against Judah' enemies. See his *Introduction to the Psalms*, 91.

population took place in when Nebuchadnezzar took Jerusalem (v. 17). The Chronicler has the massacre at Riblah eliminate Zedekiah's "official" family rather than his children (vv. 18–21).

Verse 4 describes how Judah's neighbors reveled in Judah's downfall. The psalm speaks of national humiliation and disgrace rather than any specific action that Judah's neighbors took (compare Ps 83:6–8).[38] The psalm does not name "those around us." Edom did more than taunt the prostrate Judah since it aided Babylon in its destruction of Judah (Ps 137:7; Ezek 25:12–14; 35:5–6; Obad 10–11, 13–14). The Babylonians took control of Ammon and Moab to the east and the Coastal Plain from Tyre to Gaza to the west within a few years of Jerusalem's fall.[39]

Verses 5–12: The Prayer for Deliverance

Verse 5 serves to mark the transition from the lament proper to the petition for deliverance. Instead of addressing God as אל or אלהים as is more common in the Asaphite psalms, this verse uses the distinctive יהוה[40] because the psalm calls God to redirect God's anger from Judah to the nations "who do not know you" and against kingdoms "who do not call upon your name"(v. 6), i.e., nations that can have no claim on God's protection. Of course, the psalm assumes that Judah's relationship with God is the basis for the prayer for vindication in the face of enemies. While God uses the nations as instruments of judgment, the psalmist believes that they are not merely tools. The nations have their own agenda and one day divine judgment will come to them as well. The psalms supplies the reason for this command: the enemy "has devoured Jacob." Again, the reference to Judah's enemies is vague ("nations" and "kingdoms"), making the attempt to identify 587 as the original context of this psalm speculative.

The question "How long?" (v. 5a) appears also in Pss 74:9–10; 80:5; 82:2; and 89:47. Anderson regards it as an implicit expression of

---

[38] Gunkel speaks of the "proud Jew" who felt shamed by the harassment of the nations! See his *Introduction to the Psalms*, 89.

[39] Gösta W. Ahlström, *The History of Ancient Palestine* (Minneapolis: Fortress, 1993) 801-2.

[40] יהוה appears 11 times in the psalms of Asaph; אל 23 times and אלהים 27 times.

hope.[41] It implies that while God's anger is understandable, the consequences for Judah are out of proportion to its guilt. Judah's punishment has gone on for too long.

Verse 8 reflects what became the standard explanation for the disaster described in vv. 1–4: the fall of Jerusalem was God's judgment on sin. The question that the psalm raises is "whose sin?" The NRSV, the NEB, the NJB as well as Kraus and Dahood understand the expression אונת ראשנים to refer to the disobedience of previous generations, taking ראשנים as a substantive.[42] The NAB is ambiguous as it renders v. 8a as "Do not hold past iniquities against us. . ." while Tate offers this translation: "Remember not our wayward acts of the past. . . ."[43] This translation takes ראשנים as an adjective in its usual meaning of "former" (see Gen 25:25; Deut 10:1–4; 24:10; Hos 2:9; Hag 2:3, 9). Following the NRSV and others, the sins that brought about the disaster were those of previous generations, e.g. the wilderness generation as in Psalm 78 and 81:7–12. The present generation simply shares in the consequences of this rebellion; it is the generation of the exile that is responsible for the destruction of Jerusalem. There is no attempt to evade responsibility; rather, the psalm prays that God have compassion on the people who have been subject to divine judgment. Clearly, the people have no other way to secure their future.

It is difficult to be certain about the precise referent here. Perhaps the ambiguity of the NAB is the better solution. One of the significant contributions of the Deuteronomic tradition was its demythologizing of Jerusalem's fall. It happened not because Marduk proved to be more powerful than Yahweh. Jerusalem fell because of what the Jerusalemites and Judahites did. They created and maintained a society which allowed the powerful to oppress the powerless and they found religious support for this social and economic system in the service of other gods, which was promoted by the king. The failures of the wilderness generation were simply harbingers of the failures that eventually brought down the Judahite state. If the circles that pro-

---

[41] *The Book of Psalms*, 2.578. This may be said of the entire psalm. Though it is a complaint, making such a complaint implies that one believes it will be heard.

[42] See the discussion in the notes (p. 5) and Kraus, *Psalmen II*, 713 and Dahood, *Psalms II*, 249.

[43] *Psalms 51–100*, 297.

duced this psalm had any sympathy for the Deuteronomic movement, it seems that the responsibility for the fall of Jerusalem ought to accepted by the generation of the exile and not simply relegated to their ancestors. Acceptance of responsibility for the fate of Jerusalem comes out more clearly in v. 9c. While there is no explicit assertion of confidence in being heard, calling to the "God of our salvation" (v. 9) must imply such confidence. Also, the psalmist provides God with the motive for hearing this prayer for deliverance. God should deliver Judah and forgive people's since for the glory and for the sake of God's name.

The psalm moves into a request that God taken vengeance on the invading nations of v. 1 and the scornful neighbors of v. 4 (vv. 10, 12). While vv. 8–9 ask God to forgive the sins of Judah, vv. 10–13 assume that God would not offer forgiveness to those who have pillaged Jerusalem and have thereby brought God into disrepute. Though the psalm describes in detail the affects of Jerusalem's destruction in people's lives (vv. 2–4), the impression left by v. 10 is that the most serious effect has been the insult given to God by the fall of the city. Were the atrocities described in the psalm to go unanswered, people would necessarily attribute them to the impotence of Israel's God. It is a matter of divine honor for God to take action against those who have brought disaster upon Jerusalem and its people.

Verse 13: Vow of Praise

The psalm closes with a promise to praise and thank God (v. 13) once the prisoners of war are freed (v. 11), the rest of people are saved from diaster (v. 9), Judah's neighbors are punished for their rejoicing in their neighbor's misfortune (v. 12a) and the insults to God are avenged (v. 12b). There will be an end to the disaster that vv. 1–4 describe. For that reason, the psalm can end with the word תהלתך.

Conclusion

It is an understatement to suggest that the fall of Jerusalem and the destruction of the Temple occasioned a severe religious crisis. What made this crisis so severe was that it was unexpected by most people despite the warnings issued by the prophets, e.g,. Isaiah (22:1–14;

29:1–4), Micah (3:9–12), and Jeremiah (26:1–4; 28:1–17). One achievement of the Deuteronomists was that they were able to offer an explanation for these disasters that placed the onus directly on the shoulders of the Judahite people. It was their sins that led to the destruction of their world—not any supposed weakness on the part of God. In lamenting the fall of the city and the desecration of its Temple, the psalm incorporates this perspective in vv. 8–9 while the original form of the psalm may have focused on the malevolence of the nations and the insult that this brought to God. The final form of the psalm includes a request for forgiveness along with the call for God to avenge the insults to the divine honor.

Still, it is a mistake to consider Psalm 79 to be a theological explanation for the destruction that took place in 587 B.C. It remains a prayer pleading for relief. It calls upon God to take action against both the nations that have brought this disaster about and those that use it as an occasion to deride Judah. Those who offer this prayer remind God that they belong to God as sheep belong to a shepherd and promise to exhaust themself in praising God once relief comes.

The rhetoric employed by the psalm contains elements of exaggeration ("their blood is spilled all around Jerusalem like water" v. 3) and vengeance ("Pour out your wrath over the nations that do not know you" v. 6) and as such it is not easy to appropriate. Still, it asks the same questions believers ask today: "how long" (v. 5) and "why" (v. 10). It is a prayer for forgiveness (vv. 8–9) and a promise to praise (v. 13). In this psalm, worthy and unworthy sentiments appear because it is offered by sinners–but sinners who recognize their offense, ask forgiveness and promise praise and thanks to the God who will hear them.

CHAPTER 2

The Poetics of Exodus 15 and Its Position in the Book

Mark S. Smith

It is a great pleasure to dedicate this article to Aloysius Fitzgerald whose sensitive appreciation of poetry and knowledge of Hebrew grammar have inspired me since I first took classes with him at Catholic University. His patient examinations of so many Hebrew poems have provoked searching questions and produced insightful results. His particular insight that Exodus 15 was meteorological language of the east wind (vv. 7–8; see also Exod 14:21) stands as an important corrective to interpreters who recognize only imagery of the west wind in this poem. I wish to reflect on two further aspects of Exodus 15, its poetics and its place in the final form of the book.

I. Introduction

Over the last century scholarly discussion of the poem of Exodus 15 has focused on two issues: the poem's tradition-history, especially in relation to Exodus 14,[1] and its date, specifically its place within the

---

[1] See F. M. Cross and D. N. Freedman, "The Song of Miriam," *JNES* 14 (1955) 237–50; G. W. Coats, "The Traditio-Historical Character of the Reed Sea Motif," *VT* 17 (1967) 253–65; B. S. Childs, "A Traditio-Historical Study of the Reed Sea Tradition," *VT* 20 (1970) 406–18; P. C. Craigie, "Psalm XXIX in the Hebrew Poetic Tradition," *VT* 22

corpus of "ancient Yahwistic poetry."[2] The second issue has been especially dominant in the United States, and if only as a reaction, in
Europe as well.[3] Scholarly work has generally neglected the question
of the poem's relation to the rest of Exodus, although some commentators have raised the question of late.[4] The second issue has been
posed by reference to other poems contained in narrative. Genesis 49
and Deuteronomy 32 and 33 occur toward the end of biblical books.
Judges 5 and the poems of Numbers 22–24 are dependent on the place
of the character in the narrative to whom they are attached. Deborah's
place in the book of Judges is dependent on the tribe to which she
belongs in the book's south to north framework. Balaam's poems in
the book of Numbers hinge on his place in the geographical itinerary
in Transjordan. It is arguable that the position of the poem in Exodus
15 follows a principle governing the place of the poem in Judges 5. Like
Judges 5, the poem in Exodus 15 is a victory hymn attached to the narrative of the victory.[5]

This approach is correct only in part, if only because verses 13–18
show no bearing on the victory described in the preceding narrative, as

---

(1972) 143–51; F. M. Cross, *Canaanite Myth and Hebrew Epic; Essays in the History of Religion of Israel* (Cambridge/London: Harvard University, 1973) 131–42, 310; B. Halpern, *The Emergence of Israel in Canaan* (SBLMS 29; Chico, CA: Scholars, 1983) 32–43.

[2] Cross and Freedman, "The Song of Miriam," 237–50; Freedman, "Archaic Forms in Early Hebrew Poetry," *ZAW* 72 (1960) 105; D. A. Robertson, *Linguistic Dating in Dating Early Hebrew Poetry* (Missoula, MT: Scholars, 1972); Cross, *Canaanite Myth*, 121–31; D. N. Freedman, *Pottery, Poetry and Prophecy* (Winona Lake, IN: Eisenbrauns, 1980) 187–227; C. Kloos, *Yhwh's Combat's with the Sea; A Canaanite Tradition in the Religion of Ancient Israel* (Amsterdam: G. A. van Oorschot; Leiden: Brill, 1986) 127–214.

[3] See R. Tournay, "Chronologie des Psaumes," *RB* 65 (1958) 340, 357; M. L. Brenner, *The Song of the Sea: Ex 15:1–21* (BZAW 195; Berlin/New York: de Gruyter, 1991) 11–15.

[4] J. W. Watts, *Psalm and Story: Inset Hymns in Hebrew Narrative* (JSOTSup 139; Sheffield: JSOT, 1992) 41–62.

[5] B. S. Childs, *The Book of Exodus; A Critical Theological Commentary* (OTL; Philadelphia: Westminster, 1974) 248; N. Sarna, *Exodus: the Traditional Hebrew Text with the New JPS Translation* (Philadelphia/New York: The Jewish Publication Society, 1991) 75; A. J. Hauser, "Two Songs of Victory: A Comparison of Exodus 15 and Judges 5," *Directions in Biblical Hebrew Poetry* (ed. E. R. Follis; JSOTSup 40; Sheffield: JSOT, 1987) 265–84; J. W. Watts, *Psalm and Story*, 41–62. Watts suggests that "psalm's placement here had the whole preceding account in view [13:17–14:31], and not just one or two of the sources."

J. D. Watts has recently noted.[6] These verses have been explained as anticipating events after the Egyptians' defeat. F. M. Cross and B. S. Childs note that *nāḥîtâ* (v. 13) refers to the period of the journey following the victory at the Sea.[7] R. Alter links the swallowing (**blˁ*) of Korah in Num 16:30 with the swallowing (**blˁ*) of the enemy in Exod 15:12. With little justification other than a most general thematic link, Alter adds that this motif "may also point forward, metaphorically rather than literally, to the fate of the Canaanites."[8] Watts recognizes the affinities between vv. 13–17 with passages in Deuteronomy, Joshua and Judges, and he understands that these verses "reflect the language of subsequent accounts."[9] This approach regards vv. 13–17 as anticipatory in character. The task of understanding the poem in its present context might be advanced by studying its textual relations to its immediate setting within the book of Exodus. Childs makes essentially this point: "Regardless of its prehistory, the fundamental issue is to determine the effect of joining the poem to the preceding narrative."[10] And to anticipate, to the following narrative as well.

The main purpose of this essay is to consider aspects of the "present" form of the poem which have gone largely unnoted in recent scholarly discussion. More specifically, the following discussion will address the poetics of the poem, especially its verbal word-play between its two main sections, and the poem's place in the book of Exodus. The second issue will be construed largely in synchronic terms, although some reference is made to the literary arrangement of the priestly redaction.[11] While certainly not the only plausible or valu-

---

[6] Watts, *Psalm and Story*, 41–62.

[7] Cross, *Canaanite Myth*, 141; Childs, *The Book of Exodus*, 244.

[8] R. Alter, *The Art of Biblical Poetry* (New York: Basic Books, 1985) 54.

[9] Watts, *Psalm and Story*, 41–62.

[10] Childs, *The Book of Exodus*, 248.

[11] The book of Exodus is generally regarded as containing a major priestly redaction. See J. Wellhausen, *Prolegomena to the History of Ancient Israel* (originally published in 1878; Gloucester, MA: Peter Smith, 1973) 373–74; cf. R. E. Friedman, "Torah," *The Anchor Bible Dictionary; Volume 6. Si–Z* (ed. D. N. Freedman; New York: Doubleday, 1992) 617b–618a. Most authors working on the redactional history of specific sections of the book likewise posit a major late priestly redaction. For Exod 15:22 through chapter 18, see A. Schart, *Mose und Israel im Konflikt; eine Redaktionsgeschichtliche Studie zu den Wüstenerzählung* (OBO 98; Freiburg Schweiz: Universitätsverlag; Göttingen: Vandenhoeck & Ruprecht, 1990) 23–36. For Exodus 19–24, see T. Dozeman, *God on the Mountain; A Study of Redaction, Theology and Canon in Exodus 19–24* (SBLMS 37; Atlanta, GA: Scholars, 1989). This issue is addressed within

able interpretation, the following reading has the merit of considering the two issues in tandem. Indeed, text and context constitute dual aspects of the "present" or "final" form of the poem.

II. The Poetics between the Two
Major Parts of the Song

The division of the Song is a difficult issue. N. Sarna argues for a division at the end of v. 13 and proposes four strophes: vv. 1–10, 11–13, 14–16 and 17–18.[12] A division at the end of v. 12 is proposed by D. N. Freedman.[13] The verbs *nāṭîtâ* and *nāḥîtâ* in vv. 12–13 provide syntactical, morphological and sonant connections which might appear to militate in favor of taking the two verses together as the beginning of the second half. There is nothing definitive in this criterion, however. Freedman's further suggestion that v. 12 serves as a connecting link between the two strophes may mitigate this point. Furthermore, v. 11 appears to represent a "refrain" (in Freedman's terminology), perhaps implying the end of the unit. However, the "refrain" v. 16 by no means closes the unit. As a further proposal, the poem may be divided generally into two parts consisting of vv. 1–12 and 13–18.[14] These sections mirror one another in theme and poetics. The content of v. 12 belongs with the preceding verses, as the Egyptians in the first half of the poem correspond to the enemies named in the second half.[15] The brevity of v. 12 matches that of v. 18, which closes the second half of the poem. The parallelism of sound (or "sonant parallelism"[16]) between these two verses is notable: *yĕmînĕkâ* (v. 12) and *yimlōk* (v. 18); *tiblāʿēmô* (v.

---

specific sections by B. S. Childs, *The Book of Exodus* (OTL; Philadelphia: Westminster, 1974). The basic thesis of this essay assumes a priestly redaction, and does not rely on adjudicating the complicated issues involving the nature of the pre-priestly and priestly materials. The literary plan of the priestly redaction of Exodus lies beyond the scope of this discussion, but I have addressed this question in "The Literary Arrangement of the Priestly Redaction of the Book of Exodus: A Preliminary Proposal," *CBQ* 58 (1996) 25–50; see further my *The Pilgrimage Pattern in Exodus* (JSOTSup 239; Sheffield: JSOT, 1997).

[12] Sarna, *Exodus*, 76.

[13] Freedman, *Pottery, Poetry and Prophecy*, 180, 185, 209.

[14] Childs, *The Book of Exodus*, 252; Freedman, *Pottery, Poetry, and Prophecy*, 211; Alter, *The Art of Biblical Poetry*, 54.

[15] Childs, *The Book of Exodus*, 252; Freedman, *Pottery, Poetry, and Prophecy*, 211; Alter, *The Art of Biblical Poetry*, 54.

[16] See below.

12) and *lĕʿōlam* (v. 18). In sum, the division between vv. 12 and 13 remains the most defensible. Two features might suggest a further sub-division of vv. 1–12, specifically between vv. 1–6 and 7–12.[17] The motif of *yĕmînĕkâ* in vv. 6 and 12 might suggest units of vv. 1–6 and 7–12. The hymnic character of vv. 6 and 11 noted by Muilenberg and Childs might be taken as further support for this subdivision.[18] However, theses proposed subdivisions of the two major parts appear somewhat subjective.[19]

A number of features highlights the relations between vv. 1–12 and 13–18. Although many poetic features appear within sections, there are important poetic and thematic features, especially sonant pairs, which link sections as well. A. Berlin proposes three criteria for identifying sonant pairs: (1) the words are pairs, namely words in close proximity; (2) at least two sets of consonants must be involved; and (3) the "same or similar consonant" means the identical phoneme, an allophone, or two phonemes which are articulated similarly.[20] Exodus 15 shows sonant pairs not only within close proximity, but also across verses. Identifying the pairs which meet Berlin's second and third criteria may advance the understanding of Exodus 15's poetry. The following list of sonant correspondences between vv. 1–12 and 13–18 meets the second and third of Berlin's criteria:

[17] Alter (*The Art of Biblical Poetry*, 50–54) argues for three strophes consisting of vv. 1–6, 8–11 and 12–18.

[18] J. Muilenberg, "A Liturgy on the Triumphs of Yahweh," *Studia Biblica et Semitica; Theodoro Christiano Vriezen* (Wageningen: H. Veenman & Zonen, 1966) 233–51; Childs, *The Book of Exodus*, 252. See also Freedman, *Pottery, Poetry and Prophecy*, 178–79. Muilenberg and Freedman view vv. 6, 11 and 16cd as refrains (for older views along these lines, see M. Howell, "A Song of Salvation; Exodus 15, 1b–18" [Doctorate in Sacred Theology diss., Katholieke Universiteit Leuven, 1986] 194, 197, 237 n. 51).

[19] Many commmentators propose additional delineations of smaller strophes. For a survey of late nineteenth and twentieth century views, see Howell, "A Song of Salvation," 160–212. Cross (*Canaanite Myth*, 126 n. 45) posits strophes where a change in meter occurs. Howell ("A Song of Salvation," 219–66) proposes strophes at vv. 1b, 2–3, 4–5, 6–7, 8–10, 11, 12, 13, 14–16, 17, 18. The irregularity of length in these units does not recommend this division.

[20] A. Berlin, *The Dynamics of Biblical Parallelism* (Bloomington, IN: Indiana University Press, 1985) 104–05. This approach is not intended to privilege these correspondences at the expense of others within lines or within other units smaller within the major sections of the poem. For a helpful discussion, see E. L. Greenstein, "Aspects of Biblical Poetry," *Jewish Book Annual* 44 (1986–87) 39–42, esp. 40.

Verses 1–12	Verses 13–18
ʿozzî (v. 2)	bĕʿozzĕkâ (v. 13)
wĕʾanwēhû (v. 2)	nĕwēh (v. 13)
wĕḥêlô (v. 4)	ḥîl (v. 14)
kĕmô-ʾāben (v. 5)	kāʾāben (v. 16)
tirʿaṣ (v. 6)	rāʿad (v. 15)
bāʾēlīm (v. 11)	ʾêlê (v. 15)
baqqōdeš (v. 11)	miqqĕdāš (v. 17)
ʿōśēh peleʾ (v. 11)	yôśĕbê pĕlāšet (v. 14)
nāṭîtâ . . . tiblāʿēmô (v. 12)	tĕbîʾēmô wĕtiṭṭāʿēmô (v. 17)

Other possible sonant parallels, such as gāʾô gāʾâ (v. 1)/gāʾaltâ (v. 13), milḥāmâ (v. 3)/yimlōk (v. 18), and bayyām . . . bĕyam (v. 4)/ʿām (vv. 13, 16), are distant at best, but such general sonant correspondences add to the density of other features linking the two parts.

Some of the parallels reinforce divine victoriousness in the two sections of the poem: ʿozzî (v. 2)/bĕʿozzĕkâ (v. 13); wĕḥêlô (v. 4)/ḥîl (v. 14); kĕmô-ʾāben (v. 5)/kāʾāben (v. 16); bāʾēlīm (v. 11)/ʾêlê (v. 15); ʿōśēh peleʾ (v. 11)/yôśĕbê pĕlāšet (v. 14). Other correspondences stress that the central act of the second part, though a result of the divine victory, does not involve warfare as such, but the divine establishment of a people: wĕʾanwēhû (v. 2)/nĕwēh (v. 13); baqqōdeš (v. 11)/miqqĕdāš (v. 17); nāṭîtâ . . . tiblāʿēmô (v. 12)/tĕbîʾēmô wĕtiṭṭāʿēmô (v. 17). The group of words for the divine arm show both associations. While yĕmînĕkâ (vv. 6, 12) and zĕrōʿăkâ (v. 16) refer to divine victoriousness, yādêkâ (v. 17) pertains to the creation of the divine sanctuary. The same contrast underlies the use of personal referents employed in verbs and pronominal suffixes: whereas these forms focus on Yahweh's victory in the first section, in the second section they redirect the audience's attention to the creation of the people in the sanctuary-land.[21]

One detail in the first part of the poem perhaps plays on the theme of temple-building in the second part of the poem. Following Onkelos and Rashi, NJPS translates ʾanwēhû in v. 2 as "I will enshrine him," making an explicit connection with nĕwēh in v. 13,[22] although the

---

[21] Cross, *Canaanite Myth*, 125–26, 142.

[22] See I. Drazin, *Targum Onkelos to Exodus; An English Translation of the Text With Analysis and Commentary (Based on the A. Sperber and A. Berliner Editions)* (n.p.: KTAV/Center for Judaic Studies University of Denver/Society for Targumic Studies, Inc., 1990) 152 n. 12; Sarna, *Exodus*, 77.

word refers to habitation.[23] Onkelos understands this word in the sense that "I will build for him a temple" (*wĕʾabnê-lēh maqdĕšāʾ*),[24] and in suppport of this view Rashi cites Isa 33:20 and 65:10.[25] This view would suggest that *ʾanwēhû*, at least in terms of word-play, anticipates the theme of the sanctuary in the second half of the poem. Like *ʾanwēhû*, its parallel verb in v. 2, *ʾărōmĕmenhû*, might evoke not only its literal meaning of exaltation of the deity, but also the construction of a sanctuary, as the D-stem of *rwm* shows this sense also in Ps 78:69 and Ezra 9:9 as well as the Ugaritic Baal Cycle (CTA 2.3.7 [partially reconstructed]; 4.5.114, 116).[26] In sum, the poem in Exodus 15 presents a double-image of divine victoriousness in both Egypt and in the Transjordan. Furthermore, the first part may be viewed as anticipating the theme of the sanctuary-building in the second part.

III. The Poem in the Context of the Book

The division of the poem relates more widely to the book as a whole. This question may be pursued in somewhat traditional terms, that is from the point of the priestly redaction of the poem and the book of Exodus, although the validity of this reading does not depend entirely on a correct construal of the priestly redaction. Rather, such an approach provides the inquiry with some initial road-signs familiar to biblical scholarship. To begin, the question of the poem's redactional setting needs to be addressed. While the introduction in 15:1 shows no indication of a redactional hand, the verse immediately following the poem is more indicative. A comparison of Exod 15:19 with Exod 14:29, customarily assigned to to P, indicates a priestly redactional context as noted by B. S. Childs.[27] Moreover, parts of Exodus 14 including the priestly stratum show literary dependence on the poem in Exodus 15.[28]

---

[23] Freedman (*Pottery, Poetry, and Prophecy*, 137 n. 18) cites Jer 31:23 for the parallelism between *nĕwēh* and *har*, "mountain."

[24] Drazin, *Targum Onkelos*, 152–53.

[25] See M. Rosenbaum and A. M. Silbermann, *Pentateuch with Targum Onkelos, Haphtaroth and Rashi's Commentary; Exodus* (Jerusalem: The Silbermann Family, 1930) 75b.

[26] Y. Avishur, "*RWM (RMM) - BNY* in Ugaritic and the Bible," *Leš* 45 (1981) 270–79.

[27] Childs, *The Book of Exodus*, 248.

[28] Halpern, *The Emergence of Israel*, 38 n. 66, 42–43. See also M. Vervenne, "The 'P' Tradition in the Pentateuch: Document and/or Redaction? The 'Sea Narrative' (Ex 13,17–14,31) as a Test Case," *Pentateuchal and Deuteromistic Studies; Papers Read at the*

The priestly redaction either accepted the poem in its present position or placed it there.[29]

The second question is how the priestly redaction interpreted the mountain in vv. 15–17. It is usually contended that the original referent of *har naḥălātĕkâ* was probably a sanctuary in the land; the commonest candidates besides Sinai[30] are Gilgal,[31] Shiloh,[32] Jeru-

---

XIIIth IOSOT Congress. Leuven 1989 (ed. C. Brekelmans and J. Lust; Leuven: University Press/Uitgeverij Peeters, 1990) 67–90.

[29] According to Halpern (*The Emergence of Israel*, 38–39), the J material shows literary dependence on the poem (but not vice-versa; see Cross, *Canaanite Myth*, 133–34) and the P material appears to combine details of Exodus 15 and J's notion that the sea was dried up. For Childs (*The Book of Exodus*, 245), tradition-historical grounds suggest a different relationship between the poetic and J versions. Since the crossing of the sea stands within the exodus-conquest traditions in the poetic version but in the prose context with the wilderness traditions, the poetic version represents an account parallel to J which would suggest an older tradition predating both accounts. In either reconstruction, P could draw on both the poem and J. For further discussion, see Brenner, *The Song of the Sea*, 11–15; E. Blum, *Studien zur Komposition des Pentateuch* (BZAW 189; Berlin/New York: de Gruyter, 1990) 256–62. This involves a complicated debate which cannot be addressed satisfactorily in this context, much less solved. Such a resolution is, however, irrelevant for a synchronic consideration of the priestly redaction.

[30] So J. P. Hyatt, *Exodus* (NCB; London: Oliphants, 1971) 166–67 (reference courtesy of M. Howell); Freedman, *Pottery, Poetry, and Prophecy*, 136, 141; Andersen and Freedman, *Hosea* (AB 24; Garden City, NY: Doubleday, 1980) 524. This view was anticipated by Ibn Ezra (noted by Sarna, *Exodus*, 248 n. 55). Freedman (*Pottery, Poetry, and Prophecy*, 136 n. 14) notes that in an unpublished manuscript Albright suggested either Sinai or a site in Canaan as possibilities. Howell ("A Song of Deliverance," 154) criticizes Freedman's identification of the mountain with Sinai on two grounds: (1) Freedman's identification appears prejudiced by his view that the poem is very early; (2) his argument that the poem does not mention conquest and therefore does not refer to a site in the land is irrelevant.

[31] See Cross, *Canaanite Myth*, 142; Batto, *Slaying the Dragon*, 109. Cross, followed by Batto, suggests Gilgal based largely on the combination of exodus and conquest motifs in Exodus 15 and Joshua 3–5. M. Noth (*A History of Pentateuchal Traditions* [Englewood Cliffs, NJ: Prentice-Hall, 1972] 52 n. 170) comments in a related vein: "This rejects von Rad's thesis . . . that the claim upon the land in the tradition of the occupation was formulated specifically at the sanctuary of Gilgal near Jericho. This thesis rests solely on what seems to me the untenable literary-critical presupposition that the old materials of the Book of Joshua, with their Benjaminite narratives adhering to Gilgal, constitute the continuation and conclusion of the narrative of the old Pentateuchal tradition."

[32] For this possibility, see *BDB* 874; J. Goldin, *The Song at the Sea* (New Haven, CT: Yale University, 1971) 34–58; Halpern, *The Emergence*, 35.

salem,[33] the hill-country of early Israel[34] or the land of Judah as a whole.[35] However, it is not clear that the priestly redaction interpreted the mountain in the same manner. According to B. Halpern, Sinai constitutes the referent of the mountain in the priestly reading of Exod 15:16–17:

> . . . Exodus 15 starts with two statements of the defeat of Egypt (vv. 1, 2–5); it then repeats the tidings (vv. 6–8); it then repeats the tidings again (vv. 9–10); and it repeats the tidings once more still (vv. 11–12). Only at this point, after five rehearsals of the victory over Egypt, does the poet proceeed to the migration (v. 13) and Israel's entry in Canaan (vv. 14–16). It is more than possible that in some circles, as in modern traditional circles, vv. 13–17 were seen not as an account of the conquest, but as a sixth recital of the victory at sea, and as one culminating in the arrival of Israel at Sinai![36]

For the priestly redaction, the end-point of the journey, "the mountain of your inheritance" (*har naḥălātĕkâ*)[37] in v. 17, may have been Sinai. The identification of Sinai as the mountain likely predated the priestly redaction of Exodus. For Exod 3:12, usually assigned to E in traditional source-criticism, the goal of the journey is the mountain of God which

---

[33] See Childs, *The Book of Exodus*, 252; H. Spieckermann, *Heilsgegenwart: Eine Theologie der Psalmen* (Göttingen: Vandenhoeck & Ruprecht, 1989), 113; T. N. D. Mettinger, *The Dethronement of Sabaoth; Studies in the Shem and Kabod Theologies* (ConBOT 18; Lund: Gleerup, 1982) 27; cf. 75, 109; Batto, *Slaying the Dragon*, 216–17 n. 11. This view is found also in Targum Onkelos (Drazin, *Targum Onkelos*, 158–59 at v. 17) and in traditional commentaries noted by Sarna, *Exodus*, 248 n. 57. Cf. the view of Freedman (*Pottery, Poetry, and Prophecy*, 195) that the final form of the poem is to be attributed to the Jerusalem cult under the united monarchy. See below for his two interpretations of the mountain in v. 17. In a similar vein, Mettinger and Batto see this verse as a reference to Zion, although much of the language of this verse is paralleled in the Baal Cycle; this view indicates a date from the tenth century on. The lack of an explicit reference to Zion might seem unusual for royal theology, but the same argument might levied against identifications with the other sites.

[34] For this proposal, see Halpern, *The Emergence*, 35.

[35] Freedman, *Pottery, Poetry, and Prophecy*, 214; Clifford, "Exodus," 50. See traditional commentaries noted by Sarna, *Exodus*, 248 n. 56.

[36] Halpern, *The Emergence*, 38–39. Halpern's italics.

[37] For the piling-up of epithets for the sanctuary, see CTA 3.3.26–28, 3.4.63–64, and Ps 48:2–3.

is located in the wilderness[38]: "And when you have freed the people from Egypt, you shall worship God at this mountain." That the priestly redaction could have understood Sinai as the referent of 15:17 was therefore not exceptional. In the redactional context of Exodus, the goal to which Exod 15:17 refers is more likely Sinai than a site in the land.

These are two reasons for supposing that the priestly redaction read Sinai as the referent of the mountain in Exod 15:17. The first reason is structural. The mountain may not have played such a central role in the pre-priestly strata of Exodus, but with the older mountain traditions of Exodus 3 and 32–34 now set at Sinai and the priestly insertion of Exod 19:1–Num 10:11, Sinai dominates not only the second half of the book, but also the book as a whole. The second and related reason is theological. In the priestly theology of the Pentateuch Sinai occupies an absolutely central place. With the priestly insertion of Exod 19:1–Num 10:11,[39] Sinai became the Mount Everest of priestly theology which looms larger than the cultic sites in the land such as Jerusalem. On this issue M. Noth commented:

> For the P narrative is not oriented toward an impending occupation of the land; rather, its real goal was reached with the presentation of the regulations established at Sinai, regulations which became valid immediately rather than being put off until a later occupation.[40]

Sinai not only anticipates the land. For the priestly theology Sinai defines how life inside and outside of the land is to be led. According to the priestly gloss in Exod 29:46 (see also Lev. 22:32–33; Num 15:41), Yahweh freed the Israelites from the slavery of Egypt in order "to dwell among them." This purpose is made possible only through the sacral order established at Sinai. The priestly tradition does not emphasize the land as the goal of the Exodus (cf. the deuteronomic statement in Deut 6:23). Indeed, within the priestly theology the promises of progeny and land play important roles (Gen 1:1–2:4a; 17; cf.

---

[38] McCarter, "Exodus" *Harper's Bible Commentary,* ed. J. L. Mays (San Francisco: Harper & Row, 1988) 130.

[39] J. Blenkinsopp, *The Pentateuch; An Introduction to the First Five Books of the Bible* (Anchor Bible Reference Library; New York: Doubleday, 1992) 137–38, 162–63, 191, 194.

[40] Noth, *A History of Pentateuchal Traditions,* 9.

Exodus 1), but Sinai may be regarded not only as proleptic for the land; it also defines it. For the priestly tradition Sinai would represent the site of the definitive covenant and model for later cultic remembrances in the land.

If this reading were to be placed into the historical context of the post-exilic period, Zion, perhaps the original referent of the poem, would have been understood as Sinai experienced cultically. Zion was the actual earthly location, but there Sinai's covenant and theophany was cultically experienced. Or in the words of J. Levenson,

> God's continuing availability is at Zion, not Sinai, but the canonical division of the Pentateuch from the rest of the Bible . . . insures that the heir will be eternally subordinate to the testator, Zion to Sinai, David to Moses. By limiting the concept of Torah proper to the Pentateich, the canonical process speakers more directly to an Israel on the move, its promises of land and rest as yet unrealized, than to the Israel of the Zionistic traditions. . . . The presence is the presence of Zion, but the voice is the voice of Sinai.[41]

For the priestly redactor of Exodus, this mountain was to function as the cultically pure site of Israel's God and its priesthood echoing the original place of theophany and covenant. In sum, Exod 15:17 may have referred originally to a sanctuary in the land, but it was applied secondarily to Sinai by virtue of the new interpretation of the poem in accordance with the priestly redaction of Exodus 19–40.

If this approach to Exod 15:13–17 is correct, then three further details in the poem may have been interpreted accordingly. First, the priestly redaction may have understood "it [your people] crossed" (*ya'ăbōr*) in Exod 15:16 as the crossing through the wilderness to the mountain of Sinai. The root *ʿbr* is used of crossing land in Deut 2:18, and the usage of *ʿbr b-* appears in Num 20:17, 21:22; Deut 2:4, 27, 30.[42] This view of *ya'ăbōr* in Exod 15:16 would seem to follow from the apparent refer-

---

[41] Levenson, *Sinai and Zion; An Entry into the Hebrew Bible* (New Voices in Biblical Studies; Minneapolis/Chicago/New York: Winston, 1985) 188.

[42] I wish to thank Professor Michael Fishbane who brought this usage to my attention. It is interesting to note that P. Haupt took *yʿbr* in v. 16 as a misplaced gloss from v. 8 which he believed originally referred to the crossing of the Reed Sea (see Haupt, "Moses' Song of Triumph," *AJSL* 20 [1904] 162 (reference courtesy of M. Howell). Cf. Halpern, *The Emergence*, 38–39.

ence to the wilderness journey as suggested by the verbs in Exod 15:13. Second, the reaction of the peoples in Exod 15:14–16 may have been read secondarily as the fearful response at a great distance.[43] The foreign peoples' reaction would represent a miraculous fear which the Israelite god's reputation could inspire in these peoples at such remove.[44] Other passages likewise indicate that the reputation of the Israelite victories precede them (Exod 18:1; Josh 2:9–10, 5:1; cf. Deut 2:25; Josh 9:1). Hence, the theme of fear inspired at a great distance could have been interpreted in accordance with Sinai as the referent of the mountain. Finally, *miqqĕdāš* of Exod 15:17 might be viewed as playing on the tabernacle of Exodus 25–31, 35–40 called *miqdāš* in Exod 25:8.

In sum, the victory at the sea stands at a fulcrum point in the book for the priestly redaction of the book of Exodus. The two halves of the poem in Exodus 15 recapitulate the events of the book in the priestly redaction: vv. 1–12 refer generally the events leading up to and including the victory at the Sea rendered in the first half of the book, while vv. 13–18 anticipate the events following the victory at the sea, as described in the second half of the book.[45]

---

[43] For the physical reaction of the nations, see N. M. Waldman, "A Comparative Note on Exodus 15:14–16," *JQR* 66 (1978) 189–92.

[44] Cf. Alter, *The Art of Biblical Poetry*, 54.

[45] For further discussion, see Smith, "The Literary Arrangement," 25–50.

CHAPTER 3

The Power to Endure and Be Transformed: Sun and Moon Imagery in Joel and Revelation 6

SUSAN F. MATHEWS

The prophet Joel employs earlier prophecies in his proclamation of the Day of the Lord.[1] In doing so Joel places himself squarely in the line of OT prophets and enables their imagery to speak to another generation. But Joel's dependence on earlier prophecy is a free one which is marked by preserving certain imagery without being slavish to the original contexts, so that the Day of the Lord material speaks in new ways. Joel's free rendering of some of the Day of the Lord material allows it to be transformed by later eschatology in such a way that Hans Walter Wolff can rightly claim that in his development of the theme of the Day of the Lord, "Joel stands on the threshold between prophetic and apocalyptic eschatology."[2]

If Joel adopts the traditional cosmic imagery of the Day of the Lord[3] but freely renders it in new ways, then later eschatology takes up Joel's

[1] I am delighted to be able to include this paper in a collection honoring Brother Aloysius. I hope in some tangible way it gives expression to my gratitude and love for his excellence in teaching and generous care of his students.

[2] H. W. Wolff, *Joel and Amos: A Commentary on the Books of the Prophets Joel and Amos* (Hermeneia; Philadelphia: Fortress, 1977) 12.

[3] On the Day of the Lord see especially J. Bourke, "Le jour de Yahvé dans Joël," *RB* 66 (1959) 5–31, 191–212 and G. von Rad, "The Origin of the Concept of the Day of Yahweh," *JSS* 4 (1959) 97–108.

renderings and transforms that same imagery into something utterly apocalyptic. It is Joel's developments concerning the Day of the Lord, for example, that provides the Book of Revelation with the impetus and material for its description of that Day. It is, however, the permanent vitality of OT eschatological imagery that allows for both prophets, Joel and John, to announce the Day of the Lord to their people with authority. It is the purpose of this paper to demonstrate that certain cosmic imagery associated with the Day of the Lord, in particular explicit mentions of the sun and moon, has the power to endure and to be transformed in OT prophetic eschatology and in NT apocalyptic eschatology.[4]

I. Joel's Use of Cosmic Imagery
Associated with the Day of the Lord

The Book of Joel, written around 400 BCE, is generally recognized to be a prophetic work that is eschatological in character and which contains apocalyptic imagery. Its major theme is the Day of the Lord: Joel announces its imminence while calling for his people's wholehearted return to the Lord (Joel 1–2), and describes its result for a faithful and repentant Israel as well as for the nations deserving of divine judgment (Joel 3–4). In both his announcement of the Day of the Lord and in its results Joel makes use of earlier prophecies, adopting imagery traditionally employed to describe the cosmic upheaval of that Day. Because the occasion of his prophecy is drought and economic disaster associated with a locust invasion, Joel's proclamation of the Day of the Lord is unique and unprecedented in the OT.

A. Joel's Use of Isaiah 13

Only in Joel 1:15; 2:1–2, 10–11; 3:3–4; 4:14–16 is the Day of the Lord mentioned explicitly; but the entire text is replete with descriptions of devastation and cosmic catastrophe associated with the eschatological

---

[4] This study will be directed exclusively to an examination of the explicit mentions of the sun and the moon within the context of the Day of the Lord in Joel and Revelation 6.

Day. These four explict mentions of the Day are key passages in each of the major sections of the book.[5] The first instance announces the imminent Day of the Lord as a day of ruin for Israel from the Almighty, 1:15: "Alas, the day! for near is the day of the Lord, and it comes as ruin from the Almighty." This Day of the Lord passage is situated within the descriptions of the locust invasion and drought. There is no cosmic imagery used here to describe the actual Day. In Joel 2:1–2 the Day of the Lord is again announced as coming. Here Joel elaborates, declaring the day to be a "day of darkness and of gloom" [*yôm ḥōšek waʾăpēlâ*], "a day of clouds and somberness" [*yôm ʿānān waʿărāpel*]. The description begun in 2:1–2 reaches its climax in 2:10–11 where traditional language of cosmic upheaval to convey the chaos of the Day is used. It is this passage which concerns us initially.

In Joel 2:10–11 the prophet borrows cosmic imagery and language associated with the Day of the Lord from earlier prophecy. Joel 2:10:

---

[5] Wolff calls them "eschatological catchwords" (*Joel*, 6–7). Following Wolff, who understands the Book of Joel to be a coherent whole, the outline of the Book is this:

1:1–20 Locust Invasion as Forerunner of the Day of the Lord
    1:1–4 Title and Call to Receive Instruction
    1:5–20 Call to Lamentation (communal lament)
2:1–17 Call to Return before the Day of the Lord
    2:1–11 Alarm Cry–Lament (eschatological catastrophe imminent)
    2:12–17 Call to Return to the Lord
2:18—3:5 New Life for All Who Call upon the Lord (assurance oracle answering a
    plea)
4:1–21 Judgment Oracle on the Enemies of God's people
See the outline on p. vii and his discussion, ad loc. It is not within the scope of this study to present a complete presentation of Joel. For further study of the Book of Joel see L. Allen, *The Books of Joel, Obadiah, Jonah and Micah* (NICOT; Grand Rapids: Eerdmans, 1976); J. A. Bewer, *A Critical and Exegetical Commentary on Obadiah and Joel* (ICC; New York: Scribner, 1911); S. R. Driver, *The Books of Joel and Amos* (rev. ed.; Cambridge Bible for Schools and Colleges; Cambridge: University, 1942); J. Kodell, *Lamentations, Haggai, Zechariah, Malachi, Obadiah, Joel, Second Zechariah, Baruch* (OTM 14; Wilmington, Del.: Glazier, 1982); K. Nash, S.S.N.D., "The Palestinian Agricultural Year and the Book of Joel" (Ph.D. dissertation; Washington, D.C.: The Catholic University of America, 1989); W. S. Prinsloo *The Theology of the Book of Joel* (BZAW 163; Berlin: de Gruyter, 1985); and A. Weiser *Das Buch der Zwölf Kleinen Propheten* (ATD 24/1; Göttingen: Vandenhoeck und Ruprecht, 1956).

Before them the earth trembles, the heavens shake;
The sun and the moon are darkened, and the stars withhold their
brightness.[6]
[*lĕpānāyw rāgĕzâ ʾereṣ raʿăšû šāmāyim
šemeš wĕyārēaḥ qādārû wĕkôkābîm ʾāšepû noghām*]

These signs of chaos and cosmic upheaval are typical of the Day of the
Lord, which Joel has borrowed from First Isaiah. For Joel 2:10a the
original reference is Isa 13:13:

For this I will make the heavens tremble and the earth shall be
shaken from its place. . . .
[*ʿal-kēn šāmāyim ʾargîz wĕtirʿaš hāʾāreṣ mimmĕqômāh*. . . .]

What is to be noted is that the imagery is used in its original context in
Isaiah in an oracle against Babylon. Joel has borrowed it and recontextualized it in an oracle against Israel.[7] Cleverly he has reversed the
cosmic imagery: in Isaiah it is the heavens that tremble (*rgz*) and the
earth that shakes (*rʿš*), whereas in Joel it is the earth that trembles (*rgz*)
and the heavens that shake (*rʿš*). Perhaps he has done so because it is
God's people who are addressed and not his people's enemies. In doing
so he draws closer attention to the proclamation of the Day; recontex-
tualizing the imagery to apply to Israel would make Israel take notice.
Joel's dependence on Isaiah 13, however, does not end there. In Joel
2:10b there is a borrowing of cosmic imagery from Isa 13:10:

The stars and constellations of the heavens send forth no light; the
sun is dark when it rises, and the light of the moon does not shine.
[*kî-kôkĕbê haššāmayim ûkĕsîlêhem lōʾ yāhēllû ʾôrām
ḥāšak haššemeš bĕṣēʾtô wĕyārēaḥ lōʾ -yaggîah ʾôrô*]

---

[6] The translation throughout follows the NAB (with the revised NT); the Hebrew
text is that of *Biblia Hebraica Stuttgartensia* (4th rev. ed. Stuttgart: Deutsche Bibel-
gesellschaft, 1967/77, 1990); and the text of the Septugint is that of J. Ziegler *Duodecim
Prophetae. Septuaginta: Vetus Testamentum Graecum* (vol. 13; 3rd ed.; Göttingen: Vandenhoeck und Ruprecht, 1984) and *Isaias. Septuaginta: Vetus Testamentum Graecum*
(vol. 14; 3rd ed.; Göttingen: Vandenhoeck und Ruprecht, 1983). The New Testament text
is that of Nestle-Aland, *Novum Testamentum Graece* (26th ed.; Stuttgart: Deutsche
Bibelstiftung, 1989/1979).

[7] Wolff, *Joel*, 47.

Thus Joel's description of the Day of the Lord corresponds to that of Isaiah, in theme and imagery, but not in slavish vocabulary.[8] Joel has borrowed from Isaiah in order to convey in traditional fashion the darkness attending that Day. He has freely rendered that cosmic imagery in order to give new life to the old description. Joel further develops his own proclamation of the Day of the Lord by repeating its announcement in 1:15 verbatim in 4:14 and by repeating the description of it in 2:10a and 2:10b in 4:14–16, in reverse order:

14 ... For near is the day of the Lord ...
   [... *kî qārôb yôm YHWH* ...]
15 Sun and moon are darkened, and the stars withhold their brightness.
   [*šemeš wĕyārēaḥ qādārû wĕkôkābîm ʾāsĕpû noghām* = 2:10b exactly]
16 ... The heavens and the earth quake. ...
   [... *wĕrāʿăšû šāmayim wāʾāreṣ* ... = close to 2:10a, but not exact][9]

Typical of prophecy, Joel applies cosmic imagery of the Day of the Lord as a sign of the Lord's judgment on the enemies of God's people. But atypically, Joel applies the cosmic imagery associated with the Day of the Lord both to Israel (2:10–11) and to the nations (4:14–16). He can do so because he has a theology of reversal: once Israel returns wholeheartedly to the Lord it can bear the terrible Day (2:18–27). In fact, the

---

[8] For a fuller discussion, see Wolff's excursus on the comparison of Isaiah 13 with Joel 2:1–11, *Joel*, 47. Wolff rightly recognizes that Joel employs the common biblical imagery and language associated with the Day of the Lord, having been influenced by such passages as Amos 5:18–20; Zephaniah 1–2; Ezekiel 30; Obadiah and Malachi 3 (Wolff, *Joel*, 44–47). What is of concern here, however, is Joel's direct borrowing of cosmic imagery (especially with regard to the sun and the moon) associated with that Day. On Malachi 3, see the discussion below.

[9] It seems that in 4:14–16 Joel has adapted his own earlier allusion to Isa 13:13 because he wishes to emphasize that it is the Lord alone who judges and saves. The "Lord's roaring from Zion" and the "Lord as a refuge for his people" frame the phrase taken from Joel 2:10a (cf. Joel 4:16). Whatever the purpose for the adaptation, the result is that the pairing found in 2:10a and 2:10b is recontextualized here in an oracle of judgment against the nations so that Joel 4:14–16 in particular prepares for the climactic conclusion that the Lord alone can save his faithful people on the very Day that the unrepentant nations are destroyed (Joel 4:14–17).

Day of the Lord is turned to a day of salvation and the cosmic imagery of chaos and upheaval is then also applied to Israel's rescue by the Lord (3:1–5). Instead of doom and chaos, therefore, the cosmic upheaval is a prelude to God's recreation of Israel.

B. Joel's Use of Malachi 3

In Joel 2:10–11 the prophet has also borrowed from Malachi 3.[10] In Joel 2:11b Joel borrows Day of the Lord imagery from Mal 3:2, 23 MT [4:4 LXX]:

Joel 2:11b: . . . For great is the day of the Lord,
and exceedingly terrible; who can bear it?
[. . . *kî-gādôl yôm-YHWH wěnôrāʾ měʾōd ûmî yěkîlennû*]

Mal 3:2 But who will endure the day of his coming?
And who can stand when he appears? . . .
[*ûmî měkalkēl ʾet-yôm bôʾô ûmî hāʿōmēd běhērāʾôtô*]

3:23 MT . . . Before the day of the Lord comes,
the great and terrible day.
[. . . *lipnê bôʾ yôm YHWH haggādôl wěhannôrāʾ*]

Joel has combined both texts from Malachi in 2:11b while in Joel 3:4b MT [2:31b LXX] the prophet uses Malachi again, but this time he has only borrowed from Mal 3:23 MT [4:4 LXX]:

Joel 3:4 MT [2:31 LXX]:
The sun will be turned to darkness, and the moon to blood,
At the coming of the day of the Lord, the great and terrible day.
[*haššemeš yēhāpēk lěḥōšek wěhayyārēaḥ lědām*
lipnê bôʾ yôm YHWH haggādôl wěhannôrāʾ]

Joel 3:5 MT [2:32 LXX]:
Then everyone shall be rescued who calls on the name of the Lord;
For on Mount Zion there shall be a remnant, as the Lord has said,
And in Jerusalem survivors whom the Lord shall call.

---

10 While Joel 2:11 is not strictly cosmic in imagery, Joel 2:10–11 is of apiece and therefore should be considered together. The same is true of Joel 3:4–5 MT.

Joel 3:4b MT [2:31b LXX] is identical to Mal 3:23 MT [4:4b LXX]; Joel has borrowed directly from Malachi, but he has gone significantly beyond him. In 3:4 MT [2:31 LXX], by combining Malachi's "great and terrible day" with "who will endure it?" together with the sun and the moon upheaval, taken up and adapted from Joel 2:10–11, Joel has emphasized that the great and terrible Day of the Lord of which the prophets spoke is inescapable. The pairing of "great and terrible" and "who will endure it" occurs only in Joel 2:11b in all of the OT. While not slavishly rendering Malachi 3:2, 23 MT, Joel has combined his two distinct ideas into one aspect of his own description of the Day. This pairing heightens the catastrophic nature of the Day. There is more than a rhetorical arousal of the audience in this allusion. Joel 2:10–11 prepares the way for Joel 3:4–5 MT, where the prophet, using the adapted descriptions from both Isaiah and Malachi, illustrates that the great and terrible Day can be endured by a faithful remnant. The combining of these allusions with the mention of those rescued in place of the disturbing query of "who can bear it" suggests that Joel intends to say that a faithful Israel can escape the wrath of the Lord. Joel borrowed specific language and typical imagery associated with the Day of the Lord as they were set out by the prophetic tradition before him. In 2:10–11 and again in 3:4–5 MT Joel has combined the cosmic imagery of Isaiah 13 with Malachi's Day of the Lord material in order to suit his theology of reversal. Joel wished to convey by means of adapted allusions that it is possible to endure the great and terrible Day if Israel turns to the Lord wholeheartedly.[11]

In 3:4–5 MT [2:31–32 LXX], Joel further develops his emphasis on the chaos and upheaval of the Day by adapting anew his allusion to Isa 13:10. Instead of declaring that the "sun and moon are darkened, and the stars withhold their brightness" as in Joel 2:10 and again in 4:15–16, Joel 3:4 MT [2:31 LXX] proclaims that "the sun will be turned to darkness, and the moon to blood." Joel's mention of the moon turning to blood is unique in all of the OT.[12]

---

[11] On Joel's reversal theme, see further Wolff, (*Joel*, passim) and E. D. Mallon, "Joel, Odadiah," in *The New Jerome Biblical Commentary* (ed. R. E. Brown, J. A. Fitzmyer, and R. E. Murphy; Englewood Cliffs: Prentice-Hall, 1990) 400–403.

[12] He may have borrowed the notion of elements of nature running red with blood from stock biblical expressions for the wrathful Day, cf., for example, Isa 34:4 and Ezek 32:6–7.

C. Implications

We have seen that Joel's description of the Day of the Lord in Joel 2–3 is filled with cosmic imagery denoting darkness, chaos and upheaval; the imminent Day is both great and terrible. Yet in the climax of the description in which the very celestial array is distressed (2:10–11) there is put before the reader the question of who can endure it. Immediately there follows a new section, which begins with the divine assurance, "Yet even now, says the Lord, return to me with your whole heart . . ." (2:12). Joel 2:12 is a divine summons to return to the Lord. Wholehearted return to the Lord will enable Israel to endure the dreadful Day. The implication is that there is escape for a repentant people. Indeed, the Day of the Lord is turned from a day of destruction of God's people to one of salvation for them. Joel 2:18 is pivotal ("Then the Lord was stirred to concern for his land and took pity on his people"). The Lord reverses the misfortune of his people, restoring them to prosperity and safety (2:19–27). The oracle of doom has given way to one of salvation. The cosmic imagery and mention of the Day of the Lord repeated in 3:3–5 MT is used to announce assurance of escape to Mt. Zion for all who call upon the Lord in fidelity. Correspondingly, the Lord will work cosmic signs on behalf of his people; these signs will accompany their salvation (3:3–5 MT). The imagery used to signal chaos and doom are now used to signal the reverse; cosmic upheaval accompanies the salvation which dawns for the faithful remnant.

On one more occasion Joel uses cosmic imagery of the Day of the Lord, but in this instance to describe the doom associated with the Day. The doom is turned to the enemies of God's people, the nations. As an oracle of judgment against the nations, Joel 4:1–16 is framed by announcements of salvation for God's people and the faithful dwelling with their God on Mt. Zion (Joel 3:4–5 MT and 4:17–21). Joel 4:14–16 repeats the cosmic imagery borrowed and adapted from Isaiah 13—or more precisely, from Joel 2:10–11. Here the emphasis is on the Lord as a refuge for his faithful people amidst the destruction of his Day of wrath.[13] This conclusion of the oracle against the nations serves as a transition to the final oracle of salvation for Israel.

---

[13] This theology may account for the separation in Joel 4:15–16 of the allusions to Isaiah 13 Joel paired in 2:10, and for the alteration of the second half of that pair in Joel 4:16. In any case, the effect is an a:b:a' pattern, so that the pairing in Joel 2:10–11 and

II. Revelation's Rendering of Joel's Cosmic Imagery Associated with the Day of the Lord

In the apocalypse proper of the Book of Revelation (4:1–22:5), John[14] relates a series of visions that depicts what will happen to the faithful and the unfaithful in the final cosmic distress. This distress is that of the same great Day of the Lord of which Joel and the OT prophets spoke. In particular, John alludes to Joel's description of the Day and adapts his dual rendering of the Day. Like Joel, John's major theme is the imminent Day of the Lord, which is at once a day of salvation for God's faithful people and a Day of judgment for the enemies of God's people.[15] The focus in this section of the Book of Revelation is the divine and definitive defeat of evil, which is accompanied by cosmic upheaval but which also results in the final consummation of the Kingdom, where God dwells with His people on Mt. Zion.[16]

In the famous first four seals, the four horsemen (6:1–8), John depicts war and natural disaster that is naturally part of a fallen world.[17] These seals tell the story of the world before the eschatological distress associated with the Day. In the fifth seal (6:9–11), the souls of the martyrs under the altar in heaven cry out for justice: "How long will it be, holy and true master, before you sit in judgment and avenge our blood on the inhabitants of the earth?" (6:10). But the divine response is to give each martyr a long white robe and they are told to rest a little while longer until the number of their fellow servants and brothers to be slain (as they were) is filled up (6:11). The justice of God

---

again in Joel 4:14–16 results in highlighting the first half of that pair in Joel 3:4–5 MT where it is found without its second half, adapted, and combined with another allusion.

[14] The seer of the Book of Revelation refers to himself as John, which does not appear to be a pseudonym (cf. 1:1, 4, 9). He is at least an early Christian prophet known among the churches of Asia Minor.

[15] For a discussion of this theme, see A. Y. Collins, *The Apocalypse* (NTM 22; Wilmington: Glazier, 1979) xii–xiv and passim.

[16] Cf. Rev 1:9, the septets of the seals, trumpets, and bowls; and the final cycle of visions (Rev 19:11–22:5), which reaches its climax in the eschatological vision of Rev 21:1–22:5.

[17] This is a common interpretation of the four horsemen. See, e.g., E. Corsini, *The Apocalypse: The Perennial Revelation of Jesus Christ* (GNS 5; Wilmington: Glazier, 1983) 138–42; and C. H. Giblin, *The Book of Revelation: The Open Book of Prophecy* (GNS 34; Collegeville: Liturgical Press, 1991) 87.

also requires judging the martyrs' cause among the "inhabitants of the earth." This important group is the hostile enemy of God and his faithful people; it is always pejorative in the Book of Revelation.[18]

In the sixth seal (6:12–17) there is a depiction of the eschatological distress replete with cosmic imagery traditionally associated with the Day of the Lord, i.e, John's apocalyptic rendering of the Day of the Lord is filled with imagery taken from descriptions of the great and terrible Day of the Lord in the OT prophets.[19] The Book of Revelation's text is as follows:

> 12 Then I watched while he broke open the sixth seal, and there was a great earthquake; the sun turned black as dark sackcloth and the whole moon became like blood. 13 The stars in the sky fell to the earth like unripe figs shaken loose from the tree in a strong wind. 14 Then the sky was divided like a torn scroll curling up, and every mountain and island was moved from its place.
> 15 The kings of the earth . . . hid themselves in caves and among mountain crags.
> 16 They cried out to the mountains and the rocks, "Fall on us and hide us from the face of the one who sits on the throne and from the wrath of the Lamb,
> 17 because the great day of their wrath has come and who can withstand it?"

The primary allusions to OT prophets in this seal with regard to the upheaval associated with the sun and the moon are to Joel 2:10–11 and 3:4 MT [2:31LXX] (and only indirectly to Mal 3:2).[20]

---

[18] It is likely that John has adopted this term for the enemies of God's people from such texts as Isaiah 24.

[19] The sixth seal is clearly associated with "the end"; cf. Giblin, *Revelation*, 85 n. 66, 90.

[20] Rev 6:13 alludes to Isa 34:4 in the mention of stars falling and Rev 6:14 alludes to Isa 34:4 in the mention of the sky rolling up like a scroll; but those allusions do not concern us here. As noted above, Mal 3:23b MT [4:4b LXX] is identical to Joel 3:4b MT [2:31b LXX]. It is reasonable to conclude that John is dependent on Joel and not Malachi here because of the explicit mention of the cosmic imagery and because there is also an allusion to Joel 2:11. It is only Joel 3:4 MT [2:31 LXX] that has moon turning to blood; there is none of that in Mal 3:23 MT [4:4 LXX].

A. *Revelation's Use of Joel 3:4 MT*
[2:31LXX] and 2:11b

In Rev 6:12 there is an allusion to Joel 3:4 MT [2:31 LXX]:

> . . . *kai seismos megas egeneto kai ho hēlios egeneto melas hōs sakkos trichinos kai hē selēnē holē egeneto hōs haima* (Rev 6:12)
> *ho hēlios metastraphēsetai eis skotos kai hē selēnē eis haima prin elthein hēmeran kyriou tēn megalēn kai epiphanē* [21] (Joel 2:31 LXX [3:4 MT])

The verbal similarities between Rev 6:12 and Joel 2:31 LXX are considerable: *ho hēlios egeneto melas/ho hēlios metastraphēsetai eis skotos* and *hē selēnē . . . hos haima/hē selēnē eis haima*. The descriptions of the sun becoming black differ; Rev 6:12 simply uses *egeneto* (Revelation never uses *metastrephō*) and then adds *hōs sakkos trichinos*. There is a clear allusion here; in addition to verbal correspondence, the theme and contexts are similar. Revelation has heightened the cosmic distress by likening the sun's darkness to *sakkos trichinos*.[22] With regard to the description of the lesser heavenly body, Revelation emphasizes that it is the whole (*holē*) moon which is turned to blood and not simply the moon, as in Joel. John has obviously adopted Joel's imagery of the moon turning to blood.

The sixth seal closes with an allusion to Joel 2:11b, forming an inclusion with Rev 6:12 of imagery and language associated with the Day of the Lord. The force of the inclusion is to make it clear that John is speaking of the great and terrible Day *without ever actually naming it as such*. This allusion to Joel lends weight to John's proclamation and once again makes the power of the language and imagery of the Day present to a new generation of God's people. In Rev 6:17 John alludes to Joel 2:11b:

---

[21] For the MT and the English, see above. Joel 2:31 LXX renders the MT literally. The basis of comparison between Revelation and Joel is their common Greek texts. Whether John actually borrows from the Greek or the Hebrew cannot be determined from these texts.

[22] It is Joel's description that John will borrow and reinterpret to describe the Day of the Lord. In the Book of Revelation, however, Joel's locust invasion has been completely transformed into an apocalyptic description of the Day. See Revelation 9.

because the great day of their wrath has come, and who can withstand it?

hoti ēlthen hē hēmera hē megalē tēs orgēs autōn, kai tis dynatai stathēnai; (Rev 6:17)

. . . *dioti megalē hē hēmera tou kyriou, megalē kai epiphanēs sphodra, kai tis estai hikanos autę;*[23] (Joel 2:11b LXX)

The similarities are partially verbal and partially thematic: *hoti . . . hē hēmera hē megalē/dioti megalē hēmera* and *kai tis dynatai stathēnai/ kai tis estai hikanos autē.* The verbal descriptions of the great Day differ. There is, first of all, no mention of *epiphanēs sphodra* in Rev 6:17, and no explicit mention of wrath in Joel 2:11b. Joel's *epiphanēs sphodra*, however, suggests the divine wrath and consequent doom attending the Day. Rev 6:17 has *dynatai stathēnai* whereas Joel 2:11b has *estai hikanos autę.* Instead of *kyrios* in Rev 6:17 there is the wrath of the Lamb and the Enthroned One. While there is a distinct vocabulary in Joel and Revelation, there is an allusion to Joel 2:11 in Rev 6:17. John has freely rendered Joel's text, which is the only OT text where both the "great Day of the Lord" and "who will endure it" are mentioned together.[24] Yet Revelation may not depend solely on Joel 2:11b here. In the explicit mention of the coming of the great Day ("of the Lord" in Joel; "of their wrath" in Revelation) there may also be an additional allusion to Joel 2:31b LXX [3:4b MT]:

. . . *prin elthein hēmeran kyriou tēn megalēn kai epiphanē* (Joel 2:31b LXX)

hoti ēlthen hē hēmera hē megalē tēs orgēs autōn, kai tis dynatai stathēnai (Rev 6:17)

It is noteworthy that Revelation never explicitly refers to the cosmic events of the sixth seal as the Day of the Lord, but the day is clear from John's use of Joel.

B. Implications

We have seen, then, that John has borrowed cosmic imagery associated with the Day of the Lord from Joel. There is a certain allusion to Joel

[23] For the MT, see above. Joel 2:11 LXX is a literal translation of the MT, but with *megalē kai* added.

[24] Once again, whether John borrows from the LXX or the MT cannot be determined here.

2:31 LXX [3:4 MT] in Rev 6:12 in the sun becoming black and the moon becoming like blood. The cosmic upheaval associated with the Day is described here in the terms of the prophets: Revelation 6 uses Joel 2–3 to depict the events of the sixth seal as those of the great Day of the Lord. The inclusion made from allusions to Joel 2–3 in 6:12 and again in 6:17 emphasizes that the cosmic upheaval is that of the Day of the Lord. Thus the allusions to Joel 2–3 in Rev 6:12 and 6:17 form an inclusion while the verses that come between are John's own description of that Day. John borrowed the cosmic imagery associated with the Day in the OT prophets to depict the Day without mentioning it explicitly as such so as to evoke a strong response and to provoke repentance and return. Revelation's use of Joel also highlights the cosmic upheaval of eschatological distress to be endured by God's faithful people. John stands in the line of great prophets before him in harnessing the power of language to stir his audience's imagination and move their hearts. John never uses the precise term "the Day of the Lord." The closest he comes is in Rev 7:14 "the time of great distress" and Rev 16:14 "the great day of God the Almighty." He prefers instead to let the traditional imagery he has borrowed and adapted tell of that Day by its own power.

III. Conclusion

Joel's theology of reversal indicates that he understands one side of the Day of the Lord to be salvation, and the other side to be judgment. It is Joel's contribution to the development of thought on the Day to move in both directions at once, namely, to apply the eschatological cosmic imagery of the Day against Israel and against the nations as well.[25] Thus through traditional language, and especially the cosmic imagery associated with the Day of the Lord, Joel affirms and renews its power

---

[25] Typical of OT prophecy apart from Joel is to apply the Day of the Lord imagery either to Israel or to her enemies. See, e.g, where it occurs in oracles against Israel: Amos 5; Zechariah 1; Malachi 3; and where it occurs in oracles against the nations (or one in particular): Isaiah 13 (Bablyon); Ezekiel 30 (Egypt); Obadiah (Edom). In Zephaniah the destruction is universal. Except for Zechariah 14, only Joel applies the Day of the Lord to both Israel and her enemies. It is peculiarly Joel, however, who applies the same cosmic imagery associated with the Day of the Lord both to Israel and then to the nations.

to evoke his people's return and repentance, which is his goal in announcing and describing the Day of the Lord. He wants Israel to repent and thereby bear the great and terrible Day. For Joel, only a people which has wholeheartedly returned to the God of the Covenant can dwell in His safety and prosperity on Mt. Zion. The major theme of the Day of the Lord was borrowed and adapted from previous prophets by Joel, but what distinguishes Joel from his prophetic forebears is his new context and use of this imagery: the locust disaster and drought are the impetus and metaphor for his prophecy of the Day. Further, Joel's application of the cosmic imagery to salvation for God's people and judgment on the enemies of God's people is uniquely his in the OT.

Joel freely renders the sun and moon imagery he borrowed from Isaiah 13 to give renewed vitality to an old depiction. In Joel 2:10–11 and again in 4:14–16 Joel uses his allusion to Isa 13:10 in exactly the same way verbally, but in exactly the opposite way thematically. In these same texts Joel also makes use of an allusion to Isa 13:13, thereby setting off the third and central text, in which Joel uses only the allusion to Isa 13:10 (Joel 3:4–5 MT), which he adapts by having the moon change to blood and by combining it with an allusion to Malachi 3. In doing so Joel dramatizes the Day, resulting in a depiction of the Day as more terrible and chaotic than ever imagined. Joel has succeeded in rendering the old imagery in a way that gives it added power and new meaning. The Day of the Lord is not just characterized by dreadful darkness and gloom, but by violent destruction from which there is only the Lord's own power to save. Joel's adaptation of previous prophetic material has brought him to the realm of apocalyptic description. Joel's free rendering of Isa 13:10 in Joel 3:4–5 MT also serves to drive home his theology of reversal: there is a new era for Israel, characterized by God's creative spirit and power (cf. 3:1–2 MT), illustrated by cosmic signs. The God who can change the sun to darkness and the moon to blood can recreate and save a faithful remnant. The use of Isa 13:10 in Joel 4:15–16 without the combined allusion to Malachi 3 indicates further that for Joel the nations cannot endure the Day. It is especially Joel's free rendering of Isaiah 13 that provides John with the description of the Day as set out in the sixth seal, who takes the traditional prophetic depiction completely into the realm of apocalyptic.

Rev 6:12 certainly alludes to Joel 2:31 LXX [3:4 MT]. John's free rendering of Joel may have its impetus in Joel's own free rendering of Isaiah. John pushes the apocalyptic description begun by Joel to its completion: the whole moon becomes as (red as?) blood, and the sun becomes as black as dark sackcloth. The use of Joel 2:11b in Rev 6:17 seems to serve much the same purpose as Joel's original allusion to Mal 3:2. John wants to encourage his audience to return and repent and thereby withstand the great Day of wrath. Like Joel before him, John's question is not rhetorical (there are no such questions in this work), but it was meant to exhort the faithful to remain so and the unfaithful to (re)turn to the Lord. In this way, John too depicts the Day of the Lord as a day of salvation for the faithful and a day of doom for the enemies of God's people. This is illustrated in the interlude of Revelation 7 where the faithful are sealed (7:1–9) and there is a vision of those who have survived the great period of trial (7:14–17). The elect rejoice in salvation (7:10) and are given the reward of prosperity and safety with God and the Lamb (7:15–17). John suggests by this schema that the faithful can withstand the Day of wrath. While the idea is not John's, the recontexualized and revitalized description of it is characteristically his.

In summary, Joel's rendering of the cosmic imagery associated with the Day of the Lord (especially that concerning the sun and the moon) and Revelation's rendering of Joel's material attest to the power of this imagery to continue to speak to new generations. Both Joel and John perceive this imagery to be capable of sustaining recontextualization and transformation. Their adoption and adaption of the standard cosmic imagery gives it renewed vitality. Joel's rendering of the material assures that it will not remain in the realm of purely prophetic eschatology. John is motivated to develop the imagery to suit his apocalyptic eschatology because Joel has opened the door to that possibility by applying previous prophetic imagery associated with the Day to both Israel and the nations and by using it to signal at once both destruction and salvation. Thus the Day of the Lord is a day of doom for the unrepentant and a day of recreation of the faithful by the God of the Covenant. It would seem, then, that the cosmic imagery associated with the Day of the Lord has the vitality to be transformed by new generations and the power to continue to do so for as long as the sun and moon endure.

CHAPTER 4

Zion, the Glory of the Holy One of Israel: A Literary Analysis of Isaiah 60

GREGORY J. POLAN, O.S.B.

I. Introduction

Isaiah 60–62 stands out as an extraordinary pronouncement of divine salvation in the third and final section of Isaiah, chapters 56–66. Third Isaiah begins with God's announcement that salvation was coming soon and deliverance was about to be revealed (Isa 56:1), and Isaiah 60 describes that event in language that could only portray a deed of divine proportion. Following upon a series of judgment oracles (Isa 56:9–12; 57:3–13a; 58:1–5; 59:1–15), Isaiah 60 breaks forth with a new word, a message of deliverance and transformation. The old order has passed away and God has once again remained faithful to the promise made long ago. But the unfolding of this promise far exceeds what has been suggested in earlier prophetic utterances of Third Isaiah, and even Second and First Isaiah. The salvific language and imagery of the Isaian corpus reaches its climax in Isaiah 60–62 through poetic description which expresses brilliance, abundance, beauty, restoration, hope and joy.

This article is a study of Isaiah 60, the opening poem in this great three-chapter proclamation of divine salvation. Despite the comments of Bernhard Duhm over one hundred years ago that Isaiah 60 is a poor specimen of Hebrew poetry,[1] others such as James Muilenburg believed this same chapter is "a superb example of Hebrew literary style."[2] The purpose of this article is to consider rhetorical, literary, structural and stylistic features of Isaiah 60, and to draw attention to how this poem functions in its literary context of Third Isaiah and the whole Isaian corpus. Section II includes a translation of Isaiah 60 and an initial consideration of its structure into stanzas and how those stanzas function in relation to one another. The main section of the article is a poetic analysis of each of the stanzas with an emphasis on the various literary devices and poetic images found therein. Finally, a return to the initial proposal of the text's structure in the fourth section shows how the poetic analysis furthers an understanding of Isaiah 60.

About twelve years ago as a doctoral student I sat with my director, Leo Laberge, O.M.I., as an observer at the Task Force on Hebrew Poetry at the annual meeting of the Catholic Biblical Association and there I first met Brother Aloysius Fitzgerald, F.S.C. During the break, he saw a face he did not recognize (mine!) and came over to introduce himself and offer a word of welcome. That initiated an association which has carried on until the present. Whether it be in a colloquium or an informal discussion, I have never walked away from an encounter with Aloysius in which the inveterate teacher, the dedicated scholar, and the devoted Christian Brother were not all in evidence. This article is written in appreciation for his knowledge, wisdom and friendship.

II. Translation and Structure of Isaiah 60

The Dawning Light of Salvation upon Zion

1   Arise! Shine, for your light has come;
    the effulgence[3] of the Lord upon you[4] has dawned.

---

[1] B. Duhm, *Das Buch Jesaja* (5. Auflage; Göttingen: Vandenhoeck und Ruprecht, 1892) 447–48.

[2] J. Muilenburg, "The Book of Isaiah, Chapters 40–66," in *IB* 5 (Nashville, TN: Abingdon Press, 1956) 697.

[3] The translation of *kābôd* as "effulgence" is developed by Joseph Blenkinsopp to express "a technical expression for the visible manifestation of the invisible God." See further *The Pentateuch: An Introduction to the First Five Books of the Bible* (AB Reference Library; New York: Doubleday, 1992) 169.

[4] This translation attempts to follow closely the word order of the MT to show var-

2 Behold! Darkness[5] shall cover the earth
  and deep gloom, the peoples.
  But upon you will dawn the Lord,
  and his effulgence upon you will be seen.
3 And nations will travel to your light,
  and kings to the brightness of your dawning.

The Movement to Zion

4 Raise your eyes round about and see:
  all of them are gathered; they come to you.
  Your sons from afar shall come,
  and your daughters, on the hip, shall be carried.
5 Then as you look, so you will be radiant;
  your heart will throb and swell.

  Behold![6] It shall pour out upon you, the wealth of the sea,
  the riches of nations shall come to you.
6 Throngs of camels shall cover you,
  dromedaries of Midian and Ephah,
  cargoes[7] from Sheba shall come.
  Gold and frankincense they shall bear,
  and the renown of the Lord they shall announce.
7 All the flocks of Kedar shall be gathered for you;
  to you the rams of Nebaioth shall minister.
  They shall ascend as a favorable offering on my altar,[8]
  and my beautiful house I will beautify.

8 Who are these that like a cloud fly aloft,
  and like doves to their cotes?
9 The vessels[9] of the coastlands are gathering[10]
  with the ships of Tarshish in the lead,

---

ious points of emphasis and their effect in a given line. At times a clumsiness in reading occurs, but hopefully this approach will assist in accentuating some of the elements of Hebrew style in translation.

[5] Following the LXX which drops the definite article.

[6] Reading *ky* as an emphatic particle.

[7] Scullion suggested reading *kĕlîm* (cargoes, cf. Jonah 1:5) for MT *kullām*. The "cargoes" would serve as a parallel to "the wealth of the sea" and "the riches of nations" in v. 5b. Scullion suggests repointing *yābô'û* as a *hip'il* of *yābî'û*. See John Scullion, "Some Difficult Texts in Isaiah cc. 56–66 in the Light of Modern Scholarship," *UF* 4 (1973) 116.

[8] Reading with 1QIs[a] and several manuscripts *lrṣwn mzbḥy*.

[9] Reading *kĕlê* instead of *kî-lî*.

[10] Reading *yiqqāwû* for MT *yĕqawwû*.

To bring your children from afar,
  their silver and gold with them—
To the name of the Lord your God,
  yes, to the Holy One of Israel who has glorified you.

Service to Zion

10 The children of foreigners shall build your walls
  and their kings shall minister to you.
  Once in my anger I struck you,
  but in my goodwill I had compassion on you.
  Your gates will be open[11] always—
  day or night they shall not be shut
  To bring to you the riches of nations,
  with their kings in procession.

12 For the nation or kingdom that will not serve you shall perish;
  such nations will be utterly destroyed!

13 The splendor of Lebanon's wealth shall come to you—
  the cypress and pine and boxtree all together—
  To adorn the place of my holiness;
  and the place of my feet I will make splendid.
14 And bowing down they shall travel to you,
  the children of your oppressors;
  they shall fall down at the soles of your feet,
  all who despised you.
  And they shall name you, "City of the Lord,
  Zion of the Holy One of Israel."

The Establishment of Zion

15 Instead of your being forsaken
  and hated with none passing through,
  I will make you majestic forever,
  a joy from generation to generation.
16 And you will suck the milk of nations;
  and the breast of kings you will suck.

---

[11] Reading *ûputḥû* for the MT *ûpitḥû.*

And you will know that I, the Lord, am your Savior
and your Redeemer, the Mighty One of Jacob.

17 Instead of bronze, I will bring gold,
and instead of iron, I will bring silver.
Instead of wood, bronze;
and instead of stones, iron.
I will make your overseers "Peace"
and your rulers "Deliverance."
18 No longer shall violence be heard in your land,
waste or ruin within your borders.
And you shall name your walls "Salvation,"
and your gates "Renown."

The Eternal Light of Salvation for Zion

19 No longer shall the sun be your light by day,
nor shall the brightness of the moon give light to you.
Rather for you the Lord shall be a light forever;
yes, your God will be your glory.
20 Your sun shall set no longer, nor your moon wane.
For the Lord will be a light for you forever
and the days of your mourning shall be finished.
21 Your people shall all be righteous;
for all time they shall possess the land;
They are the shoot of my planting,
the work of my hands, in which I glory.
22 The smallest shall become a clan,
the least, a strong nation.
I am the Lord; in time I will hasten it.

The division of Isaiah 60 into five stanzas can be seen from the perspectives of both content and stylistic features. The beginning and the end of the poem repeat similar motifs about the coming of the Lord, brightness and light, the nations and the earth/land. This terminology is confined to Isa 60:1–3, 19–22. This literary device, in which a cluster of words employed at the beginning and end of a poem, is called "recapitulation."[12] These numerous repetitions demonstrate a striking

---

[12] L. Boadt, "Isaiah 41:8–13: Notes on Poetic Style and Structure," *CBQ* 35 (1973) 24–25, 30–31.

manner of inclusion. Consider the following examples from Isa 60:1–3, 19–22:

(1) *ʾwr* (light) vv. 1a, 1a, 3, 19a, 19c, 20
(2) *bwʾ* (to come) vv. 1, 20
(3) *YHWH* (The Lord) vv. 1, 2, 19, 20, 22
(4) *gwy* (nation) vv. 3, 22
(5) *ʾrṣ* (earth, land) vv. 2, 21
(6) *ngh* (brightness, radiance) vv. 3, 19.

Vv. 1–3 and 19–22 function as "bookends" of the literary unit. This example is fortified by another use of this device in Isaiah 58.[13]

R. Lack suggests that there are two inclusions in the poem which distinguish two stanzas, both built on the recurrence of *bānîm* (children): *bnyk mrḥwq* in vv. 4b, 9b, and *bny-nkr* in v. 10a and *bny-m nyk* in v. 14a. The remaining vv. 15–18 describe the reversal of the situation for City-Zion and are marked by a fivefold repetition of *tḥt* ("instead of"), uniting these verses into a stanza. Finally, at the conclusion of stanzas 2, 3 and 4, a "naming" takes place in vv. 9,[14] and 18. This repeated motif distinguishes the three stanzas within the two "bookends" (vv. 1–3 and vv. 19–22) of the poem.

From these brief stylistic observations and a consideration of the content of the stanzas, a major concentric pattern is evident.

A¹ The Dawning Light of Salvation (vv. 1–3)
  B¹ The Movement to Zion (vv. 4–9)
    C Service to Zion (vv. 10–14)
  B² The Establishment of Zion (vv. 15–18)
A² The Everlasting Light of Salvation for Zion (vv. 19–22)

In reading through Isaiah 60, A¹ (vv. 1–3) describes the coming of light/salvation upon downcast Zion. Then in B¹ (vv. 4–9) the text tells of a homecoming to Zion and of the streams of other nations who also advance there toward the light. In C (vv. 10–14), the midpoint of the

---

[13] G. J. Polan, *In the Ways of Justice Toward Salvation. A Rhetorical Analysis of Isaiah 56–59* (American University Studies, Theology and Religion 13; New York: Peter Lang, 1986) 175–77.

[14] R. Lack, *La symbolique du livre d'Isaie. Essai sur l'image litteraire comme element de structuration* (AnBib 59; Rome: Biblical Institute Press, 1973) 203.

structure, the language and imagery describe the service rendered to Zion, both in rebuilding her city walls and temple and in offering humble homage. B^2 (vv. 15–18) stands in contrast to B^1: while B^1 tells of the universal movement to Zion, B^2 describes Zion as established and stable, with overseers and rulers, walls and gates for the city. Similarly, A^2 (vv. 19–22) can be contrasted with A^1: while A^1 paints a scene of light dawning, in A^2 everlasting light comes to Zion with no more setting of the sun or the disappearance of the moon—a movement from dawn to everlasting day.

This initial reading of Isaiah 60 discloses a concentric structure based on the content of the poem. A more detailed look at the stylistic elements and poetic images in the individual stanzas will demonstrate further links within the poem and further clarify the concentric pattern.

III. Poetic Analysis

A. *Elements of Unity in Isa 60:1–22*

1. *Word Repetition.* The use of recapitulation in vv. 1–3, 19–22 has already been noted. In addition to this feature, several recurring motifs punctuate the poem. Several commentators note the motif of "movement" which continues to appear throughout the poem.[15] The first of these is *bwʾ* (to come) occuring eleven times (vv. 1, 4a, 4b, 5, 6, 9, 11, 13, 17a, 17a, 20). By means of this verb the prophet shows both divine (vv. 1, 20) and human (vv. 4–6) movement toward Zion. The *hipʿil* forms used in vv. 9, 11, 17a, 17a portray the blessings which come as the Lord and the nations bring wealth and strong metals to adorn the renewed Jerusalem. The perception given is that the whole world is coming to Zion, depicted as a royal figure who receives the tribute and homage of its vassals (vv. 11, 13–14). Equally as important, this verb tells of the return of the exiled children of Mother Zion (vv. 4, 9). Those who were in captivity, and now are returning, make Zion's heart throb and swell, so strong is the emotional joy (v. 5). The use of *bwʾ* here, similarly in Isa

[15] E. Achtemeier, *The Community and Message of Isaiah 56–66. A Theological Commentary,* (Minneapolis: Augsburg Publishing House, 1982) 83; Lack, *La symbolique,* 203; Muilenburg, "The Book of Isaiah," 697; C. Westermann, *Isaiah 40–66* (OTL; Philadelphia: Westminster Press, 1969) 356.

56:1 and 59:20, carries an eschatological tone with theophanic imagery.[16] The divine advent at Zion is coupled with a movement of universal proportion toward the brilliant light, toward salvation.

The divine name *YHWH* appears seven times (vv. 1, 2, 6, 14, 19, 20, 22).[17] A consistent image occurs with the divine name depicting the One who comes in light and glory for Zion (vv. 1, 2, 19, 20). This same Lord will be the praise of all the nations (v. 6), the One by whom Zion is named (v. 14), the Mighty Lord whose marvelous acts of salvation for the chosen people (v. 22) will bring about a change in her present condition of sorrow, distress and loneliness.[18]

Also recurring seven times is *gwy*. Almost without exception the references are to people outside Zion who come to Jerusalem, to the light. In vv. 3, 11, 12, 16, *gwy* is in parallel with a form of *mlk*. In v. 22, its seventh and final appearance, there is a play or reversal of the earlier uses of *gwy*. The nations who come to Zion bring wealth and precious objects to adorn the temple (vv. 5b, 11, 13); those nations who possessed greatness come in service (v. 12) and homage (v. 14) before Zion. And what was the smallest and least (of God's people, v. 21) shall become a strong nation (*gwy*).

The word *p'r* (to beautify, glorify, adorn) occurs six times (vv. 7b, 7b, 9, 13, 19, 21). In this poem, the word *kbwd* (effulgence, glory) appears four times (vv. 1, 2, 13a, 13b), expressing a similar idea to *p'r*. Years ago, Muilenburg stated that the central idea pervading the whole of Isaiah 60 is "glory."[19] While both of these terms can refer to a sense of "glory," there are differences in their meaning. The noun *kbwd* often expresses a theophanic sense with a manifestation of visible splendor in light, fire or cloud which is bright and dazzling. Also, *kbwd* conveys the notion of presence and nearness, representing the divine presence, as is the case in Isa 60:1. When the divine effulgence

---

[16] B. Langer, *Gott als "Licht" in Israel und Mesopotamien. Eine Studie zu Jes 60,1–3.19f* (Osterreichische Biblische Studien 7; Klosterneuburg: Osterreichisches Katholisches Bibelwerk, 1989) 150.

[17] In the context of Isaiah 56–66, it may be noteworthy that the divine name YHWH also appears seven times in the poem found in Isaiah 58.

[18] This is the seventh and climactic use of the divine name where the Lord gives his word that what has been spoken will come to pass. For further examples of the climactic occurrences in repetitions of seven, see Polan, *In the Ways*, 180–81.

[19] Muilenburg, "The Book of Isaiah," 697.

withdrew there was disaster (Exod 16:7, 10–12; Numbers 16; Ezek 11:22–25) for Israel, but when present it promised assistance in salvific proportion (Exod 29:43; Ezek 39:13, 21).[20] The *kbwd YHWH* is a life-giving force for the people of God. Thus the presence of the divine effulgence in Isa 60:1–2 tells of the divine will for new and abundant life in Zion, an expression of the faithful saving order of God's presence in the midst of the city.[21] The uses of *pʾr* give evidence of God's desire to see Zion prosper, gifting her and the temple with wealth, riches and beauty.

The last key word is *ʾwr* (light), also found five times, twice in the opening stanza (vv. 1a, 3) and three in the concluding stanza (vv. 19a, 19c, 20). "Light" and the "effulgence of the Lord" are closely related to one another in Isa 60:1. In Isa 60:1–2, "light," "the effulgence of the Lord," and YHWH merge into one another; *kbwd YHWH*, similar to YHWH, is linked with the sun/light verb *zrḥ* (to dawn, to rise).[22] This image of God and salvific presence is used differently in the beginning and at the end of the poem. In the opening verses, the light dawns upon Zion, distinguished from the darkness over the rest of the earth. But in vv. 19–20, the light comes to full splendor, dismissing even the radiance of sun and moon; the repeated refrain of vv. 19b, 20b tells of the eternal light which God will be for the people. Thus the movement from dawn (vv. 1–3) to everlasting day (vv. 19–20) frames the poem.

2. *Word Clusters.* A stylistic pattern of repeating words in close proximity to one another prevails throughout Isaiah 60. Such repetitions function as a device for centering a motif and providing clues for the thought progression of the poem.[23] Consider the following patterns.

STANZA I

(1) *ʾwr* (vv. 1a, 3); (2) *kbwd YHWH* (vv. 1, 2); (3) *zrḥ* (vv. 1, 2, 3); (4) *lyk* (vv. 1, 2b, 2b)

STANZA II

(1)   *rʾh* (vv. 4, 5); (2) *pʾr* (vv. 6, 7, 9); (3) *bwʾ* (vv. 4, 5, 6)

---

[20] Blenkinsopp, *The Pentateuch*, 169.

[21] Langer, *Gott als "Licht,"* 131.

[22] Ibid., 131.

[23] J. Muilenburg discusses this stylistic device and provides examples of it in "A Study in Hebrew Rhetoric," *VTS* 1 (1953) 99.

STANZA III

(1) *mlk* (vv. 10, 11, 12); (2) *gwy* (vv. 11, 12a, 12a); (3) *kbwd* (vv. 13a, 13b); (4) *qdš* (vv. 13, 14); (5) *rgl* (vv. 13, 14)

STANZA IV

(1) *ynq* (vv. 16a, 16a); (2) *nḥšt* (vv. 17a, 17b); (3) *brzl* (vv. 17a, 17b); (4) *tḥt* (vv. 17a, 17b); (5) *bwᵓ* (vv. 17a, 17a)

STANZA V

(1) *ᵓwr* (vv. 19a, 19c, 20); (2) *YHWH* (vv. 19, 20); (3) *ywm* (vv. 19, 20); (4) *wᶜlm* (vv. 19, 20, 21); (5) *ᶜwd* (vv. 18, 19, 20); (6) *šmš* (vv. 19, 20); (7) *yrḥ* (vv. 19, 20).

This list shows how the poet brings emphasis to the various strophic units as one reads through the poem. With as much imagery as this poem has, the repetition of words in clusters or in close proximity to one another focuses the reader/hearer on a variety of motifs as they appear and sometimes reappear throughout Isaiah 60.

3. *Sound Patterns.* The *ḥolem* and *šureq* vowels echo frequently throughout the poem. The opening verse witnesses to the *o–u* vowels and other patterns that will recur.

(v. 1) *û–î ô–î î ā ô–ē û–ĕ–ô ā–ō–ay ā–a–i ā–ā*

Alonso Schokel notes that the *o–u* vowel patterns in Isaian poetry often witness to a context of majesty and splendor.[24] In Isaiah 60 this solemnity of sound continues throughout in the various ways that God's salvation comes to Zion in light (*ᵓôr*), glory (*kābôd*), and the presence of *ᵓădōnay*. It should be noted that YHWH is the speaker throughout the poem, a voice of majesty and splendor. Also influencing the sonority of the poem is the repeated use of the second person fem. sing. pronominal suffix (*-k*). Its recurrence (fifty-one times) keeps reminding the reader/hearer of the Lord's redemptive solicitude toward the one whom he raises from a point of prostration (v. 1) to where other nations will bow before her (v. 14);[25] attention is strongly

---

[24] L. Alonso Schökel, *Estudios de Poetica Hebrea* (Barcelona: Juan Hors, 1963) 116.

[25] The second person fem. sing. pronominal suffix is absent only in vv. 8, 22, while appearing as often as three times in v. 9, four times in vv. 4, 10, 18, 20, and five times in vv. 14, 19.

focused on Zion as God (vv. 1–3), her children (vv. 4–9), and the nations (vv. 3, 5, 6, 10) stream toward her.

B. Stanza 1: The Dawning Light
of Salvation (Isa 60:1–3)

Though a poem, Isaiah 60 tells a story. It begins with a divine voice speaking to a woman who lies prostrate on the ground. She mourns in darkness and is alone. Her prostrate position distinguishes her as a woman who laments (cf. Lam 1:1–2). She is told to arise and to shine for now she is no longer alone; the divine effulgence, the Lord's presence, has dawned upon her. Though only named later in the poem, this woman is Zion, returned from captivity but alone and forsaken, humbled and in need of divine redemption.

The opening stanza is marked by an inclusion repeating the final word of each colon in the bicola of vv. 1, 3.

(v. 1) [. . .] ʾwrk   I   [. . .] zrḥ
(v. 3) [. . .] lʾwrk   I   [. . .] zrḥk

This sequence of repetitions frames the stanza with the motif of the light's dawning. Lack notes that the union of YHWH and the woman is expressed in a plan of sonority which repeats and echoes vowel sounds, especially in vv. 2b, 3.[26]

(v. 2b) wěʿālayik yizraḥ ʾădōnay / ûkěbôdô ʿālayik yērāʾeh
(v. 3)   wěhālěkû gôyim lěʾôrēk / ûmělākîm lěnōgah zarḥēk

The emphasis which comes from the inclusion and the echoing sound pattern affirms that the dawning of light is the coming of divine presence in majestic splendor.

Beyond the inclusion, a chiasm appears in vv. 1–3.

A ʾwrk (v. 1aa)
   B wkbwd YHWH (v. 1ab)
   B wkbwdw (v. 2bb)
A lʾwrk (v. 3a)

26 Lack, La symbolique, 202.

Consider the progression of thought here. The opening bicolon has ʾ*wrk* and *wkbwd YHWH* in parallel construction. In v. 2, a strong contrast is introduced by *ky-hnh* and then *hḥšk* ("darkness") and *wᶜrpl* ("deep gloom"), describing what covers the earth. Then again a contrast follows immediately in v. 2b with *wᶜlyk* ("but upon you"), to show the situation is different for Zion. To further heighten the impact of the reversed condition of Zion, the opening words expressing God's presence in light and effulgence are reversed in vv. 2b and 3a from their ordering in v. 1. Here the inverting of key words functions to support the impact of the transformation expressed in the vocabulary.[27] While the rest of the earth remains in darkness, the woman shines with the light of divine glory toward which the nations and kings come.

Is it possible to define more clearly what is meant by "light" in this passage? In examining the two preceding chapters, Isaiah 58–59, the motif of "light" is an important part of the imagery used there. In Isa 58:8, 10b, the words ʾ*wrk* (your light) and *kbwd YHWH* (the effulgence of the Lord) describe an act of God's blessing that will come to the people when they carry out deeds of justice and righteousness (Isa 58:6–7, 9b–10a). God had withdrawn divine favor from the people (Isa 58:3a) because they were not walking in the ways of *mšpṭ* and *ṣdqh* (Isa 58:2b, 2c, 3b–4), only feigning uprightness. However, the Lord tells them that when they learn the meaning of fasting (which leads to justice and righteousness), then their light (ʾ*wrk*) will dawn, they will know vindication (*ṣdqh*) and the effulgence of the Lord (*kbwd YHWH*) will be their rear guard. Thus in Isa 58:8–10, the "light" symbol is linked with divine deliverance (*ṣdqh*) which flows from a way of life grounded in justice (*mšpṭ*) and righteousness (*ṣdqh*).[28] In Isa 59:9–10, a similar vocabulary and setting are found.

v. 9   Therefore, justice (*mšpṭ*) is far from us
   and righteousness (*ṣdqh*) does not reach us.
   We look for light (*lʾwr*), but behold, darkness;
   for brightness, but walk in gloom.

[27] W. G. E. Watson, *Classical Hebrew Poetry. A Guide to its Techniques* (JSOTSup 26; Sheffield; JSOT Press, 1984) 206. Here the author points out how a chiasm can function to express antithesis.

[28] Langer, *Gott als "Licht,"* 127–28; O. H. Steck, *Studien zu Tritojesaja* (BZAW 203; Berlin: de Gruyter, 1991) 104.

v. 10 We grope like the blind for a wall, like those without eyes
        we grope.
        We stumble at high noon as if at twilight;
        among the vigorous, we are like the dead.

This passage confirms a similar correlation between light and justice:
when the people do not live just lives, the light is absent and they are
like the blind, or worse, the dead.

Also in Isa 62:1b–2a, the passage is similar to what we have just considered, especially in relation to Isa 58:8, 10. In Isa 62:1b–2a, what shines
forth is Zion's vindication (ṣdqh), with salvation (wyšwʿth) as a burning torch; the nations shall behold Zion's vindication (ṣdqk) as well as
the kings gazing upon her glory (kbwdk). Combining the examples of
Isa 58:8, 10b and Isa 59:9–10 with Isa 60:1–3 and Isa 62:1b–2a, we see that
"light" in the context of Third Isaiah is a symbol of both just action
and at the same time deliverance by YHWH who establishes this norm
and comes to Zion as divine presence, divine effulgence.[29] Thus, the
description of the dawning light in Isa 60:1–3 is a metaphorical illustration of the relationship between YHWH and the woman, Zion. Light
and divine effulgence are symbols of salvific deliverance which suggest
a social order of justice and righteousness which are also being established by divine action.[30] The theophanic imagery describes a redemptive action on the part of God which alters the difficult situation of
Zion to salvific proportions.

In Isa 60:3, the close of the stanza makes note of the nations and
kings that will come to the light of Zion. They are part of the glory
that is given to Zion;[31] they come because of the brightness of her
dawning. The next stanza continues to unfold the message of glory
and salvation/deliverance that come to Zion.

C. Stanza 2: The Movement to Zion (Isa 60:4–9)

The repetition of bnyk mrḥwq in vv. 4b, 9b functions as more than an
inclusion for the stanza. In vv. 4–5a the text describes the sons and
daughters coming from exile and the joy of Mother Zion in seeing

[29] Langer, Gott als "Licht," 141.
[30] Ibid., 131.
[31] Steck, Studien zu Tritojesaja, 95–96.

their return. In v. 5b the thought seems to change since an account of the riches of nations and the wealth of the sea approaching Zion follows. But in v. 9 it is clear that the exiled children of Zion are the ones who bring the wealth of nations back with them in addition to others who come bearing gifts (v. 6). This is an example of delayed identification;[32] at the end of the stanza we discover that it is the children of Zion who bear silver and gold, the riches of the nations.[33]

This stanza is begun in a similar fashion to the first, again with two imperatives (*śᵓy* [. . .] *wrᵓy* v. 4a). The following bicolon in v. 4b indicates that all (*klm*) are converging upon Zion; the verification of this opening remark continues throughout the succeeding verses. There is a build-up of imagery which names the children, the nations and the animals streaming to Zion by sea (v. 5), by land (vv. 6–7), and even by air (v. 8); this added dimension of movement by air suggests the rapidity and the suppleness of the grand procession toward the light.[34] While it is difficult to give an accurate sense of direction of all the places converging on Zion as given in vv. 5–9, one is led to believe they are coming from all directions. The "wealth of the sea" in v. 5 probably refers to the northern maritime nations of Lebanon and Cyprus.[35] Midian and Ephah are regions known for camel bedouins, an area lying east of the Gulf of Aqabah. While Sheba refers to a location in southern Arabia (v. 6), Kedar and Nebaioth are regions in northern Arabia. Finally, the ships of Tarshish come from the West, probably southern Spain, a long-time Phoenician stronghold. All converge upon Zion.

In v. 6a the description of the throngs of camels covering (*tksk*) Zion has a contrasting use in the opening stanza. While darkness covers (*yksh*) the earth (v. 2), a multitude of camels with gold and frankincense cover (*tksk*) Zion (v. 6a). Blessings of prosperity come to the once-mourning woman.

---

[32] For a description and example of this device, see M. Dahood, "Poetry, Hebrew," in *IDBSup*, 671–72.

[33] In his study on "merism," J. Krašovec mentions Isa 60:9 as an example of how *zhb* and *ksp* depict the totality of riches and wealth. See *Der Merismus im Biblisch Hebraischen und Nordwestsemitischen* (BibOr 33; Rome: Biblical Institute Press, 1977) 113–14.

[34] Lack, *La symbolique*, 203.

[35] J. F. A. Sawyer, *Isaiah* (2 vols.; Philadelphia: Westminster Press, 1986) 2.181–82.

In the opening stanza, *kbwd YHWH* and *ʾwr* give witness to the glory which has come upon Zion. In the second stanza, the build-up of images—sons and daughters, dazzled eyes and throbbing heart, travel by land and voyage by sea, wealth and riches, beasts of burden and flocks, precious metals and incense, ships and vessels—all speak of another kind of glory. The destroyed temple is now having accouterments being brought so that sacrificial worship can be resumed. The once desolate Zion is now being filled with wealth and riches, with other signs of glory.[36] The restoration of glory to Zion is taking place with the homecoming and the movement of the nations to Zion.

D. Stanza 3: Service to Zion (Isa 60:10–14)

The story of this poem continues. With the coming of the nations to Zion (vv. 4–9), they then participate in the rebuilding of her walls (vv. 10–11). What is striking is that foreigners (v. 10), kings (v. 11), and even the descendants of their oppressors (v. 14) are involved in the work of construction and in acts of homage (v. 14).[37] Early in the stanza (v. 10b) this unbelievable procession of the world toward Jerusalem is explained: the Lord has turned from anger to compassion. This recalls a similar expression in Isa 57:17–18 where the relationship between divine punishment and restoration is straddled between the two verses. In both instances there is the mention of anger (*wʾqṣp* in 57:17; *bqṣpy* in 60: 10b) and striking (*wkhw* in 57:17; *hkytyk* in 60: 10b). While Isa 57:18 describes the reconciliation in terms of healing (*wʾrpʾhw*) and comfort (*nhmym*), Isa 60:10b speaks of it as goodwill (*wbrṣwny*) and compassion (*rhmtyk*). The coming of light and salvation, the movement of the nations to Zion, and the subsequent rebuilding are all the dynamic effect of the Lord's redemptive action toward Zion.

A number of commentators feel that v. 12 is out of place in the poem. They claim its almost prosaic style breaks the rhythm and its thematic

---

[36] Muilenburg notes how riches and expressions of abundance carry the biblical notion of glory, of heaviness, honor, rewards and beauty; see "The Book of Isaiah," 700.

[37] Several commentators remark on the significance of the nations and their actions toward Zion. See Muilenburg, "The Book of Isaiah," 703; J. Vermeylen, *Du prophète Isaïe à l'apocalyptique: Miroir d'un demi-millenaire d'experience religieuse en Israel* (T. 2; Paris: Gabalda, 1977–78) 472–73; Westermann, *Isaiah 40–66*, 360.

content does not appear to be strongly consonant with the rest of the chapter.[38] However, this verse's distinctiveness, its placement in Isaiah 60, and its poetic characteristics all recommend that it is hardly out of place. First, v. 12 appears to be the midpoint of the poem, thus strategically placed. In this twenty-two verse poem, forty-one cola both precede and follow v. 12. In addition to this point of symmetry, vv. 1–11 contain 313 syllables and vv. 13–22 have 306 syllables. Second, within v. 12, the repetition of the word *gwy* (nation) signals a key word recurring seven times in the poem (vv. 3, 5, 11, 12a, 12a, 16, 22). The repetitions of *gwy* before v. 12 depict the movement of the nations toward the light of Zion; the repetitions after v. 12 portray a way in which the nations will honor Zion by giving suck at royal breasts (v. 16) and how the once-meager Israel is now formed into a strong nation. Third, the thought of v. 12 is strongly expressed by playing with repeating sounds, similar to punning. For example, in the expression *lōʾ-yaʿabdûk yōʾbēdû* an ultimatum is issued in similar sounds saying—serve or perish![39] The repeated gutturals and the radicals *b* and *d* connect the motifs of "service" and "destruction." Also in the same verse, the use of the infinitive absolute with the Qal imperfect (*ḥārōb yeḥĕrābû*) repeats the verbal roots to highlight the utter destruction of such nations.[40]

Although some suggest that thematically v. 12 does not fit in the poem, the whole stanza tells about the service which is being offered to Zion. It should be noted that the verb *ʿbd* (to serve) used in v. 12, functions quite well in this stanza as the foreigners, kings, and even oppressors of Zion assist in rebuilding the walls and offer homage to her.

[38] L. Alonso Schökel, "Isaias III," in *Profetas I: Introducciones y commentarie*, (Madrid: Ediciones Cristiandad, 1980) 366; Muilenburg, "The Book of Isaiah," 703; K. Pauritsch, *Die neue Gemeinde: Gott sammelt Ausgestossene und Arme* (AnBib 47; Rome: Biblical Institute Press, 1971) 126; Sawyer, *Isaiah*, 182–83; Westermann, *Isaiah 40–66*, 360.

[39] There is a similar example of punning with *ʾbd* and *ʿbd* in Ps 2:11–12. For comments on this, see A. A. Anderson, *Psalms* (Vol 1; New Century Bible Commentary; London: Oliphants, 1972) 69. Another classic example of similar punning, however with the same verbal root, is found in Isa 7:9, reading "if you do not believe (*tʾmynw*), you will not stand firm (*tʾmnw*)."

[40] J. C. Exum speaks of the connection between "thought rhythm" and "sound rhythm" which figures into the interpretation of Hebrew poetry. See her essay "Of Broken Pots, Fluttering Birds and Visions in the Night: Extended Simile and Poetic Technique in Isaiah," *CBQ* 43 (1981) 340.

Further, the vocabulary and imagery of the whole stanza describe a reversed situation for Zion: She who once was servant to the nations and in exile is now being served by them in her own land. This stanza explains in another way the tremendous transformation that is taking place in Zion throughout Isaiah 60: the divine effulgence returns to Zion; the nations march to the light; and now they serve the once-humbled Zion. And v. 12 stands at the center of the poem and in that position provides the main counter-message: You nations, dare not tread on Zion, or else!

As in the conclusion of the previous stanza, Zion's identity is linked with that of YHWH. This is climactically brought out in v. 14 where the identity of the once-prostrate (v. 1) but now exalted one is made evident: She is Zion of the Holy One of Israel. This is the first time the name of the recipient of God's salvific action is mentioned. This example of delayed identification further highlights the announcement of the one who has received God's goodwill and compassion (v. 10b), the Lord's own city.

E. Stanza 4: The Establishment of Zion (Isa 60:15–18)

In the fourth stanza, the imagery tells of Zion who is now built-up, prosperous, and settled: She has overseers and rulers (v. 17c), walls and gates (v. 18b); she is cradled and nourished by royalty (v. 16);[41] she will be a center of commerce and trade (v. 15a).[42] As Westermann comments, these verses describe not merely a divine act of God, but rather the condition under which Jerusalem will abide in future genera-

---

[41] Here we are reading with Scullion the uncommon image of a nursling at the breast of a king as a metaphor of prosperity and blessing. Scullion draws on and adapts Ugaritic literature, showing that those who are suckled at the breast of a goddess enjoy divine nourishment and riches. Though the image in the Ugaritic text is feminine (i.e. a goddess) and the Isaian text is masculine (i.e., kings), Scullion suggests that there are similarities with the descriptions of the "suckling" and the "royalty" found in both texts, helping to understand the unusual image in Isa 60:16a. See, *Isaiah 40–66*, 174.

[42] Sawyer reads the image of "none passing through" in parallel with "being forsaken." Once Zion was a desolate city following the exile, forsaken by God and unvisited by neighbors. But now with the divine visitation, the nations come; she is once again a place where trade and commerce take place—another restoration that takes place in Zion. See *Isaiah*, 184–85.

tions.[43] This is Zion in a new age, established as the city of the Lord, where peace and deliverance are the ruling forces.

Within the stanza itself, there is a relationship between the opening (v. 15a) and closing (v. 18b) bicola. The opening bicolon announces the reversal of an old situation where Zion was forsaken, desolate, having none passing through her ("gates" implied).[44] In v. 18a, this motif is repeated with the proclamation that no longer shall waste or ruin exist in her borders; then in v. 18b, those very borders for the city are designated by redemptive names. The climax of the line focuses on "gates" (*wš'ryk*) which are called "praise." In contrast to an opening description which saw the gates vacant or unused (v. 15), now they stand as the entrance-way into the walled city of salvation, calling forth praise (*thlh*) to all who enter (v. 18). This echoes vv. 5b–6 which describes the universal movement toward Zion, where those who come are bearing gifts and praising the Lord (v. 6c, *wthlt YHWH*).

T. D. Anderson discusses the varying metaphorical images used to describe the "restored Zion."[45] The author notes that while at first glance the images employed by the author suggest opposing representations of Zion, further research hints that there are allusions in the passage which support greater unity of thought. In Isaiah 60 there are likewise descriptions of Zion which seem difficult to reconcile within the context of one poem. In vv. 4b–5a and v. 9, Zion is portrayed as a mother who joyfully awaits the return of her exiled children; in v. 16a, she is depicted as an infant nursed at the breast. There seems to be a kind of merismic portrayal of Zion as "mother" and as "child." The expression in v. 10b further supports the description of Zion as a child, telling of God's compassion (*rḥmtyk*) toward her after having struck her in anger. The root *rḥm* has references to an expression of pity which a parent has for his or her child (cf. Ps 103:13; Isa 49:15).[46] This

---

[43] Westermann, *Isaiah 40–66*, 362.

[44] The context of Isaiah 56–66 has another example of where the description of "passing through the gates" of the city is an expression for entry. See Isa 62:10, reading *'brw 'brw bš'rym*.

[45] T. D. Anderson, "Renaming and Wedding Imagery in Isaiah 62," *Bib* 67 (1986) 75–80.

[46] For further explanation of this, see L. J. Coppes, "*raham*," in *Theological Wordbook* 2.841; P. Trible, *God and the Rhetoric of Sexuality* (Overtures to Biblical Theology 2; Philadelphia: Fortress Press, 1978) 45–53, 64–67.

image of Zion as "mother" and "child" brings into focus the marvelous manner in which God offers salvation to Zion: the one whom YHWH has brought into being will always be a child to be cared for with a parent's love, with the favor of covenant loyalty.

F. Stanza 5: The Eternal Light of Salvation for Zion (Isa 60:19–22)

This stanza concludes the poem, recalling and expanding upon the motifs of vv. 1–3. A refrain is repeated twice (the Lord shall be a light for you for ever, vv. 19ba, 20ba), highlighting the final development of the poem: from the dawning of light (vv. 1–3) to its everlasting radiance and splendor (vv. 19–22). The eternal character of the light is further distinguished by the merism *šmš* ("sun") – *yrḥ* ("moon") in vv. 19–20. Those forms of light which God created and set in place to guide the days, seasons, and the course of time are replaced with the eternal light of the divine presence (cf. Gen 1:14–18; Ps 136:7–9).

Three sounds dominate in vv. 19–20, the *o, a,* and *e*.[47] The effect of these recurring vowels prolongs the key words, especially *lō² ʿôd* ("no longer"), *haššemeš* ("sun," twice), *lĕ²ôr* ("light," thrice), *yômān* ("day," twice), *lāk* ("to you," four times), and *ʿôlām* ("everlasting," twice). Lack points out a relation between the *o – a* sounds in *yômām* (v. 19a) and *ʿôlām* (vv. 19c, 20b).[48] For him, the repeated *ʿôlām* takes up the sound pattern and transcends *yômām*; the barriers of time limitation designated by "day" are expanded to exceed any restrictions, for God has come to be the everlasting (*ʿôlām*) light.

As already noted in the analysis of Isa 60:1–3, the image of light was used there as a metaphor of the relationship between YHWH and the woman, Zion. Further, the dawning of the light for Zion told of the return of justice (*mšpṭ*) and righteousness (*ṣdqh*) which had been absent (Isa 58:8,10b; 59:9–10). In Isa 60:19–20, the light imagery intensifies. In Isa 60:19c, *l²wr* ("light") is parallel with *ltp²rtk* ("glory"). Not only does the light assure divine presence for Zion, but it also characterizes the new life of Zion in terms of prosperity and abundance (cf.

---

[47] Lack, *La symbolique,* 205.
[48] Ibid., 205.

Isa 60:4–9, 10–14, 15–18).[49] And in Isa 60:19b, God *becomes* the eternal light for Zion. The eternal presence of God assures Zion of salvation and deliverance, a life-giving and life-preserving presence for all time.[50] And finally, as the absence of righteousness (*ṣdqh*) once brought on darkness and gloom (Isa 59:9–10), so does the return of light transform the people into a righteous (*ṣdqh*) nation (Isa 60:21) that will come to possess the land. Life is characterized here as an endless blessing, bringing deliverance (*ṣdqh*) and protection, and transforming Zion into a people of righteousness (*ṣdqh*).

In Isa 60:21b, an image is found of the people of Zion as "the shoot" of God's "planting." A similar motif also occurs in Isa 61:3 where the people are named "oaks of righteousness, the planting of the Lord." Not only is the "planting" a recurring motif, but there are also references to the motif of "righteousness" (cf. Isa 60:21a; 61:3c). B. Batto touches on these passages in Third Isaiah while looking at the larger question of the "covenant of peace" theme in the Scriptures.[51] In describing the covenant of peace, Batto notes how a "planting" motif is also present in the texts (biblical and extrabiblical) dealing with this topic, often the planting of peace. Frequently the context of the planting is linked to a situation where divine authority has overcome human sinfulness as a means of restoring wholeness to a broken situation.[52] Similarly in Isa 60:21–22, we see how the hand of YHWH has accomplished the planting, transforming the people of Zion from a state of lowliness to strength (60:22), from being an unjust to a righteous people (60:21). Drawing on an earlier image in Isa 6:13 of the "oak whose stump remains standing when it is felled," Isa 60:21–22 envisions the restored people of Zion: once forsaken but now glorified, once with nothing but now possessing the land as God's righteous ones (60:21).[53]

---

[49] Langer notes that the prosperity which is symbolized by the light in this passage is especially manifested in the dual use of the sun and moon; everything else which comes to Zion as a result of the light reaches its climactic expression by the two elements of God's created light, sun and moon. See *Gott als "Licht,"* 135.

[50] Ibid., 141, 153.

[51] B. Batto, "The Covenant of Peace: A Neglected Ancient Near Eastern Motif," *CBQ* 49 (1987) 187–211.

[52] Ibid., 211.

[53] Ibid., 206–7.

The chapter ends solemnly with YHWH's proclamation of covenant fidelity: I am the Lord. Not only does God assure the preceding word with the proclamation of the divine name, but also the divine will to see this accomplished soon: In time I will hasten it.

IV. Final Considerations

This literary analysis of Isaiah 60 has shown that this poem is an excellent example of Hebrew rhetorical style. Inclusions, chiastic structures, word clusters, sound patterns, merisms and strategically placed word repetitions all function to tell a vivid and hope-filled story of a Zion-renewed. It is a tale which moves from lowliness to exaltation for Zion. Throughout, Isaiah 60 uses imagery which describes a reversal of her previous condition: she who once was led off to captivity now has the nations coming to her; she who once was exiled is now established in majestic splendor; she who once was a servant to foreigners now receives their service and homage. At the center of the poem (Isa 60:12) stands its counter-message, a warning to the nations, "serve Zion or prepare for divine wrath." And in its context of Third Isaiah, the "light" motif is here understood as justice (*mšpṭ*) and uprightness (*ṣdqh*) coming to Zion, transforming her people into a righteous (*ṣdq*) and strong nation.

Our poetic analysis enables us to see with greater clarity and with expanded perspectives the concentric structure of Isaiah 60. The description of glory and transformation is distinct in each stanza.

A^1 The Dawning Light of Salvation; the Return of Glory (vv. 1–3)
   B^1 The Movement to Zion Restores Glory (vv. 4–9)
      C Service to Zion Restores Glory (vv. 10–14)
   B^2 The Establishment of Zion Restores Glory (vv. 15–18)
A^2 The Eternal Light of Glory and Salvation for Zion (vv. 19–22)

In A^1 we find the return of God's effulgence upon Zion; she who is alone and downcast receives the divine presence. Even the nations are drawn to the light, Zion's glory. What was dark is now light; the glory has returned. In B^1 Zion's glory is expressed in the form of children, wealth, ships and cargoes from afar, and precious metals. What had been lost with the invasion and exile is now restored. The nations bring what will renew life and prosperity in Zion. In C, the midpoint of the chiasm, the glory of Zion is renewed as foreigners rebuild the walls of the city and express their servitude toward Zion. These foreigners name Zion as being in full relationship with YHWH: City of the Lord, Zion of the Holy One of Israel. And finally, the counter-message reads boldly: Serve Zion or perish, you nations! In B^2 Zion is depicted as being firm and stable with walls and gates, overseers and rulers. Once forsaken, it is Zion's glory to be visited by the nations, with wealth and prosperity passing through. The precious metals of gold, silver, bronze and iron replace wood and stones—all gifts from the hand of God. And in A^2, Zion's glory is the eternal light of YHWH, the everlasting presence of God which promises a righteousness people and a nation of strength.[54]

Isaiah 60 stands as a testimony to the author's vision of faith and hope, salvation and redemption. The combined elements of glory and transformation which pulsate through each line of this poem tell of the prophet's vision of God —a God who comes to grieving Zion in order to exchange her mourning for joy, her dark gloom for brilliant light, her loneliness for eternal divine presence, and her nothingness for strength. Not only is Zion renewed, but she is given signs of the reversal accomplished by God on her behalf: Once humbled before the nations, she is now the recipient of the nations' homage and praise. The nations are drawn by the divine light to behold what God has done for this chosen one, blessed beyond measure. The light toward which the nations process is none other than the eternal YHWH whose life-giving presence remains as the eternal pledge of fidelity to Zion. The eternal light over Zion draws the nations to behold for themselves what the Mighty One of Jacob has recreated and made new. In beholding the effulgence of the Lord, they behold the glory of Zion—redeemed, delivered and made righteous forever.[55]

---

[54] Langer, *Gott als "Licht,"* 135.

[55] I want to acknowledge my appreciation to the editors of this volume, Lawrence Boadt, C.S.P., and Mark Smith, whose suggestions and insights have enriched this article. My sincere thanks to them.

CHAPTER 5

A Closer Look:
Isaiah 35:1–10

Maribeth Howell

As a perusal of recent literature on the book of Isaiah demonstrates, current scholarship has taken tremendous interest in the unity of this most favored prophetic work.[1] While it is difficult to avoid completely

[1] For some of the most recent studies that address this topic, see: R. E. Clements, "The Unity of the Book of Isaiah," *Int* 36 (1982) 117–29; W. Brueggemann, "Unity and Dynamic in the Isaiah Tradition," *JSOT* 29 (1984) 67–87; R. E. Clements, "Beyond Tradition History: Deutero-Isianic Development of First Isaiah Themes," *JSOT* 31 (1985) 95–113; C. A. Evans, "On the Unity and Parallel Structure of Isaiah," *VT* 38 (1988) 128–47; C. R. Seitz, "Isaiah 1–66: Making Sense of the Whole," *Reading and Preaching the Book of Isaiah* (ed. C. R. Seitz; Philadelphia: Fortress, 1988) 105–26; J. Vermeylen, "L'unité du livre d'Isaïe," *The Book of Isaiah* (ed J. Vermeylen; BETL 81; Leuven: Leuven University Press, 1989) 11–53; E. W. Conrad, *Reading Isaiah* (Overtures to Biblical Theology; Minneapolis: Augsburg Fortress, 1991); R. Rendtorff, "The Book of Isaiah: A Complex Unity. Synchronic and Diachronic Reading," *SBL 1991 Seminar Papers* (ed. E. H. Lovering; Atlanta: Scholars, 1991) 8–20; C. R. Seitz, *Zion's Final Destiny: The Development of the Book of Isaiah, A Reassessment of Isaiah 36–39* (Minneapolis: Augsburg Fortress, 1991) especially 1–35 and 193–208; G. T. Sheppard, "The Book of Isaiah: Competing Structures according to a Late Modern Description of Its Shape and Scope," *SBL 1992 Seminar Papers* (ed. E. H. Lovering; Atlanta: Scholars, 1992) 549–82; D. Carr, "Reaching for Unity in Isaiah," *JSOT* 57 (1993) 61–80; R. Rendtorff, "The Composition of the Book of Isaiah," *Canon and Theology* (Overtures to Biblical Theology; Minneapolis: Augsburg Fortress, 1993) 146–69; C. R. Seitz, "On the Question of Divisions Internal to the Book of Isaiah," *SBL 1993 Seminar Papers* (ed. E. H. Lovering; Atlanta: Scholars, 1993) 260–73; J. Van Ruiten and M. Vervenne (eds.), *Studies in the Book of*

the use of the now commonplace terminology of "first," "second," and "third" Isaiah, the tendency among many Isaiah specialists is to pay far less attention to clearly defined lines which have served to identify several distinct periods in Judah's history, and to focus instead upon texts which function as links within the Isaiah corpus, underscoring some of the common themes of the book.

In this essay we will examine Isaiah 35, a text that often has received significant recognition from scholars particularly concerned with the book's unity. Appearing in "first" Isaiah, and considered by some to be the conclusion of this collection, it has long been identified as having a rather special function within the book.[2] While many have acknowledged that its language bears close resemblance to that of "second" Isaiah, this has not resulted in unanimity of opinion. Rather, a variety of proposals have been advanced: (a) the text comes from the same hand or school as those chapters attributed to Deutero-Isaiah; (b) the text is the product of an author familiar with Deutero-Isaiah, and is thus to be associated with Trito-Isaiah; (c) the text was composed by a later redactor.

With repeated reference to and examination of the function of our text within the Isaiah corpus, it is somewhat surprising that in recent years so few studies have closely examined the ten verses which com-

---

Isaiah: Festschrift W. A. M. Beuken (Leuven: University Press, 1997); W. Brueggemann, *Israel 1–39* (Westminster Bible Companion; Louisville: Westminster John Knox Press, 1998) 1–7; B. S. Childs, *Isaiah: A Commentary* (Old Testament Library; Louisville: Westminster John Knox Press, 2001) 3–5.

[2] C. C. Torrey, *The Second Isaiah* (New York: Scribner's Sons, 1928); R. B. Y. Scott, "The Relation of Isaiah 35 to Deutero-Isaiah," *AJSL* 52 (1935/1936) 178–91; M. Pope, "Isaiah 34 in Relation to Isaiah 35, 40–66," *JBL* (1952) 235–43; J. D. Smart, *History and Theology of Second Isaiah* (Philadelphia: Westminster, 1965) 292–94; J. L. McKenzie, *Second Isaiah* (AB 20; Garden City: Doubleday, 1968) 12; C. Stuhlmueller, *Creative Redemption in Deutero-Isaiah* (AnBib 43; Rome: Biblical Institute, 1970) 12–13; O. Kaiser, *Isaiah 13–39* (OTL; Philadelphia: Westminster, 1974) 362; R. E. Clements, *Isaiah 1–39* (NCBC; Grand Rapids: Eerdmans, 1980) 275; idem, "The Unity of the Book of Isaiah," 121; J. Blenkinsopp, *A History of Prophecy in Israel: From the Settlement in the Land to the Hellenistic Period* (Philadelphia: Westminster, 1983) 209–10; O. H. Steck, *Bereitete Heimkehr: Jesaja 35 als redaktionelle Brücke zwischen dem Ersten und dem Zweiten Jesaja* (SBS 121; Stuttgart: Katholisches Bibelwerk, 1985); B. Gross, "Isaïe 34–35: Le chatiment d'Edom et des nations, Salut pour Sion," *ZAW* 102 (1990) 396–404; D. Carr, "Reaching for Unity in Isaiah," 65–71; B. S. Childs, *Isaiah*, 253 and 255–56.

prise chapter 35.[3] Thus, our immediate purpose is to examine the dynamic of this chapter: What takes place within the poem itself? What are some of the poetic qualities of this text? What is the significance of the dynamic within the text? Does this dynamic reflect the broader function of our text within the Isaiah Book? Having examined the first three of these questions, it is hoped that some insight might be provided to other authors for the continued examination of the final question.

We begin our study with a segmentation of the text into strophes. We will present a brief examination of the dynamic within the strophe, followed by an identification of some of the key poetic elements within that unit before proceeding to the next strophe of our poem. While proposals for strophic division range from three to six, we support the four part structure employed by Leupold and Wildberger,[4] and translate the text in the following manner:

A

1 The wilderness and dry land shall exult
    the desert shall rejoice and blossom;
    like the crocus, it shall bloom luxuriantly,
    it shall rejoice, with gladness and shouts of joy.
    The glory of Lebanon shall be given to it,
    the majesty of Carmel and Sharon.
    They shall see the glory of the Lord,
    the majesty of our God.

B

3 Strengthen the heavy hands
    and make firm the knocking knees.
4 Say to the pounding heart:
    "Be strong, fear not.

---

[3] To our knowledge, in the past fifteen years, the only articles to appear in the literature are the following: J. Kleinig, "The Holy Way: An Exegetical Study of Isaiah 35:1–10," *LTJ* 17 (1983) 115–20; F. M. Cross, "The Redemption of Nature," *PBS* 10 (1988) 94–104; J. N. Oswalt, "God's Determination to Redeem His People (Isaiah 9:1–7; 11:1–11; 26:1–9; 35:1–10)," *REx* 88 (1991) 153–65.

[4] C. H. Leupold, *Exposition of Isaiah* (vol. 2; Grand Rapids: Baker, 1968) 536; H. Wildberger, *Jesaja* (Teilband 3; Neukirchen-Vluyn: Neukirchener, 1982) 1352–53.

Behold, your God!"
With vengeance God comes,
with divine recompense
God comes and will save you.

C

5 Then, the eyes of the blind shall be opened,
the ears of the deaf unstopped.
6 Then, the lame shall leap like a deer,
and the speechless tongue cry out with joy!
For waters shall burst forth in the wilderness,
and streams in the desert.
7 The parched earth shall become a pool of reeds,
and the thirsty ground, springs of water.
The haunt of jackals, their lair,
shall become a home for reeds and papyrus.

D

8 A highway shall be there,
it shall be called the holy way.
The unclean shall not travel upon it
it is for those who walk the way,
(and fools shall not stumble upon it).
9 No lion shall be there,
nor beast of prey come upon it.
(They shall not be found there).
The redeemed shall walk there,
10 and the ransomed of the Lord shall return.
They shall enter Zion in song,
everlasting joy shall cover them.
They shall acquire joy and gladness,
while grief and groaning vanish away.

Strophe A

Strophe A, verses 1–2, makes a bold announcement: a drastic change is
to take place in the barrens. Not only will the wilderness (*mdbr*), dry
land (*ṣyyh*), and desert (*ʿrbh*) break forth in bloom, but they will do so
in great abundance (*prḥ tprḥ*). This phenomenal transformation of the

desert places is described with multiple words of exultation and rejoicing (*śwś, gyl, rnn*). Not only will these wastelands become luxuriant, but they will receive the glory (*kbwd*) and majesty (*hdr*) of Lebanon, Carmel, and Sharon, places renowned for their lush green growth. The strophe concludes with the proclamation: "They shall see the glory (*kbwd*) of the Lord, and the majesty (*hdr*) of our God."[5]

In this strophe the poet matches the threefold reference to the arid places (*mdbr, ṣyyh, ʿrbh*) with vocabulary that emphasizes the singing and rejoicing that will take place there (*śwś*, 1x; *gyl*, 3x; *rnn*, 1x). While *gyl* does not make another appearance in our text, noun forms of both *śwś* and *rnn* do recur in the concluding verse of the poem, along with a double usage of the noun *śmhh*. Furthermore, *rnn* again appears in verbal form at the very center of the poem, verse six, where "the speechless tongue cries out with joy."

A chiastic arrangement of rejoice/blossom//blossom/rejoice (*gyl/ prh//prh/gyl*) is found in the first half of Strophe A, while parallel usage of glory (*kwbd*) and majesty (*hdr*) appears twice in the latter half of the strophe.

Strophe B

The subject of the second strophe, verses 3–4, is no longer the arid lands, but people. Commanding words of encouragement are addressed to those whose hands are heavy (*ydym rpwt*), whose knees knock (*brkym kšlwt*), and whose hearts pound (*nmhry lb*). "Be strong, fear not. Behold, your God!"

It seems quite obvious that the poet's audience is paralyzed by fear. Heavy hands, knocking knees, and pounding hearts are vivid and effective descriptions of a fear so intense that it may require startling words to jolt the listeners to action. And that is precisely what the poet commands. Unlike the arid lands in Strophe A, the audience here is ordered, commanded to take an active part in their transformation. This is clearly demonstrated by a series of four imperatives: strengthen (*hzqw*), make firm (*ʿmṣw*), say (*ʾmrw*), and be strong (*hzqw*). The first

---

[5] As Oswalt notes in his commentary: "*They will see* does not have a clear antecedent. The LXX makes it clear by reading 'my people' and the Targum does similarly with 'the house of Israel.'" See J. N. Oswalt, *The Book of Isaiah, Chapters 1–39* (NICOT; Grand Rapids: Eerdmans, 1986) 623.

two imperatives are in the *Piel* form, while the second two are in the *Qal*. Before verse four continues with the formal announcement of God's coming (*ybw*ᵓ occurs twice), a comforting and encouraging pronouncement is made: "Fear not!"

Strophe C

The delimitation of Strophes C and D, particularly where C ends and D begins, is the subject of disagreement among authors. We propose that the third strophe consists of verses 5–7, while the final strophe is comprised of verses 8–10. That verse 5 tells us something new, can hardly be disputed. Most works that employ strophic divisions recognize this by placing the verse at the beginning of a new strophe, regardless of whether it be identified in the second or third strophe of the poem. The appearance of ᵓ*z* in the first position of verse 5, as well as in verse 6, indicates that we are about to be told something more — what will happen *as a result of the coming of God* announced in the previous verse. What we are told is nothing less than incredible.

We contend that this strophe proceeds through verse 7 precisely because verses 6c–7 continue to speak of the miraculous transformation associated with the advent of God. The entire strophe is concerned with the reversal of current circumstances. Verse 6c, which begins with the particle *ky*, shifts our attention away from those who will experience physical transformation (who might be understood as the fearful people addressed in Strophe B), and back to the wilderness areas referred to in Strophe A (*mdbr* and ᶜ*rbh* occur in both verses 1 and 6). Human persons and the arid earth will both be changed. The known world will be drastically transformed. It is interesting that in both instances, people and land, there are four sets of changes that occur. We shall return to this point below.

Another possible indicator that verses 5–7 form a distinct unit within our poem is the occurrence of the verb *wtrn* in verse 6b. As mentioned above, the same root, *rnn*, appears in two other places in our text, verses 2 and 10. While the *Piel* infinitive construct in verse 2 refers to the "shouts of joy" that will be proclaimed by the desert, in verse 6b, it is the speechless tongue that will "cry out with joy" (*wtrn*), and in verse 10, those who return to Zion will do so "in song" (*brnh*). Thus, *rnn*, might serve as a unifying link throughout the poem.

We noted previously that Strophe C contains four sets of changes for both people and land. Those human transformations are detailed as: the eyes of the blind shall be opened (*ʾz tpqḥnh*), the ears of the deaf unstopped (*ʾz tptḥn h*)[6], the lame shall leap like a deer (*ᶜz ydlg kʾyl psḥ*), and finally, the speechless tongue cry out with joy (*wtrn lšwn ʾlm*)[7]. The fourth and climactic transformation is located at the center of the poem. The tongue that had been silent will jubilate (*rnn*)!

We find it striking that this final transformation identified with persons is the change from being mute to shouting with joy. Most certainly the movement from being blind to seeing, from being deaf to hearing, and from being lame to leaping are remarkable, indeed miraculous. However, the poet identifies the speechless tongue crying out with joy as the climax of these physical transformations.[8] Those whose

---

[6] Berlin has observed the *abab* patterning of the sound pairs in these lines, and has written that "Sound pairing enhances the perception of correspondence between the lines. When the sound pair is also a lexical-semantic pair, the bond between them is reinforced; when the sound pair is not a lexical-semantic pair, it can be said to replace such a pair." A. Berlin, *The Dynamics of Biblical Parallelism* (Bloomington: Indiana University, 1985) 111 and 116.

[7] Berlin has used the whole of verse 6 as an example of *aabb* patterning. Of the first two lines of this verse, those noted in our text, she writes: "The first pair, *ʾyl* (deer) and *ʾlm* (dumb [*sic*]), are a sound pair, not a semantic pair. . . ." In reference to the next two lines of verse 6, "For waters shall burst forth in the desert; and streams in the wilderness," she states: "the second pair, *mdbr* (desert) and *ᶜrbh* (wilderness), are both a semantic and a phonetic pair." A. Berlin, *The Dynamics of Biblical Parallelism*, 114.

[8] A number of my young adult years were devoted to teaching hearing impaired children in the inner-city of Detroit. As a result of their hearing loss, every one of these children exhibited some degree of speech impairment. I happily recall the day that through the generosity of an anonymous donor, a new auditory system replaced the antiquated system that had been used throughout the school. The new system was cordless. The children wore walkman like units around their waists with wires that trandsmitted sound through their earmolds. Supposedly, the voice of the teacher speaking through the microphone could be transmitted to the students across the distance of two football fields. The first day that we "experimented" with the new equipment, one of the children who had "excused himself" seemed to me to be taking an unusually long time in returning to class. I had suspected that Jack had not remembered to change the dial on his personal unit from "classroom" to "other" mode, and decided to give him a little message. I spoke clearly into my microphone: "Jack Holland, get back here." Moments later, an astounded little nine-year-old bolted into the classroom and shouted with joy: "Howell, I hear!" It was one of my most memorable moments of teaching. A miraculous event had occurred, and Jack could not help but shout for joy!

fears had paralyzed them from speaking are made bold at the coming of their God. At this point in our study, we would simply draw attention to the fact that Clements has demonstrated that blindness and deafness appear as a significant theme in the material identified with 'second' Isaiah, and we should like to return to this point in our conclusion.[9]

The second half of Strophe C returns to the theme introduced in the opening strophe, the transformation of the desert lands. As in verse 1, wilderness (*mdbr*) and desert (*ᶜrbh*) are parallel. However, in verse 6, these places are now identified as being water rich. Verse 7 continues to describe this changed land by employing an abundance of rare words. Parched earth (*šrb*) and thirsty ground (*ṣmʾwn*) only occur here and in one and two other texts, respectively,[10] while pool of reeds (*ʾgm*) and springs (*mbwᶜy*) are also quite rare.[11] Finally, two other rare words, lair (*rbṣh*) and papyrus (*gmʾ*) appear in the last two lines of verse 7.[12] Thus, this most unusual event, the transformation of the desert into a land where waters flow and plants flourish, is depicted by like vocabulary.

Strophe D

This strophe is not without textual difficulties. However, neither is it within the scope of this work to examine and deliberate upon each of those problems here. Thus, for a critical presentation of the text, we recommend that the technical commentaries be consulted.

The final strophe, verses 8–10, speaks of a highway (*mslwl*), a way (*drk*) for the redeemed (*gʾl*) and ransomed (*pdh*) of the Lord. This way, which will be free of all beasts of prey, will lead to Zion, where the transformation spoken of earlier will be fulfilled. The possessions of the people who enter there will be joy (*śwś*) and gladness (*śmḥh*), while their grief (*ygwn*) and groaning (*ʾnḥh*) will vanish.

---

[9] R. E. Clements, "Beyond Tradition-History," 101–4.

[10] *šrb* also occurs in Is 49:10, while *ṣmʾwn* is found in Deut 8:15 and Ps 107:33.

[11] *ʾgm* also appears in Exod 7:19; 8:1; Isa 14:23; 41:15; Pss 107:35; 114:8; and Jer 51:32. *mbwᶜy* is only found in two other texts, Isa 49:10 and Qoh 12:6.

[12] *rbṣh* is also found in Prov 24:15; Isa 65:10; and Jer 50:6. *gmʾ* also appears in Exod 2:3; Isa 18:2; and Job 8:11.

Concluding Remarks

At the beginning of our study we expressed concern over the dynamic and poetic features of this text. We also stated that we hoped our examination might provide some insight or direction for the continued study of the unity of the Isaiah Book. Having taken a closer look at chapter 35, we can definitely state that the poem speaks clearly and eloquently of transformation of a changed world order, of healing, of abundant growth, and of homecoming.

We are reminded of the insightful and reflective contributions that Walter Brueggemann has made in regard to the poets of the exile, and particularly to those texts located in this prophetic book[13]. It would seem that the community to whom the poet of chapter 35 announced these words, was indeed a people who had "embraced the pain" of past and present, and who had expectantly yet fearfully longed for a new future and new words of hope that might jar them out of their paralysis, and into new ways of living and proclaiming the faithfulness of their God.

Well aware of the limits and limitations of this work, and mindful of some of the many and outstanding studies of this prophetic book, we would like to conclude by raising several questions: (1) Is there any relationship between blindness, deafness, and speaking/rejoicing in the Isaiah Book? (2) To what degree is transformation a significant theme within the book? And (3) To what extent is the community/listener encouraged to enter into the transformation process?

[13] See W. Brueggemann, "Unity and Dynamic in the Isaiah Tradition"; idem, *Hopeful Imagination: Prophetic Voices in Exile* (Philadelphia: Fortress, 1986).

CHAPTER 6

Sense Relations in the "Rain" Domain of the Old Testament

MARK D. FUTATO

Aloysius Fitzgerald has taught many students that "it is possible to analyze and make distinctions in the language of storms and particularly storm theophanies in the OT and to show that Palestinian, or better Syro-Palestinian, meteorology is the ultimate source of these presentations."[1] The primary intention of the present study is to show that it is possible to analyze and make distinctions in the vocabulary of rain in the OT and to show that Syro-Palestinian meteorology is the source of these distinctions.

The OT vocabulary for rain has been the subject of study in the past. In 1952 R. B. Y. Scott treated the OT words for rain, along with other weather terminology, in their meteorological context.[2] Since only a single page was given over to defining the senses of the various words for rain,[3] a lack of precision is not surprising. For example, questions as to the difference between *māṭār* and *gešem*, if there is any, are not addressed. Four years latter P. Reymond discussed the OT vocabulary for rain as part of a broader treatment of the significance of water in the OT.[4] While six pages are given over to rain, only two

---

[1] A. Fitzgerald, *The Lord of the East Wind* (unpublished manuscript) xii.

[2] R. B. Y. Scott, "Meteorological Phenomena and Terminology in the Old Testament," *ZAW* 64 (1952) 11–25.

[3] Scott, "Terminology," 23.

[4] P. Reymond, *L'eau, sa vie, et sa signification dans l'Ancien Testament* (VTSup 6; Leiden: Brill, 1958).

focus on the senses of the various words.[5] And all the reader is told about *gešem*, e.g., is that it, like *māṭār*, has a "very general sense."[6] In 1970 L. Stadelmann dealt with the vocabulary for rain in *The Hebrew Conception of the World*, but his analysis does not cover the complete domain of rain and has other shortcomings.[7] More recently H.-J. Zobel analyzed the words in the semantic domain of rain as part of an article on *māṭār*.[8] This is the best treatment to date, but several problems remain.[9]

The semantic domain under examination here is the narrow field of rain proper, so words for other kinds of precipitation, e.g., *bārād* ("hail") and *šeleg* ("snow"), are excluded. Included are: *māṭār* (38x), *gešem* (35x), *zerem* (9x), *malqôš* (8x), *ṭal* (perhaps 10x with the sense of rain), *rĕbîbîm* (6x), *môreh* (3x), *yôreh* (2x), *zarzîp* (1x), *sagrîr* (1x), *sĕpîaḥ* (1x), *śĕʿîrîm* (1x), and *šeṭep* (1x with the sense of rain).[10]

The Relation of *māṭār* and *gešem*

A distinction is commonly made between the senses of *māṭār* and *gešem*, *māṭār* being taken as the general term for "normal" rain, while *gešem* is understood as a specialized term for "abnormal" rain, i.e., heavy or violent rain. Commenting on Gen 7:12, E. A. Speiser translates *gešem* by "heavy rain" and says, "Heb. *gešem*, unlike *māṭār*, signifies abnormal rainfall."[11] No supporting evidence is given. Other commentators offer the same sense for *gešem* and support their comment simply by quoting Speiser.[12]

[5] P. Reymond, *L'eau*, 22–23.

[6] P. Reymond, *L'eau*, 22.

[7] L. Stadelmann, *The Hebrew Conception of the World* (AnBib 39; Rome: Pontifical Biblical Institute, 1970) 114–26. As will be shown Stadelmann misconstrues the relation between *māṭār* and *gešem*, and misunderstands the sense of *rĕbîbîm*.

[8] H.-J. Zobel, *"māṭār,"* TWAT 4 (1984) 827–42; the first part of the article is devoted to the various words for rain (pp. 827–31).

[9] The term *ṭal*, which I will argue is used in the sense of "rain" as well as the traditionally understood "dew," is omitted; an unwarranted distinction is drawn between *māṭār* and *gešem*; *sagrîr* is inadequately nuanced.

[10] *ʿărîpîm* (Isa 5:30) may be a term for rain, but difficulties in the text preclude establishing the sense of this word.

[11] E. A. Speiser, *Genesis* (AB 1; Garden City, NY: Doubleday, 1964) 53.

[12] C. Westermann, *Genesis 1–11: A Commentary* (trans. J. Scullion; Minneapolis, MN: Augsburg, 1984) 392; G. Wenham, *Genesis 1–15* (WBC 1; Waco, TX: Word, 1987) 181.

The standard lexica also seem to distinguish *māṭār* from *gešem*. While they gloss *māṭār* with the unqualified "rain,"[13] they qualify *gešem* in various ways: "downpour" > "rain,"[14] "rain, especially violent or prolonged,"[15] "rain, shower."[16]

H.-J. Zobel maintains that the semantic content of *gešem* is easily distinguished from that of *māṭār*. The distinction offered is that *gešem*, in addition to parallel uses with *māṭār*, is used for winter rains.[17]

The following considerations, however, lead to the conclusion that *māṭār* and *gešem* are absolute synonyms,[18] i.e., the two words are interchangeable in all contexts, the sense of each term itself consistently being "rain." (1) Both *māṭār* and *gešem* are used as terms for rain in general. (a) The lack of rain in general as the result of sin is expressed in terms of no *māṭār* or no *gešem*. In 1 Kgs 8:35 Solomon prays, "When the sky is shut up *wĕlōʾ yihyeh māṭār* ("and there is no rain") because they have sinned against you. . . ." Jer 14:1-9 is an oracle concerning drought (v. 1). The drought is the result of sin (v. 7) and is expressed in v. 4 with the same vocabulary as in 1 Kgs 8:35 except for the substitution of *gešem* for *māṭār* — *lōʾ hāyâ gešem* ("there is no rain").

(b) Rain in general is referred to throughout the narrative unit 1 Kings 17-18,[19] sometimes by *māṭār* and sometimes by *gešem* with no difference in sense. The crisis that sets the narrative in motion is this word from Elijah: "Over the next few years there will be neither dew nor *māṭār* except at my word" (17:1). Elijah then goes into hiding in Wadi Cherith, and his word comes true: "After a period of time, the wadi dried up, since there was no *gešem* in the land" (17:7). Moving on to Zarephath, Elijah encounters the widow to whom he gives this

---

[13] *HALAT*, 544, "rain;" F. Zorell, *Lexicon hebraicum et aramaicum Veteris Testamenti* (Rome: Pontifical Biblical Institute, 1963) 430, "rain;" BDB, 564, "rain."

[14] *HALAT*, 197.

[15] F. Zorell, *Lexicon*, 160.

[16] BDB, 177.

[17] Zobel, "*māṭār*," 828.

[18] I am using "synonym" to refer to "words that overlap in sense;" see M. Silva, *Biblical Words and Their Meaning: An Introduction to Lexical Semantics* (Grand Rapids, MI: Zondervan, 1983) 121.

[19] S. DeVries, *1 Kings* (WBC 12; Waco, TX: Word, 1985) 211–19, understands the Elijah versus Baal unit to be 17:1–16; 18:1–18, 41–46 rather than the whole of chaps. 17–18. But this issue is moot for my purpose, because the shifting of vocabulary from *māṭār* to *gešem* all takes place within the narrative as delineated by DeVries.

promise: "The jar of flour will not run out and the jug of oil will not run dry until the day the LORD gives *gešem* on the land" (17:14). After three years the story takes a turn at this word from the Lord to Elijah: "Go show yourself to Ahab, that I might send *māṭār* on the land" (18:1). Finally the initial crisis of no *māṭār* (17:1) is resolved with the coming of *gešem* (18:41, 44, 45).

(c) The rain in general that results from Israel's covenant loyalty and fructifies the land is referred to by *māṭār* or *gešem* with no difference in sense. "If you carefully obey my commands . . . *wěnātattî ʾarṣěkem běʿittô* ("I will give rain to your land in its time") and you will gather your grain, your new wine, and your oil" (Deut 11:13-14). "If . . . you obey my commands . . . *wěnātattî gišmêkem běʿittām* ("I will give rain to you in its time") and the land will yield its produce" (Lev 26:3-4). Both texts use *wěnātattî* + noun for rain + genitive for the dative[20] + *běʿitt* + suffix. The same slot is filled in one case by *māṭār*, in the other by *gešem* with no difference in sense.

(d) The generic and synonymous sense of *māṭār* and *gešem* is also clear from their identical collocation with *běʿittô/ām* ("in its/their time"). "I will give *māṭār* to your land *běʿittô*, both the fall rain and the spring rain" (Deut 11:14; see also Deut 28:12). "Let us fear the LORD our God, who gives *gešem*, fall rain and spring rain, *běʿittô* (Jer 5:24; see also Ezek 34:26). Collocated with *běʿittô/ām* the scope of both *māṭār* and *gešem* is extended to include the fall rain and the spring rain.

(e) As is clear from the two previous texts, both *māṭār* and *gešem* are used as general terms for the more specific *malqôš* (fall rain) and *yôreh/môreh* (spring rain).[21]

(2) Neither *māṭār* nor *gešem* has the lexical sense "heavy rain," or the like, but both are used to refer to heavy rain when further qualified. For example, one who oppresses the poor is like a *māṭār sōḥēp* ("a driving rain") that destroys crops (Prov 28:3). Here *māṭār* itself signifies nothing more than "rain;" the added signification, "driving," comes from the added qualifier, *sōḥēp*. Similarly, *gešem* refers to heavy rain when qualified. Ezekiel refers to "torrential rain" (*gešem šōṭēp*,

---

[20] P. Joüon and T. Muraoka, *A Grammar of Biblical Hebrew* (subsidia biblica 14; Rome: Pontifical Biblical Institute, 1991) §129h.

[21] See below under "Sense distinctions based on time of year."

Ezek 13:11, 13; 38:22), the psalmist refers to "abundant rain" (*gešem nĕdābôt*, Ps 68:10), and Elijah refers to the "sound of heavy rain" (*qôl hămôn haggāšem*,[22] 1 Kgs 18:41) that is a harbinger of "heavy rain" (*gešem gādôl*, 1 Kgs 18:45). So both *māṭār* and *gešem* when further qualified in context are used to refer to the heavy rains of severe storms,[23] but neither has the lexical sense "heavy rain."

(3) Forms of *mṭr* and *gšm* are collocated in ways that are most readily explicable if there is no difference in sense. (a) First to consider are *māṭār* and *gešem* collocated with the hiphil of *mṭr*. In Isa 5:6 *māṭār* is used as the cognate internal accusative[24] of the hiphil of *mṭr*. The Lord threatens to command the clouds not to let their rain fall on his vineyard (*wĕ'al he'ābîm 'ăṣawweh mēhamṭîr 'ālāyw māṭār*). Given that the result will be the vineyard become a waste land (v. 6), the rain in view is that of an entire year or more. In Ezek 38:22 *gešem* is the non-cognate internal accusative[25] of the hiphil of *mṭr*. The Lord promises to execute judgment on Gog: "I will pour down torrential rain on him" (*wĕgešem šôṭēp . . . 'amṭîr 'ālāyw*). As shown above, the sense of *gešem* here is simply "rain;" the nuance "torrential" stems from the added *šôṭēp*.[26] In Isa 5:6 and Ezek 38:22 there is no difference in sense between *himṭîr māṭār* and *himṭîr gešem*.

In Amos 4:7 the Lord says, "I also withheld rain (*gešem*) from you . . . I sent rain (*himṭartî*) on one city, but on another city I did not send rain (*lō' himṭartî*). . . ." The implicit direct object of the hiphil of *mṭr* is the non-cognate internal accusative, *gešem*. There is no difference in sense between *māna'tî . . . gešem* ("I withheld rain") and *lō' himṭartî* ("I did not send rain").

(b) Second to consider are the construct chains *mĕṭar gešem* (Zech 10:1) and *gešem miṭrôt* (Job 37:6). The MT of Job 37:6 reads *kî laššeleg yō'mar hĕwē' 'āreṣ wĕgešem māṭār wĕgešem miṭrôt 'uzzô*. The first

---

[22] Since at this point in the narrative (v. 41) not even a small cloud could be seen on the horizon (see v. 43), *qôl hămôn haggāšem* probably refers to the sound of the wind that blows before the onset of a storm.

[23] Such storms are most frequent at the beginning and end of the rainy season; see E. Orni and E. Ephrat, *Geography of Israel* (Jerusalem: Israel University Press, 1976) 147.

[24] B. Waltke and M. O'Connor, *An Introduction to Biblical Hebrew Syntax* (Winona Lake, IN: Eisenbrauns, 1990) §10.2.1g.

[25] Waltke and O'Connor, *Syntax*, §10.2.1g.

[26] See 2) above.

colon is easily rendered, "For to the snow he says, 'Fall[27] to the earth'."[28] The second colon, however, is problematic. *wĕgešem māṭār* is probably a dittography.[29] *gešem miṭrôt ʿuzzô* can then be understood as filling the same slot as is filled by *šeleg* in the previous colon and as having the sense "his heavy, drenching rain"[30] This sense would derive from understanding the construct chain *gešem miṭrôt* as the genitive for the intensive/superlative[31] further modified by *ʿuzzô* ("his strength"). *gešem miṭrôt* as "the rainiest of rains" or "drenching rain" would be a singular noun in construct with a synonymous plural for the intensive/superlative. This construction would stand in a mediating position between intensive/superlatives like *šîr haššîrîm* ("the best song," Cant 1:1), where a singular is in construct with the plural of the same noun, and *mibḥar qĕbārênû* ("the best of our graves," Gen 23:6), where a singular is in construct with the plural of a different noun.

The reverse chain *mĕṭar gešem* is used in a similar fashion in Zech 10:1. The audience is instructed to ask the Lord for *māṭār* in the spring and is assured that the Lord is the one who sends *mĕṭar gešem*. *mĕṭar gešem* is the singular of one noun in construction with the singular of a second noun to express the intensive/superlative,[32] and is best rendered with a phrase like "pouring rain."[33] The use of *mĕṭar gešem* (Zech 10:1) and the reversed *gešem miṭrôt* (Job 37:6) with the same sense, "heavy rain," argues for the two terms being interchangeable.

The evidence does not warrant making any distinction between the

---

[27] For this sense of *hĕwēʾ* see *HALAT*, 231, I *hwh*.

[28] See the *NAB* and the *NRSV*.

[29] Several MSS omit *wĕgešem māṭār*, and the Syriac does not translate *gešem miṭrôt*; see J. Hartley, *The Book of Job* (Grand Rapids, MI: Eerdmans, 1988), 478; see also N. H. Tur-Sinai, *The Book of Job: A New Commentary* (Jerusalem: Kiryat Sepher, 1967) 509. The *NAB* presumes this dittography. The *NRSV* retains *wĕgešem māṭār* and takes *gešem miṭrôt ʿuzzô* as explanatory: "the shower of rain, his heavy shower of rain." Retaining *gešem māṭār* would provide a better parallel to *māṭār gešem* than does *gešem miṭrôt* but is not essential for the present argument.

[30] So the *NAB*. The *NRSV* renders *gešem miṭrôt ʿuzzô* by "his heavy shower of rain."

[31] Waltke and O'Connor, *Syntax*, §9.5.3j; Joüon and Muraoka, *Grammar*, §129k.

[32] For the intensive/superlative expressed by a singular noun in construction with a second singular noun see *rāʿat rāʿatkem* ("your utter wickedness," *NAB*, Hos 10:15) and *GKC* §133i.

[33] So the *NAB*.

sense of *māṭār* and *gešem*.[34] Both terms simply mean rain in general, and more specific nuances are owing to additional contextual elements.[35]

Sense Distinctions Based on Time of Year

While "synonym" is a familiar term,[36] the terms "superordinate," "hyponym," and "cohyponym" have not graced the titles of many articles in biblical studies.[37] What the terms lack in felicity, however, they gain in precision.[38] "Hyponomy" refers to the inclusive relations between the senses of genus and species, e.g., the relation between the senses of "dog," "collie," and "schnauzer." "Dog" includes "collie" and "schnauzer;" "dog" is the superordinate of "collie" and "schnauzer;" "collie" and "schnauzer" are hyponyms of "dog;" "collie" is a cohyponym of "schnauzer," and vice versa. Hebrew has three words inclusively/hyponymously related to *māṭār* and *gešem*: *malqôš, môreh,* and *yôreh*.[39]

[34] I agree with P. Cotterell and M. Turner that "Absolute synonymy hardly ever occurs (for there is little point in a language retaining two words with exactly the same range of senses, connotations, habitual collocations, and social register);" see P. Cotterell and M. Turner *Linguistics and Biblical Interpretation* (Downers Grove, IL: Intervarsity, 1989) 159; see also M. Silva, *Biblical Words*, 121, n. 6. It is possible that *māṭār* and *gešem* could have had some different senses at an earlier point in the history of the language or even that there were differences in Biblical Hebrew. The burden of the above argument is that the extant literature does not warrant our making any distinction between the senses of the two words.

[35] *HALAT*, 197, understands the plural of *gešem* in Ezra 10:9 as "down pour" and in Ezra 10:13 as "rainy season." While the *NRSV* renders *gĕšāmîm* in 10:9 by "heavy rain," nothing in the context warrants such a nuance, and it would not take heavy rain to make a crowd in Jerusalem uncomfortable on the twentieth day of the ninth month (v. 9), i.e., in early December. Ezra 10:13 does use *gĕšāmîm* in the expression "rainy season," but the sense of "season" comes from *hāʿēt* ("the time"), with which *gĕšāmîm* is in apposition.

[36] Though a familiar term, "synonym(ous)" is, nevertheless, often used imprecisely, resulting in confusion; see M. Silva, *Biblical Words*, 121–22.

[37] For one example, see D. Tsumura, "A 'Hyponymous' Word Pair: *ʾarṣ* and *thm(t)* in Hebrew and Ugaritic," *Bib* 69 (1988) 258–69.

[38] See J. Lyons, *Semantics* (2 vols.; Cambridge: Cambridge University, 1977) 1.291–95; M. Silva, *Biblical Words*, 126–29; and Cotterell and Turner, *Linguistics*, 157–58.

[39] *môreh* and *yôreh* are biforms from II *yrh*, "give to drink;" see *HALAT*, 386, 416, 531; and S. Wagner, "*yārâ* II," *TDOT* 6 (1990) 337.

The senses of *malqôš*, *môreh*, and *yôreh* are correlated with the time of year during which the rain referred to by each word falls. This can be established by their use with *ʿēt* ("time"). In Zech 10:1 the audience is instructed to ask the Lord for rain (*māṭār*) *bĕʿēt malqôš* ("in the time of *malqôš*"). In Deut 11:14aα the Lord promises to send rain (*māṭār*) *bĕʿittô* ("in its time"); what this time is finds clarification in v. 14aβ by the addition of *yôreh ûmalqôš*.[40] While use establishes a general temporal sense, nothing in the use establishes the precise sense of *môreh* and *yôreh* as "fall rain" or of *malqôš* as "spring rain."

For the precise sense of *malqôš* as "spring rain" we are cast upon etymology.[41] *malqôš* is related to Arabic *laqasa* ("to be late"), Aramaic *lqaš* ("to do x late"), and Hebrew *leqeš*, which has the sense "late/spring grass."[42] Since use has established a general temporal sense for *malqôš*, etymology can be safely drawn upon to provide the further precision "late/spring rain."

The precise sense of *yôreh* and *môreh* as "fall rain" can be established by their use with *malqôš*. *yôreh* occurs only twice, both times in the expression *yôreh ûmalqôš* (Deut 11:14; Jer 5:24). Similarly, *môreh* occurs in the expression *môreh ûmalqôš* (Joel 2:23). The fixed order in the expressions is owing to the fixed order in the annual cycle of the rains: first comes *yôreh/môreh* then, *malqôš*.[43] The fixed order and the opposition of *yôreh/môreh* to *malqôš* warrants the precise sense of "fall rain" for *yôreh/môreh*.[44]

---

[40] In Jer 24:5 the Lord sends rain (*gešem*) *bĕʿittô*, the sense of which is then specified by *yôreh ûmalqôš*.

[41] While synchronic considerations have the priority in determining the sense of a term, there are times when diachronic considerations must be brought into play; see M. Silva, *God, Language, and Scripture: Reading the Bible in Light of General Linguistics* (Foundations of Contemporary Interpretation 4; Grand Rapids, MI: Zondervan, 1990) 66 and 87.

[42] See *HALAT*, 509; and G. Dalman, *Arbeit und Sitte in Palästina* (7 vols.; Gütersloh: Evangelischer Verlag, 1928–42) 1.411–12.

[43] An analogy is provided by the fixed order in the expression "grain, wine, and oil," e.g., Deut 11:14, which is owing to the fixed order in the agricultural cycle: first the grain is harvested, then the grapes, and finally the olives; see M. Futato, "A Meteorological Analysis of Psalms 104, 65, and 29" (Ph.D. diss., The Catholic University of America, Washington, D.C., 1984) 42–44.

[44] Double entendre is at work in Joel 2:23a, where *hammôreh liṣdāqâ* means first "the teacher of truth," and second "the early rain in abundance;" see the work of a stu-

The expression *yôreh/môreh ûmalqôš* is consistently used to add specificity to the general terms *māṭār* (Deut 11:14) and *gešem* (Jer 5:24; Joel 2:23), thus establishing the hyponymous relations: *yôreh/môreh* and *malqôš* are hyponyms of the synonymous superordinates *māṭār* and *gešem*, and are thus cohyponyms.

Sense Distinctions Based on Intensity

Hebrew has two words for rain in general (*māṭār* and *gešem*) and three words for distinct kinds of rain based on the time of year during which the rain falls (*yôreh*, *môreh*, and *malqôš*). The intensity of the rain is not part of the semantic content of any of these words. Hebrew has eight words with sense distinctions based on the intensity of the rain that falls.

Words for "Heavy Rain"

The most frequent word for heavy rain is *zerem*. *zerem* occurs in contexts which require the sense "heavy rain." One such use is in Isa 30:30. The meteorology of Isa 30:27-33 has already been analyzed by A. Fitzgerald in *Lord of the East Wind*.[45] The text describes the coming of the wrath of God as a combined sirocco-rain storm theophany.[46] In v. 30 the arm of the Lord descends with furious wrath (*zaʿap ʾap*), lightning (*lahab ʾēš ʾôkēlâ*),[47] a cloud burst (*nepeṣ*),[48] *zerem*, and hail stones. In this context *zerem* as a manifestation of the wrath of God cannot have the sense "light rain." A sense like "down pour" is required.

An analogous use of *zerem* is found in Hab 3:10. Hab 3:2-19, like Isa 30:27-33, describes the wrath of God in terms of a combined sirocco-rain storm theophany.[49] Verses 8-11 and vv. 12-15 describe a rainstorm

---

dent of A. Fitzgerald: K. Nash, "The Palestinian Agricultural Year and the Book of Joel" (Ph.D. diss., The Catholic University of America, Washington, D.C., 1989) 105–6, 127–28.

[45] Fitzgerald, *East Wind*, 100–104.

[46] Verses 27–28 — sirocco; vv. 30–31 — rain storm; v. 33 — sirocco; see Fitzgerald, *East Wind*, 102–3.

[47] For *lahab ʾēš ʾôkēlâ* as lightning see Fitzgerald, *East Wind*, 252–57.

[48] BDB, 658.

[49] Fitzgerald, *East Wind*, 104–20.

that will destroy the enemy: this storm is accompanied by lightning (v. 11) and has wind strong enough to blow away[50] the warriors (v. 14). The mountains, where the heaviest rains fall,[51] see this storm theophany and tremble (v. 10aα). Then we read *zerem mayim ʿābār* (v. 10aβ). If the MT is correct, *zerem* used with *ʿbr* would be used by metonymy for a torrent of ground water that results from the falling of torrential rain. It may be better, however, to emend the text to *zōrĕmû mayim ʿābôt* ("clouds poured down water") in light of *zōrĕmû mayim ʿābôt* in Ps 77:18.[52] In either reading *zrm* has "heavy rain" in view.

The sense "heavy rain" explains the use of *zerem* in other texts. There are several texts where shelter must be sought because of the intensity of the rain, e.g., Isa 25:4, where the Lord is said to have been a "a shelter from the heavy rain" (*maḥseh mizzerem*; see also Isa 4:6 and 32:2). In Isa 28:2 the Assyrian king[53] is said to be "strong and powerful" (*ḥāzāq wĕʾammîṣ*) and is immediately likened to a *zerem bārād* ("a hailstorm"). Since the adjectives *ḥāzāq wĕʾammîṣ* correlate with *zerem*, a severe storm is in view.

The noun *šeṭep* occurs 6x. The primary sense is "flood."[54] But in Job 38:25 Job is asked if he knows who cuts (*plg*) a channel (*tĕʿālâ*) for the *šeṭep*. Since *šeṭep* here is parallel to *ḥāzîz qōlôt* ("cloud of thunder"[55]) and comes to earth through a channel, as does the rain in Ps 65:10,[56] *šeṭep* is here used by metonymy for heavy rain.[57]

Hebrew has three other words for heavy rain, each occurring one time. *sagrîr* is used only in Prov. 27:15, where a quarrelsome wife is

---

[50] Verse 14 is extremely difficult. Following the initial reference to God piercing the head of the enemy, *przw ysʿrw* should refer to something negative experienced by the enemy. Read *yĕsōʿărû*; see *HALAT*, 720; and Fitzgerald, *East Wind*, 107, 109.

[51] See D. Baly, *The Geography of the Bible* (New York: Harper, 1957) 53–66. Note also the expression *zerem hārîm* in Job 24:8, which would refer to the heavy rains of the mountains.

[52] The suggested emendation finds support in the use of *ntn qwl* for "thunder" immediately following *zōrĕmû mayim ʿābôt* in both texts.

[53] Either Shalmaneser or Sargon II; see J. Watts, *Isaiah 1–33* (WBC 24; Waco, TX: Word, 1985) 362–63.

[54] *HALAT*, 1367; BDB, 1009.

[55] Zobel, "*māṭār*," 830; *HALAT*, 290, "thunder clap."

[56] The channel in Ps 65:10 is referred to by *peleg*; see Futato, "Analysis," 175–76.

[57] Zorell, *Lexicon*, 837, "meton. violent storm."

likened to rain that constantly drips through the roof and into the house. Such a constant dripping could only be the result of heavy rain.[58]

sĕpîaḥ is used only in Job 14:19, where God's power to destroy hope is likened to the power of water to erode stone (*ʾăbānîm šāḥăqû mayim*) and to the power of *sĕpîaḥ* to wash away soil (*tištōp-sĕpîḥêyhā ʿăpar-ʾāreṣ*). The translation of *sĕpîaḥ* here by "floods" (*NAB*) or "torrents" (*NRSV*) may be based on an emendation to *sĕpîaḥ*, supported by Arabic *saḥîfah* ("torrential rain").[59] We have met *shp* in the expression *māṭār sōḥēp* ("a driving rain;" Prov. 28:3) and the semantic shift "torrential rain" > "torrent" in the expression *zerem mayim ʿābār* ("a torrent of water passed by;" Hab 3:10), so this emendation and interpretation are credible. The MT may, however, be correct, and *sĕpîaḥ* may be a noun with the sense "torrential rain" or the extended sense "torrent."[60] In either reading the rain in view must be heavy enough to cause erosion.

śĕ ʿîr is used only in Deut 32:2 as one of four words for precipitation to which Moses' teaching is likened: his sayings are like *śĕ ʿîrim* on new grass. The sense "heavy rain" is probable but not certain, since the primary evidence is the etymological connection of *śĕ ʿîr* to *saʿar* ("storm").[61]

Words for "Light Rain"

There is a wide divergence of opinion on the sense of *rĕbîbîm*: "spring rain,"[62] "heavy rain,"[63] or "light rain."[64] "Spring rain"[65] is not possi-

---

[58] See Dalman, *Arbeit und Sitte*, 1.189.

[59] See D. Clines, *Job 1–20* (WBC 17; Waco, TX: Word, 1989) 284–85, who, however, disputes the Arabic etymology.

[60] *sĕpîaḥ* would be related to Arabic *safaḥa* ("pour out"); see Zorell, *Lexicon*, 559; and M. Futato, "*sĕpîaḥ*" in *The New International Dictionary of Old Testament Theology* (ed. W. VanGemeren; Grand Rapids, MI: Zondervan, 1997) 3.280.

[61] See *HALAT*, 1250; and N. Snaith, "The Meaning of 'ś^eʿîrim'," *VT* 25 (1975) 116.

[62] Scott, "Terminology," 23; Stadelmann, *Hebrew Conception*, 116.

[63] BDB, 914; Snaith, "*ś^eʿîrim*," 116.

[64] Reymond, *L'eau*, 22; T. Hartmann, "*rab*," *THAT* 2 (1976) 722–23.

[65] The collocation *rĕbîbîm ûmalqôš* (Jer 3:3) lies at the root of *rĕbîbîm* = "spring rain." But the collocation is better understood as "light rain (in general, that is more typical of the fall and spring rains than of the heavy rains of December through February) and (in particular) spring rain;" see below.

ble based on the use in Ps 65:11 — "You moistened its furrows, smoothed its ridges, softened it with rĕbîbîm, blessed its new growth." Here rĕbîbîm refers to the fall rains that soften the soil hardened by five months of drought and that allow for plowing and planting.[66] "Heavy rain" is based on the presumed etymology from I rbb ("numerous/much/many").[67]

While certainty is not possible, both synchronic and diachronic considerations lead to the conclusion that the sense of rĕbîbîm is "light rain." Synchronically, one text that sheds some light on the intensity of rĕbîbîm is Mic 5:7, where the remnant of Jacob is likened to dew and to rĕbîbîm on grass, which dissipate quickly. Both the parallel with dew and the quick dissipation would indicate that "light rain" is in view. A second text is Ps 72:6, where the righteous king is compared to rĕbîbîm in the expression kirbîbîm zarzîp ʿāreṣ. zarzîp is hapax and problematic. If zarzîp is retained, zarzîp ʿāreṣ ("a dripping on the earth") in apposition to rĕbîbîm would seem to favor the sense "light rain" for rĕbîbîm. If, however, zarzîp is emended to zirzĕpû ("sprinkle"),[68] the sense of rĕbîbîm would still seem to be "light rain." The text seems to refer to the slow steady rains that fructify the land.[69]

Diachronically, rĕbîbîm as "light rain" seems to be anticipated at Ugarit in the word rbb. In CTA 3.2.38-41 Anat washes herself in ṭl ("dew") and rbb. Because of the use of rbb with ṭal, J. C. de Moor understands the sense of rbb to be "rain-like dew."[70] L. Grabbe has rightly criticized de Moor for offering no evidence for this sense.[71] The use of rbb with ṭl at Ugarit and in the OT is, however, significant, but in the opposite direction from that taken by de Moor. As in Mic 5:7, cited above, the juxtapositioning of rbb with ṭl would seem to favor

---

[66] See Futato, "Analysis," 176; Zobel, māṭār, 830.

[67] The etymological connection with I rbb is the only evidence offered by Stadelmann, Hebrew Conception, 116; HALAT, 1099, says the etymology is uncertain.

[68] So H.-J. Kraus, Psalmen (BKAT 14/1-2; 2nd ed.; Neukirchen: Neukirchener Verlag, 1972) 656; and HALAT, 272.

[69] One might argue that Ps 65:11, cited above, requires "heavy rain" to soften the soil, but the initial downpours tend to run off more than soak in. The slow steady rains are the most effective softeners.

[70] J. C. de Moor, New Year with the Canaanites and Israelites (2 parts; Kampen: Kok, 1972) 1.6, 2.11.

[71] L. Grabbe, "The Seasonal Pattern and the 'Baal Cycle'," UF 8 (1976) 61.

the sense "dew-like rain" or "light rain" at Ugarit.[72] At the other end of the temporal continuum is *rĕbîbîm* with the sense "light rain" in Modern Hebrew.[73]

The semantic range of *ṭal* includes "light rain"[74] as well as "dew," as has been recognized by some lexicographers,[75] though not by all.[76] Translators (e.g., the *NAB*, *NRSV*, and *NIV*) have not recognized "light rain" as part of the range of *ṭal*, as they have translated every occurrence with "dew." It remains to identify the texts where "light rain" is the sense.[77]

The first text[78] is Deut 32:2, "May my teaching drip (*yaʿărōp*) like *māṭār* and my word trickle (*tizzal*) like *ṭal*, like *śĕʿîrim* on new grass, and like *rĕbîbîm* on green plants." Both the use of *ṭal* as a parallel term with three other words for rain, and its collocation with the verb *nzl*, which is elsewhere used for the falling of rain (see Job 36:28) argue for the sense "rain" here.[79]

A second text is Prov 3:20, "by his knowledge the deeps were divided, and the clouds dripped *ṭal*." Arguments for *ṭal* as rain here include the following: (1) *ṭal* is collocated with the verb *rʿp*, which is elsewhere used for the falling of rain (see Job 36:28). (2) *ṭal* falls from

---

[72] "Drizzle" is the sense of *rbb* in CTA 3.2.39 according to J. Aistleitner, *Wörterbuch der Ugaritischen Sprache* (Berlin: Akademie Verlag, 1967) 286.

[73] R. Sivan and E. Levenston, *The Megiddo Modern Dictionary* (2nd ed.; Tel Aviv: Megiddo Publishing, 1975) 626.

[74] The sense *light* rain is based on the use of *ṭal* as a parallel term for *rĕbîbîm* in Hebrew and Ugaritic (see above), and the fact that *ṭal* is used for dew, a modest amount of water.

[75] *HALAT*, 358–59, gives "dew, soft rain," but lists no specific texts where "soft rain" is the sense. Zorell, *Lexicon*, 284, says "the word in its broader sense includes rain," and lists Isa 18:4; Gen 27:28, 39; Deut 33:28; Zech 8:12; and Prov 3:20 as examples. See also J. Katsnelson, "Dew," *EncJud*, 5.1601, "It should be noted, however, that in Biblical Hebrew *ṭl* may also refer to rain."

[76] BDB, 378, does not give "(light) rain" as part of the range of *ṭal*. Zobel, "*māṭār*," *TWAT*, 827; Scott, "Terminology," 23; and Reymond, *L'eau*, 18–24; do not include *ṭal* in the semantic domain of "rain."

[77] See M. Futato, "*ṭal*," in *The New International Dictionary of Old Testament Theology* (ed. W. VanGemeren; Grand Rapids, MI: Zondervan, 1997) 2.363–64.

[78] This text is not included in Zorell's list.

[79] In Deut 33:28 *ṭal* is collocated with *ʿrp*, which is also used for the falling of *māṭār* in Deut 32:2.

šĕḥāqîm, which are rain clouds, as is clear from Job 36:28, where šĕḥāqîm appears in the context of a rain storm (vv. 27-30).[80] (3) ṭal is contrasted with tĕhômôt. In the context of v. 19, which speaks of the initial setting in place of the earth and the heavens, tĕhômôt would correlate with terrestrial waters and ṭal with celestial waters or rain.[81]

A third text is Hos 14:6. In the broader context Israel's covenant loyalty is like ṭal/dew which disappears quickly (6:4), so with poetic justice Israel will disappear quickly like ṭal/dew (13:3). But this is not the final word, for in poetic mercy the Lord will be like ṭal to Israel (14:6). Here the sense of ṭal switches to "rain" for the following reasons: (1) The result of the coming of ṭal is the blossoming of the šûšannâ. šûšannâ refers to the same flower as does ḥăbaṣṣālet,[82] which in Isa 35:1 does not bloom in the presence of dew but at the coming of the fall rains, as argued by A. Fitzgerald.[83] 2) The image unfolds in terms of the flourishing of cedars (v. 6), olive trees (v. 7), grain and grapes (v. 8), a flourishing that concords with rain but not dew alone.[84]

To summarize: (1) Hebrew has two words for rain in general, māṭār and gešem. (2) These two are synonymous superordinates of three words for rain distinguished by the time of year during which the rain falls, malqôš, môreh, and yôreh. (3) There are eight words for rain that focus on the intensity of the rain that falls: (a) five used for heavy rain, zerem, šeṭep, sagrîr, sĕpîaḥ, and śĕʿîr, and (b) three used for light rain, rĕbîbîm, zarzîp, and ṭal.

---

[80] Further support that ṭal collocated with clouds is used for "rain" is the fact that dew forms mainly on clear nights when exposed surfaces more readily lose heat by radiation; see J. Neumann, "Dew," Encyclopedia Britannica: Macropeadia, 5.679; and Katsnelson, "Dew," 5.1600.

[81] A striking parallel is Prov 8:27–28, where celestial waters, referred to by šĕḥāqîm, are contrasted with terrestrial waters, referred to by ʿînôt tĕhôm ("springs of the deep").

[82] M. Zohary, Plants of the Bible (Cambridge: Cambridge University, 1982) 176.

[83] Fitzgerald, East Wind, 134, n. 4.

[84] Other texts where ṭal may have the sense "light rain" are Gen 27:28, 39; Deut 33:13, 28; Isa 18:4; Hag 1:10; and Zech 8:12. Space precludes an examination of these texts.

CHAPTER 7

Singing in the Rain:
A Meteorological Image
in Isaiah 42:10–12

JOHN J. FERRIE, JR.

One contribution Aloysius Fitzgerald has made to the study of biblical Hebrew poetry is his analysis of images based on the meteorology of the fall interchange period in ancient Palestine.[1] At that time of year, the long, dry summer comes to a dramatic end in the onset of fierce desert winds, known as the *hamsin* in modern Israel and as the *qādîm* (the "sirocco") in the Bible. They are the harbingers of the vitally important fall rains on which the success of the agricultural cycle depends; to quote a Palestinian proverb, "The east wind brings rain."[2]

In this paper I hope to show that rain is the reason for the "new song" of praise in Isa 42:10-12. Yahweh comes in a rainstorm theophany to prepare the road home from Babylon to Zion in anticipation of the liberation of the people by Cyrus. The image has an emotional appeal based on the exiles' traditions of the fall festival celebrated in their homeland at the time of the advent of the life-giving rain, the feast of Sukkoth. The anonymous author uses the image as part of the

---

[1] A. Fitzgerald, *Lord of the East Wind* (unpublished manuscript).

[2] See J. H. Eaton, "The Origin and Meaning of Habakkuk 3," *ZAW* 76 (1964) 162-63, and G. Dalman, *Arbeit und Sitte in Palästina* (7 vols.; Gütersloh: Evangelischer V., 1928-42) 1.105, 107.

"rhetoric of persuasion," eliciting a nostalgia aimed at convincing the people to undertake the difficult journey home.[3]

I. Sirocco and Rain in Second Isaiah

Second Isaiah has several examples of both sirocco and rain imagery; important as they are for understanding these chapters, here I can point to only a few of the clearest ones.[4] A good example of sirocco imagery is found in 40:7, where the grass and the flowers wilt "for Yahweh's wind (*rûaḥ Yhwh*) has blown on them." In 40:24, the princes and rulers of the earth, conceived of as newly planted crops, wither when Yahweh blows on them and are carried off by the storm wind (*sĕʿārâ*). In 42:14-15, Yahweh's breath, figured as the breath of a woman in labor, withers the vegetation on the hillsides and dries up pools of water. All of these passages describe phenomena characteristic of the sirocco.

On the other hand, rain imagery appears in Isa 41:17-20, where the desert (*midbar*) is turned into pools of water, and trees that normally do not grow there suddenly sprout up. A similar image is found in 43:19b-20; there the animals praise God for the gift of rivers of water in the desert. In 44:3-4a water is once again poured out on the dry land, and the people grow like trees beside channels of water. In 45:8, "salvation" (*yešaʿ*) and justice (*ṣĕdāqâ*) sprout like vegetation when the rains come.

The key image for beginning to understand Isa 42:10-12 occurs at the end of Second Isaiah, in 55:12-13:

---

[3] See Y. Gitay, *Prophecy and Persuasion: A Study of Isaiah 40-48* (Forum theologiae linguisticae 14; Bonn: Linguistica Biblica, 1981) and R. J. Clifford, *Fair Spoken and Persuading: An Interpretation of Second Isaiah* (New York/Ramsey/Toronto: Paulist, 1984).

[4] Both R. Lack, *La symbolique du livre d'Isaïe* (AnBib 59; Rome: Biblical Institute, 1973) and J. H. Eaton, *Festal Drama in Deutero-Isaiah* (London: SPCK, 1979) recognize the importance of rain imagery in these chapters. For more theoretical discussions of imagery, see K. Nielsen, *There is Hope for a Tree: The Tree as Metaphor in Isaiah* (JSOTSup 65; Sheffield, JSOT, 1989) 25-67 and K. P. Darr, *Isaiah's Vision and the Family of God* (Literary Currents in Biblical Interpretation; Louisville: Westminster John Knox, 1994) 36-45.

(12) Yes, in joy you will leave
and you will be led along safely.
The mountains and hills will peal
with ringing sounds before you,
And all the trees of the field
will clap their hands.
(13) Instead of thorns the juniper will grow,
instead of briars the myrtle will grow.

The effectiveness of God's word is compared to the rain coming down and making the earth fertile (Isa 55:10). The mountains and hills are pictured as shouting for joy (*yipṣĕḥû rinnâ*; cf. 44:23; 49:13) at the return of the exiles (Isa 55:12b). Trees grow where they could not before (v. 13). In light of the importance of the comparison in 55:10 and the images in 41:19, 43:19b-20, 44:3-4a and 45:8, Isa 55:12-13 is a rain image.

II. Rain Theophanies in Psalms 96 and 98

To move from Isa 55:12-13 to the image in Isa 42:10-12 requires an excursus through Pss 96 and 98.[5] Language similar to Isa 55:12b is found in Pss 96:12 and 98:9, where nature rejoices at a theophany of Yahweh (Pss 96:13; 98:9) who comes to "order" (*lišpōṭ*) the earth. If the rejoicing of nature in Isa 55:12b is in the context of rain, then the same may be true in Psalms 96 and 98. But nature is called on to praise God in a particular order in these psalms, a sequence of praise that follows the course of a rainstorm theophany.[6] Affinities between the sequence of praise Psalms 96 and 98 with Isa 42:10-12 will indicate that a rainstorm image is likewise operative there.

---

[5] The question of literary dependence cannot be addressed here. I prefer to think of the language and images of the psalms and of Second Isaiah as coming from a common, cultic source; see J. M. Vincent, *Studien zur literarischen Eigenart und zur geistigen Heimat von Jesaja, Kap. 40-55* (Beiträge zur biblischen Exegese und Theologie 5; Frankfurt/Bern/Las Vegas: Lang, 1977) 54.

[6] For a study of the movement of a rainstorm in Psalm 29, see M. Futato, "A Meteorological Analysis of Psalms 104, 65, and 29" (Ph.D. diss., Washington: The Catholic University of America, 1984) 204-55.

The images that connect Isa 55:12b with Psalms 96 and 98 are auditory. In Isa 55:12b, the mountains and hills "peal with ringing sounds" (*yipṣĕḥû rinnâ*) and the "trees of the field" (*ʿăṣê haśśādeh*) "clap their hands" (*yimḥăʾû kāp*). In Ps 98:8, the rivers "clap their hands" (*yimḥăʾû kāp*) and the mountains rejoice (*yĕrannēnû*). In Ps 96:12, the fields exult and the "trees of the forest" (*ʿăṣê yaʿar*; cf. Isa 49:13) rejoice (*yĕrannĕnû*). These are auditory images of the sound of falling rain: a running stream or rain falling on tree leaves does sound like clapping, and wadis newly filled with rain make the mountains and hills echo with their sound.

A closer look at the psalms shows that the sequence of praise found there provides an important clue in understanding that the theophany in those psalms is a rainstorm theophany. The last verses of Psalm 98 describe the movement of an autumn rainstorm moving from the Mediterranean towards and across the Palestinian littoral, the normal track of such storms:

(7)   Let the sea roar, and what fills it,
        the dry land and its inhabitants;
(8)   Let the rivers clap their hands,
        and all the mountains ring out
(9)   Before Yahweh, for he comes
        to order the earth.
        He will order the dry land justly
        and the peoples rightly.

The progress of a rainstorm from west to east is reflected in the sequence of praise in vv. 7-8. As the storm Palestine from the Mediterranean the sea "roars" (v. 7a); the sea and its creatures are imagined to be roaring their praise for Yahweh, but at the same time the auditory images of rain pouring on water and wind stirring up the waves are present. In v. 7b the storm moves east over "dry land." The *tebel* and its inhabitants are also subjects of the jussive *yirʿam*; the storm crashes across the land while the land creatures again roar their praise of Yahweh. In v. 8a the rivers of the littoral, their waters increased by the runoff and tossed by the storm, "clap." The sound of running water in a stream or river or the sound of rain falling on water may at times be similar to the sound of clapping. This becomes the basis for the personification of the rivers as giving praise to Yahweh by clapping. Then in v. 8b the storm moves further east to the mountains. The mountains are likewise personified as ringing out with joy, while the echoing of cataracts of water is the auditory image that forms the basis for the personification.

In Psalm 96 the image works in the same way and in the same context as the rainstorm image in Psalm 98:

(11) Let the sky rejoice, and the earth be glad;
       let the sea and what fills it roar.
(12) Let the fields exult, everything in them,
       then let all the trees of the forest ring out
(13) Before Yahweh, for he comes,
       for he comes to order the earth.
      He will order the dry land justly,
       and the peoples in his faithfulness.

In Ps 96:11a, the "sky" and "earth" represent the created universe, as in Gen 1:1 and especially Gen 2:1, where the phrase sums up all of creation. The storm stirs up the sea (Ps 96:11b), and then passes on to the land where the fields and trees join in the rejoicing. The west to east progression, though the sequence is brief here, is clear. In Ps 96:13, as in Ps 98:9, Yahweh comes to order the land *běsedeq*, "justly," by giving it rain. His "faithfulness" (*bě'ěmûnātô*) refers in part, at least, to Yahweh's having supplied the earth with the first rains every fall in the past, and his reliability to do so again in the future.

III. The Progress of Yahweh's Rain
Theophany in Isa 42:10-12

Like Psalms 98 and 96, Isa 42:10-12 begins with the command to "sing to the Lord a new song":

(10) Sing to Yahweh a new song,
       his praise from the end of the earth.
      Let the sea roar (rd *yir'am hayyām*) and what fills it,
       the coastlands and their inhabitants.
(11) Let the desert and its cities lift up their voices,
       the encampments where Kedar dwells;

> Let the inhabitants of the crags cry out,
> let them shout out from the tops of the mountains!
> (12) Let them give Yahweh glory
> and tell he praise among the coastlands.

There is disagreement among commentators as to the relationship of these verses to the following 42:13-17; some include v. 13 with vv. 10-12.[7] Several stylistic features, however, argue for limiting the unit to vv. 10-12. The five lines of vv. 10-12 (emended) begin with verb forms, all of them volitives. This series ends abruptly at v. 12, suggesting that the break should occur between vv. 12 and 13. Further, there is an inclusion based on the words *lyhwh* ("to Yahweh") and *těhillātô* ("his praise") in vv. 10a and 12b. Finally, the root *yšb* occurs three times in these verses (*wěyōšěbêhem, tēšēb, yōšěbê*), thus reinforcing their cohesiveness.

The sequence of praise in Isa 42:10-12 is more detailed in mentioning both geographical places and their inhabitants than the sequences in the psalms.[8] The sequence of praise in Psalm 98 is sea, dry land, rivers, mountains; in Psalm 96 it is sea, fields, trees. In each psalm the sequence describes the progress of a rainstorm coming from the Mediterranean moving from west to east. In Isa 42:10-12, the sequence is extended in both directions, extending from the far western "end of the earth" (*miqṣēh hāʾāreṣ*, v. 10a) to the coastlands of the eastern sea (*bāʾiyyîm*, v. 12b), but the essential west-to-east progress of the storm is clear, from sea to coastal plain to mountains. Each element in this sequence needs to be examined in detail.[9]

The sequence of praise in Isa 42:10a begins with the "end of the earth," representing, in this case, the far west (cf. 43:5-6). Jer 10:13 gives a picture of a rainstorm in which the clouds arise "from the end of the earth" (cf. Jer 51:16; Ps 135:7). Reymond suggests that the *něśîʾîm* may be thunder-clouds appearing over the horizon as one looks out to

---

[7] See C. Westermann, *Isaiah 40-66: A Commentary* (OTL; Philadelphia: Westminster, 1969) 101-06; Y. Gitay, *Prophecy and Persuasion*, 123-24; and R. F. Melugin, *The Formation of Isaiah 40-55* (BZAW 141; Berlin/New York: de Gruyter, 1976) 98-99, 102.

[8] C. C. Torrey (*The Second Isaiah: A New Interpretation* [New York: Charles Scribner's Sons, 1928] 328) notices the structure in each line from v. 10b to v. 11b of the shout raised first by "a great division of the earth," and then by "its inhabitants."

[9] J. M. Vincent (*Studien*, 51) is wrong in dismissing the precision of these verses as "typical poetic style" with no particular geographical references intended.

sea.[10] This is precisely the picture in Isa 42:10; the rainstorm appears from the west, ascending from the horizon, and is imagined to have begun its course from "the end of the earth." The phrase "the coastlands and their inhabitants" refers to those who dwell in the westernmost Mediterranean coastlands or islands.

The usual emendation of the first half of Isa 42:10b, from *yôrĕdê hayyām* ("those who go down to the sea") to *yirʿam hayyām* ("let the sea roar"), brings the language of this passage even closer to that of the psalms (see Pss 96:11; 98:7). Although there is virtually no textual evidence to support the emendation, it makes better sense with the following *ûmĕlōʾô*, "and its fullness." Psalm 107:23, where the phrase *yôrĕdê hayyām* also occurs, is followed by a description of a storm at sea (vv. 25-26), which could explain the presence of the phrase in Isa 42:10b. At any rate, for the purposes of my argument, either reading establishes the movement of the rainstorm over the sea.

From the far west, across the sea, to the coast—but in Isa 42:11a the rainstorm does not stop in the forested hill country as it does in Ps 98:8. It is typical that ranges of hills tend to wring the moisture out of rainstorms, creating "rain shadows" on their leeward side. A glance at a rainfall map of Palestine reveals that this is precisely what happens there—the hill country on either side of the Jordan receives far more rain than the land to the east.[11] In contrast to ordinary rainstorms, the storm in Isa 42:10-12 continues on into the *midbār*, causing the steppeland east of the hill country "and its cities," "the encampments where Kedar dwells," all to rejoice.[12] The word *midbār* occurs in Isaiah 40-55 eight times (40:3; 41:18, 19; 42:11; 43:19, 20; 50:2; 51:3), and in all of the texts but 50:2 (where its reference is indeterminate) and 51:3 (*midbārâ*, referring to the wilderness around Jerusalem) *midbār* refers to northern Arabia Deserta. The road home crosses this *midbār* (40:3; 43:19); abundant water will be provided for the road through the *midbār* (41:18, 19; 43:20).

---

[10] P. Reymond, *L'eau, sa vie, et sa signification dans l'Ancien Testament* (VTSup 6; Leiden: Brill, 1958) 13, 17. Cf. 1 Kgs 18:44; Lk 12:54.

[11] See the map in H. G. May, *The Oxford Bible Atlas* (2d ed.; London: Oxford, 1974) 51.

[12] J. L. McKenzie (*Second Isaiah* [AB 20; Garden City, NY: Doubleday, 1968] 43) recognizes the movement from the Palestinian littoral to the eastern steppes.

The mention of the Kedarites 42:11ab strengthens the image of the rain theophany moving from west to east. The Kedarites live in tents (Cant 1:5). Their flocks supply sacrificial animals for the Jerusalem temple (Isa 60:6-7). Jer 49:28-29, in an oracle against Arabia, describes them as having tents and camels. The term that parallels Kedar is běnê qedem, "sons of the east." The latter term is used in the OT exclusively for nomads living east of the Jordan.[13] In Jer 2:10 Kedar is opposed to Cyprus (kittiyyîm) to designate east and west. The OT leaves the impression that the Kedarites are a tribe or confederation of tribes of Bedouin, Arab pastoralists whose territory was the northern reaches of the great Arabian desert east of Amman and the strip of agricultural land to the east of the Jordan. Granted the type of life lived by these Bedouin, it is strange to find them described as living in "cities" (42:11aa), but in Assyrian sources they are associated with the oasis of Tema and with Dumah, an oasis town at the end of the Wadi Sirhan on the principal route through the desert from Amman to Babylon. The ʿārîm and ḥăṣērîm where Kedar dwells are probably references to oasis "towns" and unfortified temporary camps.[14] In Isa 42:11a the rainstorm has crossed over the Jordan out into the desert east of Amman.

Crags and mountains are mentioned next in Isa 42:11b. The hill country of the southern or northern Syro-Palestinian littoral is not in the picture here, nor even the mountains of Edom, since the storm has already moved further east. Selaʿ ("craggy land") is thus not Petra, nor any other particular town. The suggestion of R. Levy quoted by Elliger, that what is meant by hārîm is the Zagros Mountains that form the eastern border of Babylonia, is likely correct.[15] The Zagros Mountains marked the border between Babylonia and Elam. This rainstorm has swept far eastward over the desert from the Mediterranean to the mountains of eastern Babylonia.

The second reference to "coastlands" in 42:12 fits this picture. There was an awareness among the Israelites that they existed between two seas; the phrase "from sea to sea" occurs in Ps 72:8, Amos 8:12, and

[13] J. Simons, *The Geographical and Topographical Texts of the Old Testament* (Leiden: Brill, 1959) 13.

[14] See I. Eph'al, *The Ancient Arabs: Nomads on the Borders of the Fertile Crescent, 9th-5th Centuries B. C.* (Jerusalem/Leiden: Magnes/Brill, 1982) 223-27 and K. Elliger, *Deuterojesaja* (BKAT 11/1; Neukirchen-Vluyn: Neukirchener, 1978) 246-47.

[15] K. Elliger, *Deuterojesaja*, 248.

Zech 9:10. Although it is often claimed that the second sea is the Gulf of Aqaba (the first, of course, being the Mediterranean), in Isa 42:12 it seems that the "coastlands" are the shores of the Persian Gulf, a border of Babylon. In fact, southern Babylon stretching along the northwest coast of the Persian Gulf was a marshy region called the "Sealand" by the Babylonians.[16] The view of the known world presented in 42:10-12 as extending from the western edge of the earth (*miqṣēh hā'āreṣ*), the Mediterranean (*hayyām*) and its islands/coastlands (*'iyyîm*, v. 10), to the islands/coastlands (*bā'iyyîm*, v. 12b) at the eastern end of the earth may be a calque of an Akkadian expression: from the upper sea (*tiamtim elītim*, the Mediterranean) to the lower sea (*tiamtim šaplītim*, the Persian Gulf).[17]

This completes the picture of a storm of such range that it begins far out over the western ocean and sweeps across the desert to Babylon and beyond to the eastern ocean, the Persian Gulf. No ordinary Palestinian rainstorm is described in Isa 42:10-12; rather, the author traces the extraordinary range of this storm to make a particular point. The storm moves from the far west to the remote east and includes in its path the road from Babylon to Zion. Yahweh will pass over Zion, creating the garden-like conditions described in Isa 51:3:

> When Yahweh has comforted Zion,
>   has comforted all her ruins,
> When he has made her steppe-land like Eden
>   and her desert like Yahweh's garden,
> Then joy and rejoicing will be found in her,
>   thanksgiving and the sound of song.

On returning home to these (metaphorical) conditions the returnees will flourish like plants with plenty of water (44:1-5). Yahweh will water the desert between Babylon and Zion, making the road safe for travel (49:8-13; 41:17-20; 43:16-21). Then he will arrive at Babylon to lead the people home on the abundantly watered road through the desert to

---

[16] *mat tiamti*, cf. *AHW*, 1354a. The Sealand was the place of origin of the Chaldeans and their dynasty. See J. Oates, *Babylon* (London: Thames and Hudson, 1979) 83, 112, 115-17.

[17] The expression is still attested in neo-Babylonian inscriptions. For texts see *CAD*, E.113 and *AHW*, 1354a.

Zion (49:9b-12; 40:9-11). The language of praise originating in the image of the rainstorm theophany marks his progress (44:23; 49:13; 55:12b).

IV. Conclusion

The imagery of Isa 42:10-12 is, in a sense, "once removed." Though originally used of nature rejoicing at the coming of the fall rains, as in Psalms 96 and 98, it has an added referent here. In these verses the motif of rejoicing at the coming of the rains in the fall has been extended metaphorically to a particular historical event: the liberation of Israel by Cyrus' victory over the Babylonians. But Cyrus is merely Yahweh's agent (41:2-3), the "bird of prey" he has called from the east (46:11). It is the advent of Yahweh, metaphorically described by the rainstorm theophany, and not the will of Cyrus that will result in the release of the people.

The rain theophany image in Isa 42:10-12 functions to evoke an emotional response from its hearers, based on their treasured traditions of the great fall pilgrimage festival in Zion. All that is necessary for agricultural success was provided annually by the coming of the fall rains. All that is required of the people is to have faith sufficient to venture on the return journey, joining the song of renewed creation in praise of God.

CHAPTER 8

Psalm 88:
A Lesson in Lament

IRENE NOWELL

There is a story told of Teresa of Avila who, having one day been unceremoniously dumped in a creek when her carriage turned over, complained to the Lord. He answered her, "This is the way I treat my friends." She snapped back, "It's no wonder you have so few."

The story illustrates a relationship to God which is witnessed frequently in the psalms. Complaining to God, even being angry and demanding, is not only all right, it is necessary if we are ever to have a full, healthy relationship with the living God. Psalm 88 is an example of this kind of prayer, this kind of relationship with God.

I. Genre

Psalm 88 is a lament. Laments are not only complaint; they are a protest to God that things should not be this way. Laments are not only petition; they are insistent demand that God change the situation. Psalm 88 is a lament in this tradition. The blame for the psalmist's distress is laid squarely at the feet of God. Many of the elements found in standard laments are missing. Psalm 88 has a compelling simplicity. God is at once the only enemy and the only hope for rescue. There is just one cry, "Listen." There is no distraction: no claim of innocence or plea for forgiveness. The reasons for the psalmist's distress have to do solely with God. There is no relief in the accusation, no turn to praise and thanksgiving. The psalm ends in darkness.

II. Text and Translation

שִׁיר מִזְמוֹר לִבְנֵי קֹרַח לַמְנַצֵּחַ עַל־מָחֲלַת לְעַנּוֹת מַשְׂכִּיל לְהֵימָן הָאֶזְרָחִי׃ 1

יְהוָה אֱלֹהֵי יְשׁוּעָתִי יוֹם־צָעַקְתִּי בַלַּיְלָה נֶגְדֶּךָ׃ 2

תָּבוֹא לְפָנֶיךָ תְּפִלָּתִי הַטֵּה־אָזְנְךָ לְרִנָּתִי׃ 3

כִּי־שָׂבְעָה בְרָעוֹת נַפְשִׁי וְחַיַּי לִשְׁאוֹל הִגִּיעוּ׃ 4

נֶחְשַׁבְתִּי עִם־יוֹרְדֵי בוֹר הָיִיתִי כְּגֶבֶר אֵין־אֱיָל׃ 5

בַּמֵּתִים חָפְשִׁי כְּמוֹ חֲלָלִים שֹׁכְבֵי קֶבֶר 6

אֲשֶׁר לֹא זְכַרְתָּם עוֹד וְהֵמָּה מִיָּדְךָ נִגְזָרוּ׃

שַׁתַּנִי בְּבוֹר תַּחְתִּיּוֹת בְּמַחֲשַׁכִּים בִּמְצֹלוֹת׃ 7

עָלַי סָמְכָה חֲמָתֶךָ וְכָל־מִשְׁבָּרֶיךָ עִנִּיתָ סֶּלָה׃ 8

הִרְחַקְתָּ מְיֻדָּעַי מִמֶּנִּי שַׁתַּנִי תוֹעֵבוֹת לָמוֹ 9

כָּלֻא וְלֹא אֵצֵא׃ 10 עֵינִי דָאֲבָה מִנִּי עֹנִי

קְרָאתִיךָ יְהוָה בְּכָל־יוֹם שִׁטַּחְתִּי אֵלֶיךָ כַפָּי׃

הֲלַמֵּתִים תַּעֲשֶׂה־פֶּלֶא אִם־רְפָאִים יָקוּמוּ יוֹדוּךָ סֶּלָה׃ 11

הַיְסֻפַּר בַּקֶּבֶר חַסְדֶּךָ אֱמוּנָתְךָ בָּאֲבַדּוֹן׃ 12

הֲיִוָּדַע בַּחֹשֶׁךְ פִּלְאֶךָ וְצִדְקָתְךָ בְּאֶרֶץ נְשִׁיָּה׃ 13

וַאֲנִי אֵלֶיךָ יְהוָה שִׁוַּעְתִּי וּבַבֹּקֶר תְּפִלָּתִי תְקַדְּמֶךָּ׃ 14

לָמָה יְהוָה תִּזְנַח נַפְשִׁי תַּסְתִּיר פָּנֶיךָ מִמֶּנִּי׃ 15

עָנִי אֲנִי וְגֹוֵעַ מִנֹּעַר נָשָׂאתִי אֵמֶיךָ אָפוּנָה׃ 16

עָלַי עָבְרוּ חֲרוֹנֶיךָ בִּעוּתֶיךָ צִמְּתוּתֻנִי׃ 17

סַבּוּנִי כַמַּיִם כָּל־הַיּוֹם הִקִּיפוּ עָלַי יָחַד׃ 18

הִרְחַקְתָּ מִמֶּנִּי אֹהֵב וָרֵעַ מְיֻדָּעַי מַחְשָׁךְ׃ 19

1 Song. Psalm of the sons of Korah. For the director. Concerning the heartsickness of affliction.* *Maskil* of Heman the Ezrahite.

I

2 Yahweh, my saving God,
  by day I cry out,
  by night in your presence.
3 Let my prayer come before you;
  incline your ear to my cry.

4 Indeed my soul is sated with misery;
  my life has drawn near to Sheol.
5 I am reckoned with those who go down to the Pit;
  I am like a man[1] without might.
6 My bed* is among the dead,
  I am like the slain,
  sleepers in the grave.
 Whom you remember no more,
  who are cut off from your hand.

7 You have set me in the lowest Pit,
  in dark places, in the depths.
8 On me your anger lies;
  with all your breakers you humble me.* Selah.
9 You have removed my friends from me;
  you have made me an abomination* to them.
 Imprisoned I cannot escape;*
10 my eye fails me because of affliction.

II

 I call to you, Yahweh, every day,
  I stretch out to you my hands.
11 Do you work wonders for the dead?
  Do the shades rise up to praise you?
12 Is your love recounted in the grave?
  Your fidelity in Abaddon?
13 Are your wonders made known in the dark?
  Your righteousness in the land of forgetting?

---

[1] Ironically, *geber* carries the connotation of strength.

III

14 Yet I, Yahweh, cry out to you;
   in the morning my prayer comes to you.
15 Why, Yahweh, do you reject me?
   Why do you hide your face from me?
16 Afflicted, I have been perishing since my youth.
   I have borne your horrors, I am numb.*
17 Over me have swept your furies;
   Your terrors have silenced me.*
18 They surround me like water all day;
   they close in together against me.
19 You have removed from me
   dear one and neighbor.
   My only friend is darkness.

Textual Notes

v. 1 *māḥalat* is ordinarily transliterated and understood as a melody indication. *ʿal-māḥalat* occurs only one other place, Ps 53:1. Dahood derives it from *ḥwl* and translates "dancing," an odd note in this somber psalm.[2] I suggest it be read as the hiphil participle of *ḥlh*, "to make sick" (cf. Prov 13:12; compare also the noun *maḥălâ*, Exod 15:26; 23:25; 1 Kings 8:37; 2 Chr 6:28). *lĕʿannôt* is commonly translated "for singing" from *ʿnh* IV. The only other occurrence of the piel infinitive of *ʿnh* IV, however, is in Exod 32:18, a dubious text. I propose that *lĕʿannôt* be read as the piel infinitive of *ʿnh* II, "to afflict, oppress, humiliate" (cf. Num 30:14; Judg 16:5-6, 19; 2 Sam 7:10; Isa 58:5). This root is repeated in the psalm: *ʿōnî* (v. 10); *ʿānî* (v. 16). The resulting title certainly fits the content of the psalm.[3]

v. 6 *ḥopšî* appears to be an adjective from *ḥpš*, "to be freed" (pual). BHS proposes *napšî*, "my soul"; or *hušabtî* (*yšb*), "be made to dwell," or *ḥuppašti*, "be searched for." LXX reads *eleutheros*, "free." Syriac reads *br ḥr*, "free." Kraus points out additional suggestions: "set apart" (cf. 2 Kings 15:5), "couch" (cf. Ezek 27:20). He translates "I must dwell" (*muss ich wohnen*).[4] Dahood translates "my cot," based on Ugaritic *ḥptt* and parallel to other descriptions of beds in Sheol (Ps

[2] M. Dahood, *Psalms II: 51–100* (AB 17; Garden City, NY: Doubleday, 1968) 302.

[3] See *KB* (719-720) where this is also suggested. H.-J. Kraus (*Psalmen* [BKAT 15; rev. ed.; Neukirchen-Vluyn: Neukirchener, 1978] 1.22) suggests also that *māḥălat* is derived from the root *ḥlh*, "in affliction," which would fit the content of Pss 53 and 88. Compare the New Jerusalem Bible translation: "In sickness. In suffering."

[4] Kraus, *Psalmen*, 2.771-72.

139:8; Job 17:13; Prov 7:27).[5] Based on *šōkĕbê* in the latter part of the verse, I have opted for "bed." The reading is far from certain.

v. 8 *ʿinnîtā*. The sense of the verse calls for an object, "me." See LXX *eme* (with a different verb); Syr, *ʿly*. Because of the predilection for pronominal suffixes in this psalm, I read *ʿinnîtanî*.[6]

v. 9 *tôʿebôt*. Plural of intensity or state (cf. Joüon, §136f, h).

v. 9 *kālū*. Qal passive participle of *klʾ*, "to restrain, shut up, keep back." Cf. *keleʾ*, "prison."

v. 16 *ʾāpûnâ*. KB interprets as qal imperfect of *pwn*, "be helpless, embarrassed, stiff" (cf. LXX *exēporēthēn*), the only occurrence of *pwn* in the MT. BHK suggests *ʾăpāpûnî* from *ʾpp*, "they encompass me" (cf. the similar context in 2 Sam 22:5 = Ps 18:5; Jonah 2:7; Ps 116:3). Dahood reads "the terrors of your wheel" (cf. *ʾōpan*, "wheel").[7] BHS proposes *ʾāpûgâ* (from *pwg*, "to grow numb," cf. Gen 45:26; Hab 1:4; Ps 77:3). Syriac reads *twrt*, "dazed, shocked, confounded." Parallelism with *ṣmt* in the following verse supports the meaning, "benumbed, dazed."[8] I emend to *ʾāpûgâ*.

v. 17 *ṣimmĕtûtûnî*. There is some manuscript support to read as piel, *ṣimmĕtûnî*, rather than pilpel.[9]

III. Poetic Technique

A. Line Structure

The parallelism in the psalm is primarily synonymous. The line structure consists of bicola with three exceptions: Verses 2, 6a, and 19 are tricola. In each section of the psalm there is a verse which is chiastic (v. 4 in Ia, v. 8 in Ib, v. 17 in III):

4 (a) is-sated
   (b) with-misery
     (c) my-soul
     (c') my-life
   (b') to-Sheol
 (a) has-drawn-near.

---

[5] Dahood, *Psalms II*, 301, 303-4.

[6] Dahood (2.305) reads *ʿālay* as having a double duty suffix; Kraus (2.772) emends to *ʿinnîtā lî* with LXX (*epēgages eme*).

[7] Dahood 2.306-7.

[8] Cf. Kraus (2.773) who opts for *psn* in the sense of "stiff" (*erstarrt*).

[9] Cf. BHS, KB, Kraus (2.773). Dahood (2.307), however, reads *ṣmtwtny* as a blend of *ṣmt*, "to annihilate," and *mwtt*, "to slay."

8 (a) on-me
   (b) lies
      (c) your-anger
      (c') with-all-your-breakers
   (b') you-humble
(a') -me.

17 (a) over-me
   (b) have-swept
      (c) your-furies
      (c') your-terrors
   (b') have-silenced
(a') -me.

The greatest concentration of chiastic lines is in the central section (II). There is a chiastic arrangement (abccb) within each of the verses 12 and 13 and the two verses parallel each other.

12 (a) is-recounted
   (b) in-the-grave
      (c) your-love
      (c') your-fidelity
   (b') in-Abaddon.
13 (a) are-made-known
   (b) in-the-dark
      (c) your wonders
      (c') your-righteousness
   (b') in-the-land of forgetting.

Vv. 12 and 13 are also delineated as a unity by the rhyming of Yhwh's four virtues (c and c' in the chiasms):

12 *ḥasdekā*   *ʾemûnātĕkā*
13 *pilʾekā*   *wĕṣidqātĕkā*

In vv. 14-17 (Section III) there is a chiastic arrangement of terms referring to the two main actors in this psalm, "I" (*ʾănî*), and "Yhwh."

14 *I* (*ʾănî*), to you, *Yhwh*, cry out;
   in the morning my prayer comes to you.
15 Why, *Yhwh*, do you reject me?
   Why do you hide your face from me?

16 Afflicted am *I* (*ʾănî*) and perishing from my youth.
I have borne your horrors, I am numb.

The chiasms draw attention to the two apparent oppositions in the psalm: the psalmist's distress vs. Yhwh's goodness; the psalmist vs. Yhwh.

B. Verb Forms and Pronominal Suffixes

With few exceptions the verbs throughout the psalm are in the perfect. The psalmist's situation is virtually a foregone conclusion. Two of the three exceptions reveal the hope in the psalm. The rhetorical questions in vv. 11-13 are imperfect. Two of the three cries to Yhwh (vv. 2-3, 14-15) begin with a perfect followed by imperfect/volitive forms (*ṣāʿaqtî/ tābōʾ*, *haṭṭēh* in vv. 2-3; *šiwwaʿtî/těqadděmekkā, tiznaḥ, tastîr* in vv. 14-15). In each case the psalmist's cry is in the perfect and its hoped-for consequence in the imperfect. V. 9c, which describes an ongoing situation, is in the imperfect.

The grammatical person of the verbs and the extensive use of pronominal suffixes demonstrates that this psalm is between Yhwh and the psalmist. This psalm, which seems to recount the most desperate abandonment, grammatically is intensely personal. The first-person singular pronominal suffix, referring to the psalmist, occurs 24 times (vv. 2, 3 [2x], 4 [2x], 6, 7, 8 [2x], 9 [3x], 10 [3x], 14, 15 [2x], 17 [2x], 18 [2x], 19 [2x]). The second-person singular pronominal suffix, referring to Yhwh, occurs 19 times (vv. 2, 3 [2x], 6, 8 [2x], 10 [2x], 11, 12 [2x], 14 [2x], 15, 16, 17 [2x]). The subject of almost every verb is either first- or second-person singular. Third person verbs are predicated (a) of things belonging to Yhwh ("your love," 12; "your wonders," 13; "your furies," "your terrors," 17; "they" [2x: your terrors/furies], 18); (b) of things belonging to the psalmist ("my prayer," 3; "my soul," "my life," 4; "my eyes," 10; "my prayer," 14); or (c) of the dead (6b, 11) in whose company the psalmist feels included.

Grammatical features and repeated words link the series of questions in vv. 11-13 and the description of the psalmist's distress in vv. 4-9. In vv. 4-9, the psalmist proclaims his inclusion among the dead; in vv. 11-13 the psalmist inquires ironically concerning Yhwh's presence among the dead. In v. 6 the psalmist makes a bed among the dead (*mētîm*) and in v. 11 inquires if Yhwh works wonders among the dead (*mētîm*). In v. 6 the psalmist joins those who sleep in the grave (*qeber*) and in v. 11 inquires if Yhwh's love is recounted in the grave (*qeber*). In v. 7 Yhwh is accused of setting the psalmist in darkness (*maḥăšakkîm*); in v. 13 the psalmist inquires if Yhwh's works are known in darkness (*ḥôšek*). In v. 9 Yhwh is accused of separating the psalmist from friends (*měyuddāᶜay*); in v. 13 the psalmist asks if Yhwh's works are known (*yiwwādāᶜ*) in darkness.

Vv. 4-6a focus on the psalmist with the repeated "I," "my." Vv. 4-6a are the only verses in which there are no second person suffixes or verbs. In vv. 7-9a the action belongs exclusively to Yhwh who is the subject of all the verbs. The demanding questions of vv. 12-13 concentrate on Yhwh with four second-person suffixes, "your." Vv. 11-13 are the only verses in which there are no first-person suffixes or verbs.

Thus the description of distress in vv. 4-9—I am like the dead—is linked to the rhetorical questions—Of what use am I to you dead? The grammatical link increases the power of persuasion in the questions.

The accusations of vv. 17-19 parallel vv. 7-9a with four more second-person suffixes and a second-person verb. (The other sections of the psalm alternate between first- and second-person verbs and suffixes.) In vv. 8 and 17 in which the psalmist seems surrounded by Yhwh's afflictions, the grammatical structure indicates the opposite. The psalmist has surrounded and internalized Yhwh's anger:

> 8 On-*me*
> lies
> *your*-anger
> with-all-*your* breakers
> *you* humble
> -*me*.
> 17 Over-*me*
> have-swept
> *your*-furies
> *your*-terrors
> have-silenced
> -*me*.

C. Word Choice

Word selection also highlights significant concepts. The words referring to Yhwh's anger in vv. 8 and 17 (*ḥămātekā . . . mišbārêkā; ḥărônêkā . . . biᶜûtêkā*) and the words describing Yhwh's covenant virtues in vv. 12-13 (*ḥasdekā* . . . *ʾĕmûnātĕkā*; *pilʾekā* . . . *wĕṣidqātĕkā*) are rhymed, calling attention to the seeming disjunction. Other rhymes emphasize the meaning in key verses: end rhymes of "my prayer" and "my cry" in v. 3 (*tĕpillātî* . . . *lĕrinnātî*; cf. *yĕsûʿātî* in v. 2); "grave" and "man" in vv. 5-6 (*kĕgeber* . . . *qeber*). Puns highlight the psalmist's affliction: *ʿênî/ʿōnî* in v. 10 ("my eye . . . "afflicted") and *ʿānî/ʾănî* in v. 16 ("afflicted" . . . "I"). The punning of "eye" and "afflicted" is particularly significant in a psalm in which darkness is the symbol for affliction. There are also two paradoxical juxtapositions of the root *ydʿ* ("know") with *ḥōšek/maḥšāk* ("darkness") In v. 13 the psalmist asks Yhwh if his wonders are known in the dark; in v. 19 the only friend (*mĕyuddāʿay*, "one known") of the psalmist is darkness.

Noteworthy also is the extensive list of synonyms. The place of the dead is referred to as: *šĕʾôl* (4); *bôr*, "the Pit" (5, 7); *qeber*, "the grave (6, 12); **maḥšak*, "darkness" (7, 19); *ḥōšek*, "dark" (13); *mĕṣōlôt*, "depths" (7); *ʾăbaddôn* (12); *ʾereṣ nĕšiyyâ*,"land of forgetting" (13). The psalmist is indicated by *ʾănî* (14, 16), *napšî* (4, 15), *ḥayyay* (4); as well as by parts of the body, i.e., *ʿênî* (10), *kappāy* (10); and personification of the cry, *tĕpillātî* (3, 14), and *rinnātî* (3). Yhwh is indicated by the name Yhwh (2, 10, 14, 15); *ʾĕlōhîm* (2); "bodily" parts, i.e., *ʾoznĕkā* (3), *pānêkā* (15, cf. 3), *yādĕkā* (6); characteristic virtues, i.e., *ḥesed* (12), *ʾemûnâ* (12), *ṣĕdāqâ* (13), *peleʾ* (11, 13); and personified actions, i.e., *ḥămāteḵā* (8), *mišbārêkā* (8), *ʾēmêkā* (16), *ḥărônêkā* (17), *biʿûtêkā* (17). The three main subjects of this psalm are Yhwh, the psalmist, and the place of the dead. All three are indicated by numerous synonyms.

An important set of words refers to inclusion or exclusion. Words connoting presence or approach are: *negdekā* (2), *lĕpānêkā* (3), *ʾēlêkā* (10, 14), *tābôʾ* (3), *haṭṭēh* (3), *higgîʿû* (4), *tĕqaddĕmekkā* (14). The word *nehšabtî*, "reckoned" (5), connotes inclusion in a group. Yhwh's terrors surround (*sabbûnî*) or close in on (*hiqqîpû*) the psalmist (18). In contrast one finds these words of exclusion or separation: *miyyādĕkā* (6), *mimmennî* (9, 15, 19), *minnî* (10), *nigzārû* (6), *hirḥaqtā* (9, 19), *tiznaḥ* (15), *tastîr* (15).

The approach words refer primarily to the psalmist's approach to Yhwh, with the exception of *haṭṭēh*, in which the psalmist asks for Yhwh's approach in return, and *higgîʿû* in which the psalmist mourns the imminent approach to Sheol. The words of exclusion refer primarily the psalmist's separation from friends, dear ones, neighbors, vision, even Yhwh. The psalmist is included with those who go to the Pit, the dead, the slain, sleepers in the grave (5-6). This same group is excluded from Yhwh (6, cf. 11-13). Yet Yhwh's terrors surround the psalmist; Yhwh's presence is constantly in evidence. The words of inclusion and exclusion touch the basic paradox of the psalm: presence or absence.

IV. Structure

A. Thematic Units

In light of the various poetic devices in the psalm, the thematic units can be outlined as follows:

1	Title
2-3	Call to Yhwh: Petition
4-6	Description of distress: I am like the dead.
7-10a	Description of distress: You have done this to me.
10b	Call to Yhwh
11-13	Persuasion: I am no use to you dead.
14	Call to Yhwh
15	Complaint: Why are you doing this?
16-19	Description of distress: I am dying at your hand.

B. Structure of the Psalm

The psalm can be divided into three major sections by the repeated call to Yhwh (2-3, 10b, 14). Several repeated words link these three calls to one another. Most notable is the repetition of the name "Yhwh" (vv. 2, 10, 14) which is found otherwise only in v. 15. Other repeated words refer to the paslmist's prayer (*tĕpillātî*, vv. 3, 14), its persistence ("day," *yôm*, vv. 2, 10), and its direction ("to you," *ʾēlêkā*, vv. 10, 14). Synonyms and parallels emphasize the same elements: the psalmist cries out (*ṣāʿaqtî*, v. 2; *qārāʾtî*, v. 10; *šiwwaʿtî*, v. 14) night and morning (*ballaylâ*, v. 2; *babbōqer*, v. 14), in hopes that the cry (*lĕrinnātî*, v. 3) will reach Yhwh (*negdekā*, v. 2; *lĕpānêkā*, v. 3; *tābôʾ*, v. 3; *tĕqaddĕmekkā*, v. 14). The psalmist stretches out his hands (*šiṭṭaḥtî kappāy*, v. 10) and begs Yhwh to incline an ear (*haṭṭēh-ʾoznĕkā*, v. 3). Thus these four verses form a kind of refrain for the psalm, introducing rather than concluding each section.

Section I can be further subdivided by the two descriptions of distress, one which focuses on the psalmist (4-6) and the other which focuses on Yhwh (7-10a). The final bicolon of each of these two subdivisions turns to the other party: Yhwh in v. 6b, the psalmist in v. 10a. Section II continues the focus on Yhwh, with no first-person suffixes or verbs in vv. 11-13. Section III begins by referring to both parties: "I to you, Yhwh" (*ʾănî ʾēlêkā yhwh*, v. 14). There is no verse in the rest of Section III that does not refer both to the psalmist and Yhwh.

Thus the following structure can be determined:

Title (1)
I. First Petition
   A. Call to Yhwh: Petition (2-3)
   B. Description of distress: I am like the dead (4-6)
   C. Description of distress: You have done this (7-10)
II. Second Petition
   A. Call to Yhwh (10b)
   B. Persuasion: I am no use to you dead (11-13)
III. Third Petition
   A. Call to Yhwh (14)
   B. Complaint: Why are you doing this? (15)
   C. Description of distress: I am dying at your hand (16-19)

There is a symmetry in the number of cola in each section:

I. vv. 2-10a, 10 cola (2 + 4 + 4)
II. vv. 10b-13, 4 cola
III. vv. 14-19, 6 cola

V. Content

A. Title

The psalm is included in the collection of the Sons of Korah (Pss 2, 44-49, 84-85, 87-88). It is the only psalm attributed to Heman the Ezrahite (see, e.g., 1 Kgs 5:11; 1 Chr 2:6; 6:18). It is a *šîr* ("song," cf. Ps 46), a term which is often connected with psalms about the temple and about Yhwh's presence (cf. Pss 120-134; 137; 1 Chr 6:16; 25:6),[10] an ironic note in the psalm about absence. The phrase *ʿal-māḥălat lěʿannôt*, "the heartsickness of affliction," sets the tone for the rest of the psalm. The situation of the psalmist seems to be grave illness.

B. Section I: Description of Distress (2-10a).

The call (vv. 2-3) indicates the major themes of the psalm and forms the model for vv. 10 and 14. The psalmist addresses Yhwh by name and

---

[10] Kraus 1.15.

then by title: "my saving God."[11] Thus this psalm, which ends on such a dismal note, begins with a strong statement of hope.[12] The one on whom the psalmist calls continually is one, indeed the only one, who can be counted on to save. After this expression of confidence, the psalmist pleads with urgency and persistence. He sets himself in Yhwh's presence and announces the arrival of his prayer before Yhwh. The repetition of the cry in vv. 10 and 14 continues this claim on Yhwh's presence. In a prayer which bewails the apparent absence of Yhwh, the psalmist stands firmly in God's presence throughout.[13]

The next three verses (4-6) declare the extent of the psalmist's distress. He is literally at death's door (cf. Ps 107:18). He has already been listed with those destined for the Pit, those whom Yhwh has cut off and forgotten. To be cut off from Yhwh's hand, Yhwh's power, is to become powerless oneself, a strong one without strength. To be forgotten by Yhwh is death.

Worse than the fear of being forgotten by Yhwh, however, is the psalmist's conviction that it is Yhwh's action which has inflicted this distress on him (vv. 7-10a). It is Yhwh who has set him in the darkest deepest pit. It is Yhwh who has set him up with anger and thrown him down with shattering waves. It is Yhwh who has left him utterly alone, like a corpse, abominable to those who know him. He is caught without escape, blinded by affliction.

C. Section II: Challenge to Yhwh (vv. 10b-13)

Section II begins with another cry. The psalmist, in mortal distress caused by Yhwh, calls out again to Yhwh, the only one who can save, the only one left in this abandonment. The cry will not cease. The psalmist calls every day.

The three verses which follow (vv. 11-13) consist entirely of rhetorical questions. These questions come where, in a lament, we might expect

---

[11] *yĕšûʿātî*, "my salvation," is often emended to *šiwwaʿtî*, "I call out," to parallel *ṣāʿaqtî* in the second colon.

[12] It is frequently pointed out that this is the only psalm in the psalter which does not end on a note of hope. It should be noted that it begins with one.

[13] In this assertion of presence, Psalm 88 differs from the first section of Psalm 22, which it resembles in so many other ways. In Ps 22:2, the psalmist complains that Yhwh is far (*rāḥôq*) from his cry.

a confession of guilt or a protestation of innocence. Instead the psalmist focuses entirely on Yhwh. The psalmist who seeks Yhwh's presence has been set by Yhwh at the edge of the abode of death and now asks, "Is this where you are?" The psalmist is in the Pit, in the dark, among the forgotten dead, in the grave (cf. vv. 4-6). Is this where Yhwh is to be found? Is this where Yhwh displays the covenant virtues of love (*ḥesed*) and fidelity (*ʾĕmûnâ*)? Is this where one experiences Yhwh's righteousness (*ṣĕdāqâ*), a virtue which demands relationship,[14] and benefits from Yhwh's mighty deeds (*pĕlāʾîm*), deeds which save the people (cf. Exod 15:11; Ps 77:15)? The psalmist will not let go of Yhwh's presence and with high irony demands to know: "Are you present in this place where you have put me?"

D. Section III: Yhwh and the Psalmist (vv. 14-19)

After inquiring ironically concerning Yhwh's presence among the dead, the psalmist lays hold of that presence with the prayer of the refrain. The psalmist has suggested the covenant by naming covenant virtues. Now the refrain is followed by an inquiry about the psalmist's personal experience of Yhwh. This section focuses on the relationship between the two.

Yhwh's covenant virtues are *ḥesed* and *ʾĕmûnâ*. The covenant relationship between Yhwh and the people is one of *ṣĕdāqâ*. It is for the chosen that Yhwh works mighty deeds (*pĕlāʾîm*) to save them. The psalmist recognizes all this in Section II. Yet the psalmist's own experience, recounted in Section III, is of Yhwh's horrors (*ʾēmêkā*, v. 16), Yhwh's furies (*ḥārônêkā*, v. 17), Yhwh's terrors (*biʿûtîm*, v. 17). These manifestations of Yhwh mark the psalmist's experience even though his knowledge of Yhwh leads him to anticipate *ḥesed*, *ʾĕmûnâ*, *ṣĕdāqâ*, *pĕlāʾîm*. His response is the cry: "Why?"

The final statement of the psalm is one of presence and absence. What Yhwh has sent—horrors, furies, terrors—surround the psalmist and are inescapably present. Because of Yhwh's presence he is perishing! There are no enemies in this psalm. Only Yhwh and darkness. Yhwh has removed from him everyone else, dear one and neighbor. Even Yhwh's own presence is hidden. No one is known to the psalmist; no one is present but darkness. The last word is darkness.

---

[14] See E. R. Achtemeier, "Righteousness in the OT," *IDB* 4.80.

The question raised by the ending of the psalm is: Is Yhwh present or absent? That is the major issue of the psalm. The only plea of the psalm is "listen." There is no plea that the pain be taken away. The plea is rather, "Don't abandon me; don't leave me!" The psalmist has clung to Yhwh's presence throughout the psalm. Yet there is a thick irony in the continued statements that Yhwh is the cause of the pain and affliction. There is no one else. Yhwh's actions surround the psalmist. Yhwh's presence is killing the psalmist, yet the psalmist feels rejected and abandoned by Yhwh. Yhwh is hidden. The covenant virtues which one would hope for cannot be found in the realm of the dead where Yhwh is exiling the psalmist. Still the author of this prayer will not let go of Yhwh.

This plea for presence implies that perhaps God could change the situation. Or that even if God does not change the situation, the presence of Yhwh—which is causing the pain—is still better than the absence of Yhwh. This psalmist refuses to let go of the relationship.

The psalm ends in darkness. Is there no hope? The psalmist has no one else, recognizes no one else. Yet there is hope even in the cry. The cry itself maintains the relationship. The question remains: Can Yhwh be found even in the darkness?

Christian Postscript

We should leave the cry in darkness, sit with the pain as the psalm does, but the story doesn't end there. The act of crying out already changes the situation. In Christian belief it is precisely the word, God's Word, who relieves our suffering, gives meaning to its absurdity, ultimately liberates us from its power. What a wonderful irony to realize God's answer to the questions of Psalm 88: Do you work wonders for the dead? Do the shades rise up to praise you? Is your faithful love made known in the land of death? The psalmist who asked those questions assumed the answer was no. With what awed delight do we proclaim that the answer is yes! God does work wonders for the dead; God's faithful love is indeed made known in the land of death. With what gratitude do we praise the God who willed to go with us into the shadow of death so that we might be alone in the dark no longer.

A lesson in the power of lament.

CHAPTER 9

Anti-monarchical Ideology in Israel in Light of Mesopotamian Parallels

DALE LAUNDERVILLE

According to 1 Samuel 8-12, kingship was born in Israel in the midst of controversy. 1 Samuel 8 portrays the elderly judge Samuel as opposing the introduction of kingship in Israel since it will constitute a rejection of the Lord's kingship and will make Israel like the other nations. When Samuel speaks to the Lord about Israel's request for a king, the tradition reports the Lord as saying: "They have not rejected you but they have rejected me as king over them" (1 Sam 8:7). Such extreme anti-monarchical sentiment is rare in the ancient Near East. Most explanations of the relationship between divine and human kingship in the ancient Near East allow for tension between them, but they usually see the two forms of kingship in a symbiotic relationship. It has been claimed that there is no knowledge of a nation in the environs of Israel which characterized earthly kingship as incompatible with the kingship of the divine realm.[1] But the extremely negative attitude toward kingship in 1 Sam 8:7 which tries to reserve the title of king to the Lord and thereby prevent the transformation of the judgeship into

---

[1] F. Crusemann (*Der Widerstand gegen das Königtum* [WMANT 49; Neukirchen: Neukirchener Verlag, 1978] 76) claims: "Jedenfalls kann man mit Sicherheit davon ausgehen, dass Israel nirgends in seiner Umwelt auf ein göttliches Königtum traf, das in einem ausschliessenden Gegensatz zum irdischen stand. Nach all unserer Kenntnis handelt es sich hier um eine ganz eigene Leistung Israels."

the kingship is not as novel as it might appear at first glance. For Israel is not the only nation in the ancient Near East where there was an effort to reserve the title of king exclusively for a ruling deity. On the basis of a limited number of royal inscriptions and seals, it is clear that a few Mesopotamian cities in the late third and early second millennium BC restricted the title of "king" to the ruling deity. While it is undeniable that the theocratic ideal of recognizing the existence of authentic kingship only in the divine realm was rare in the ancient Near East and was apparently unknown among Israel's neighbors in the late second millennium, I would contend that such an ideal is not a unique creation of Israel such that it sets Israel apart as its only source in the history of the ancient Near East. After recounting briefly the theology of kingship promoted by Samuel in 1 Samuel 8, I will first show that such a theology finds an analogue in a few Mesopotamian royal inscriptions in the early second millennium and then compare Samuel's theology of kingship with the more widespread royal theology favorable to earthly kingship to point out the continuity between the two theologies.

According to the tradition recorded in 1 Samuel 8, the people requested that a king rule over them (1) because Samuel's corrupt sons were ineffective rulers (v. 3) and (2) because they wished to have a king lead them in battle and rule over them like the other nations (vv. 5, 20). By such a request for a king, the people are portrayed as vainly overstepping their boundaries and forfeiting their uniqueness.[2] The Lord's jarring response to Samuel that the people have rejected his leadership and not Samuel's (1 Sam 8:7) finds an echo in 1 Sam 12:12 where Samuel reminds the people: "When you saw that Nahash the king of the Ammonites was coming against you, you said to me, 'No, rather let a king rule over us,' but the Lord your God was your king." Although it is debated, it seems that 1 Sam 8:7 and 12:12 are pre-deuteronomistic.[3]

---

[2] P. K. McCarter, Jr., *1 Samuel* (AB 8; Garden City, NY: Doubleday, 1980) 160.

[3] Crusemann, 83 and D. J. McCarthy, "The Inauguration of the Monarchy in Israel: a Form-Critical Study of 1 Samuel 8-12," *Int* 27 (1973) 403. M. Noth (*Überlieferungsgeschichtliche Studien: Die sammelnden und bearbeitenden Geschichtswerke im alten Testament* [3rd ed.; Tubingen: Max Niemeyer, 1967] 57, 59-60) regarded 1 Samuel 8 and apparently 1 Samuel 12 as deuteronomistic. R. E. Clements ("The Deuteronomistic Interpretation of the Founding of the Monarchy in 1 Sam. VIII," *VT* 24 [1974] 399, 408-9.) and A. D. H. Mayes ("The Rise of the Israelite Monarchy," *ZAW* 90 [1978] 11) argue that 1 Samuel 8 is deuteronomistic.

For the deuteronomist, who sees a tension between the Lord's kingship and the way royal rule has been exercised in Israel and Judah, does not go so far as to see earthly and heavenly kingship as incompatible.[4] Such a position would not be consonant with Israel's history where kingship was introduced and the Lord continued to rule over the Israelites. While it is difficult to determine whether these verses stem from the time of Samuel or from a later time in Israel's history, it is clear that they express the theological conviction that kingship is at odds with authentic Yahwism. Such strong anti-monarchical sentiments in support of a theocratic ideal which rejects the institution of earthly kingship come to expression in the OT outside of 1 Samuel 8-12 only in Gideon's rejection of the offer to rule over Israel: "I will not rule (*māšal*) over you and my sons will not rule (*māšal*) over you, but the Lord shall rule (*māšal*) over you" (Judg 8:23). Even though Gideon rejects the offer of dynastic kingship, he is portrayed as acquiring for himself some of the trappings of kingship: a harem (Judg 8:30) and an upperclass, ruling position for his family (Judg 9:2).[5] Those who oppose the kingship believe that it will compromise Israel's unique relationship with the Lord which in turn will undermine the social fabric of the Israelite community (1 Sam 8:11-17). In defense of the status quo, Samuel essentially enunciates a political theology which calls for expressing the subordination of the earthly ruler to the heavenly ruler through the use of different titles—*šōpēṭ,* "judge," for the Israelite ruler and *melek,* "king," for the Lord.

A few Mesopotamian cities around the turn of the second millennium BC reserved the title of *šarrum,* "king," for the deity who reigned in the city and designated the human ruler as a "governor" or "vice-regent." The cities of Assur and Ešnunna were ruled by officials entitled *iššiakkū,* "governors," and the cities of Mari and Der by officials entitled *šakkanakkū,* "governors." The *iššiakkū* in Assur and Ešnunna and the *šakkanakkū* of Der and perhaps of Mari[6] were subordinates to the Sumerian king of Ur in the imperial system of the

---

[4] Clements, "Deuteronomistic Interpretation in 1 Sam. VIII," 401, 406; Mayes, "The Rise of the Israelite Monarchy," 11.

[5] A. Soggin, *Das Königtum in Israel* (BZAW 104; Berlin: Töpelmann, 1967) 20.

[6] J.-R. Kupper ("Rois et Sakkanakku," *JCS* 21 [1967] 123) notes that there is some question of the extent of the dependence of the *šakkanakku* of Mari on the Ur III king since they do not explicitly acknowledge him as their overlord in their inscriptions.

Third Dynasty of Ur (2100-2003 BC). But when these cities gained their independence from Ur, they continued to refer to the earthly ruler in their midst as a *šakkanakkum* or *iššiakkum*.

In Assur, a number of royal inscriptions from the early second millennium BC entitled the god Assur *šarrum*, "king," and the earthly ruler *iššiakkum*, "governor, vice-regent." This hierarchy in the government of Assur is clearly expressed on a seal of Silulu: "Assur is king (*šarrum* [LUGAL]); Silulu is governor (*iššiakkum* [PA])."[7] In the inscriptions from the city-state of Assur, the title *iššiakum* always appears in construct with the deity Assur.[8] Functioning as an intermediary or chief priest,[9] the *iššiakkum* recognized the sovereignty of the protector deity and his subordination to him. When the *iššiakkum* Erišum recounts in an inscription his restoration of a temple for Assur, he repeatedly entitles himself the *iššiak Assur*, "the vice-regent of Assur."[10] Nevertheless, in referring to a future ruler who would again restore this temple, Erišum describes him as "a king of my rank," (*šarrum* [LUGAL] *šumšu ša kīma jāti*).[11] So while Erišum does not hold the title of *šarrum*—at least when he is considered in relation to the ruling deity—he sees himself as a royal figure who carries out royal functions such as restoring temples and maintaining justice. The distinction in title between the tutelary deity of the city and the earthly ruler would seem to have constituted a check upon the earthly ruler's tendency to expand his power.

In Ešnunna, after the collapse of Ur III (ca. 2003), the rulers retained the title of *iššiakkum* throughout the twentieth century BC. On the seals of a number of the rulers of Ešnunna, similar to the pattern at Assur, the subordination of the ruler of Ešnunna to the protector deity

---

[7] B. Landsberger and K. Balkan, "Die Inschrift des assyrischen Königs Irisum, Gefunden in Kultepe 1948," *Belleten* 14 (1950) 231.

[8] M. T. Larsen, "The City and its King: On the Old Assyrian Notion of Kingship," *La palais et la royauté* (XIX Rencontre Assyriologique Internationale; ed. P. Garelli; Paris: Geuthner, 1971) 287.

[9] Larsen ("The City and its King," 296) identifies three royal titles for the Old Assyrian ruler besides the *iššiakkum* title: *rubāʾum*, "prince," *waklum*, "deputy," and *bēlum*, "lord, master."

[10] Lines 4, 35-36 according to the collation of Landsberger and Balkan, "Die Inschrift," 225-26.

[11] Landsberger and Balkan, "Inschrift," 224-25, line 20.

Tišpak is communicated by the use of different titles: "Tišpak, the strong king (*šarrum dannum*), the king (*šarrum*) of the land of Warum. Usur-awassu, his beloved and his envoy, the governor (*iššiakkum*) of Ešnunna, his servant."[12] Among the numerous seals reported from the excavations at Ešnunna, only one seal prior to the reign of Ipiq-Adad II (ca. 1884)—that of Ilšuilija (ca. 2000 BC)—departs from the usual pattern of reserving the title of *šarrum*, "king," to the protector deity and ascribes it to the earthly ruler.[13] Without explicitly entitling the deity Tišpak as *šarrum*, a number of short royal inscriptions from Ešnunna use the same form as the following example from Bilalama (ca. 1984-75 BC): "Bilalama, the beloved of Tišpak, the governor (*iššiak [ENSI*) of Ešnunna."[14] The rulers of Ešnunna retained the title *iššiakkum* until the time of Ipiq-Adad II (ca. 1884); then they began to refer to themselves as *šarru*: "Ipiq-Adad, the strong king (*šarrum dannum*), the king who enlarges Ešnunna, the shepherd of the dark-headed people, the son of Ibalpiel."[15] It is noteworthy that Ipid-Adad II and the next two occupants of the throne of Ešnunna, Naram-Sin (ca. 1820)[16] and Dadusa (ca. 1800 BC),[17] match the prestige of the earlier kings of Ur not only by gaining the title of *šarrum* but also by claiming divine status by writing their names with the divine determinative. Such a rise in rank by Ipiq-Adad II must have been facilitated by his success in enlarging the territory under Ešnunna's control.[18]

When a king is successful in carrying out functions which he shares with the protector deity such as battling foreign foes, then it would

---

[12] H. Frankfort et al., *The Gimilsin Temple and the Palace of the Rulers at Tell Asmar* (OIP XLIII; Chicago: U. of Chicago, 1940) 147, no. 19.

[13] Frankfort et al., *The Gimilsin Temple*, 144, no. 8. D. O. Edzard (*Die "zweite Zwischenzeit" Babyloniens* [Wiesbaden: Harrassowitz, 1957] 67) regards this seal of Ilšuilija as an exception; in fact, in another of his seals Ilšuilija refers to Tišpak as "the strong king, the king of the land of Warum" and to himself as *wakilšu*, "his deputy" (Frankfort et al., Gimilsin Temple, 143, no. 6.).

[14] Frankfort et al., *The Gimilsin Temple*, 135, no. 3.

[15] Frankfort et al., *The Gimilsin Temple*, 138, no. 13.

[16] Frankfort et al., *The Gimilsin Temple*, 139, no. 14.

[17] O. Schroeder, "Zwei neue 'Könige' von Tuplias," *OLZ* 17 (1914) 246-47.

[18] C. J. Gadd ("Babylonia, c. 2121-1800 BC," *CAH*, vol I, part 2, 618) argues that the practice of divinizing the king of Ur III may well have arisen from the king's assuming the function of appointing officials in the cities throughout the empire. Previously such local rulers were regarded as appointed by the protector deity.

seem that the distinction between the king and the protector deity would blurr. For the sake of increased power and prestige, the king would obviously promote the perception of himself as a deity.

In Der (a city located east of the Tigris on the frontier between the Babylonian plain and Elam), the rulers Nidnuša and Ilum-muttabbil in the twentieth century BC were entitled *šakkanakku*. In one of his inscriptions, Ilum-muttabbil identified himself as:[19]

> the strong man, the favorite of Ištaran, the beloved of Ištar, the governor (*šakkanakkum*) of Der, the one who struck the head of the troops of Anšan, Elam, Simaškim, and the one who helped Barahsum.

In another inscription of Ilum-muttabbil, Ištaran, the tutelary deity of Der, was identified as "the strong one, the king (*šarrum*) of Der, and the king (*šarrum*) of the mountains."[20] As in the inscriptions from Assur, the tutelary deity alone bore the title of *šarrum*. Even though the earthly ruler may have carried out royal functions, he was only entitled a *šakkanakkum*. In the only known inscription of Nidnuša, this *šakkanakkum* presents himself as one who has established justice and good order in Der— an essential function of a legitimate king in the ancient Near East:[21]

> Nidnuša, the strong man, the favorite of Ištaran, the beloved of Ištar, the governor (*šakkanakkum*) of Der, the just judge (*dajjanum*) who oppresses no one, who provides justice for the oppressed man and woman, the one who establishes good order (*šākin mēšarum*), the one who destroys the wicked.

It is striking that even though Nidnuša did not take over the title of *šarrum*, he wrote his name with the divine determinative. The earthly ruler in Der then was more readily granted divine status than he was allowed to hold the title of "king." This is a reversal of the usual pat-

---

[19] F. Lenormant, *Choix de textes cuneiformes inedits ou incompletement publieés jusqua'à ce jour* (Paris: Maisonneuve et Cie, 1873-75) pl. 7, no. 5.

[20] L. Speleers, *Recueil des inscriptions de l'Asie anterieure des Musées Royaux du Cinquintenaire à Bruxelles* (Bruxelles: Musées Royaux d'Art et d'Histoire, 1925) pl. 7, no. 4.

[21] F. Stephens, *Votive and Historical Texts from Babylonia and Assyria* (YOS 9; New Haven: Yale, 1937) no. 62; D. O. Edzard, "Die 'zweite Zwischenzeit,'" 73.

tern in Mesopotamia where the rulers were regularly referred to as kings but rarely were they deified.[22] Again this practice of reserving the title *šarrum* to the tutelary deity was apparently essential to maintaining a clear governing structure in which the earthly ruler was mindful of his position subordinate to that of the tutelary deity.

In Mari, the practice of restricting the title *šarrum* to the tutelary deity seems to have been in force prior to the advent of the Lim dynasty in the nineteenth century BC. The foundation deposit of a sanctuary in Mari contained the following inscription:[23]

> Ištup-ilum, governor (*šakkanakkum*) of Mari, son of Išma-Dagan, governor (*šakkanakkum*) of Mari, built the temple of (the deity) Šarrumatim ("the king of the land").

The deity Šarrumatim in this inscription is Dagan:[24] the god whom Sargon of Akkad claimed had invited him to rule over the territory around Mari and about whom Hammurapi later made a similar claim.[25] Thus, the god Dagan was regarded as the sovereign ruler in the kingdom of Mari, and he alone seems to have been counted worthy of holding the title of *šarrum*.[26] Ištup-ilum and his father Išma-Dagan are among six known *šakkanakkū* who did not claim the title of *šarrum* for themselves.[27]

So the practice in these small Mesopotamian cities at the end of the third and the beginning of the second millenium BC of reserving the title of "king" to the protector deity of the city or territory corresponds to the practice proposed as an ideal for Israel in 1 Sam 8:7: that the Lord alone be entitled king in Israel. In Assur, Mari, and Ešnunna, this practice was in force during the relatively short time after these cities gained their independence from Ur and prior to their own growth into powerful cities rivaling Hammurapi's Babylon. So in light

---

[22] W. W. Hallo, "The Birth of Kings," *Love & Death in the Ancient Near East: Essays in Honor of Marvin H. Pope* (ed. J. H. Marks and R. M. Good; Guilford, CT: Four Quarters, 1987) 48.

[23] G. Dossin, "Inscriptions de fondation provenant de Mari," *Syria* 21 (1940) 162.

[24] Ibid., 165-67.

[25] R. Borger, "Code of Hammurapi," *Babylonisch-assyrische Lesestucke* (AnOr 54; Rome: Biblical Institute, 1972) 6, IV:24-31; J.-R. Kupper, *Les nomades en Mesopotamie au temps des rois de Mari* (Paris: Belle Lettres, 1957) 32.

[26] Kupper, "Rois et Sakkanakku," 124.

[27] Ibid.

of the practice of reserving the title of "king" to the protector deity, one can say of these polities that just as judgeship was a transitional form of government in Israel from the time of the settlement to the rise of the monarchy, so also was the governorship in Assur, Mari, Der, and Ešnunna prior to the rise of the monarchy in their respective cities. It seems reasonable that just as Samuel protested the abolition of the judgeship in Israel, so also individuals in these Mesopotamian cities would have argued in favor of retaining the governorship.

Since a king and a judge or a governor alike carry out on behalf of a polity the two essential functions of defending against foreign foes and maintaining justice, the difference between rule by a judge or governor and rule by a king often seems to be more a matter of degree than of kind. However, two new elements which a king introduces into a polity highlight the difference between kingship and judgeship or governorship: viz., a standing army and a bureaucracy. These two elements give the royal government a greater degree of stability than the looser form of organization under a judge or a governor. But as Samuel warned (1 Sam 8:11-17), this stability in government carried a price tag in the form of conscription and taxation. While the people's contribution to the government in the form of military service and of surplus goods was as necessary under a judgeship or governorship as under a kingship, the king would be able to exercise greater control over the people and be more independent from them in conscripting soldiers and collecting taxes. Thus in Samuel's protest against the kingship, he essentially argues that the people would be better off if they would simply trust in the Lord's rule and not take matters too much into their own hands by trying to establish a greater degree of visible security in the form of the kingship. Under the judgeship the Lord would have greater latitude in choosing when, where, and through whom to intervene to defend the nation and maintain justice. It is almost as if in Samuel's eyes the establishment of earthly kingship threatened to make the Lord into an otiose deity.

But theologically Samuel's argument is no more compelling than that proposed by the supporters of the kingship who claim that a symbiotic relationship between the protector deity and the king can exist. In the royal ideology spread throughout the nations of the ancient Near East, this symbiotic relationship was succinctly characterized by the shepherd image in which the earthly king was to shepherd the people who were sheep belonging to the heavenly king. This image spells out both the subordination and the accountability of the earthly king to the heavenly king; such a relationship is described in an inscription of Samsuiluna, the son and successor of Hammurapi as king of Babylon:[28]

> At that time, Marduk, the chief god of the land, the god who creates wisdom, gave me, Samsuiluna, the king of his longing, all lands to shepherd them, and indeed he instructed me in a grand fashion to bring about the settling of the pastures of the land and to lead forever his widespread people in peace.

This same shepherd imagery is used in Israel to portray David's relationship to the Lord as symbiotic:

> He [the Lord] chose David, his servant,
>   and brought him from the sheepfolds,
> From tending the ewes he brought him,
>   in order to shepherd Jacob, his people,
>   and Israel, his possession.
> He shepherded them with all his heart,
>   and with skillful hands he led them.
>   (Ps 78:70-72)

Within the use of this shepherd imagery, there is ample opportunity for criticizing a particular king. If the king does not promote the well-being of the people, there are grounds for calling the legitimacy of his rule into question. By increasing the authority of the human ruler from that of a judge to a king, the protector deity does not forfeit his position as sovereign. Rather the granting of the title of king to the earthly ruler constitutes a promotion in rank for such a ruler. The fact that the protector deity allows both the judge or governor and the king to act on his behalf shows that each rules by divine appointment; such rule by divine right is a significant point of continuity between the judge-ship/governorship and the kingship. Thus, the theocratic ideal of the league or of the city-state where the protector deity is sovereign is not discarded but rather adapted. However, if a king does become a tyrant and the protector deity remains silent, then it may appear as if the pro-

---

[28] L. Messerschmidt and A. Ungnad, *Inschriften historischen Inhalts und anderer Urkunden* (VAS 1; Leipzig: Hinrichs, 1907) 33:17-30.

tector deity has lost his position as sovereign. In such an extreme position one could plausibly make the claim that heavenly kingship and earthly kingship have proven themselves to be incompatible over against the more usual response of demanding that a particular king be removed. However, earthly kingship does not need to be either a tyranny or a rejection of the sovereignty of the protector deity as Samuel attempts to portray it in 1 Samuel 8.

While the tension between human and divine kingship is stated in more uncompromising terms in 1 Samuel 8 than in the Mesopotamian inscriptions cited above, this difference is most likely due to the fact that the genre of 1 Samuel 8 is narrative and lends itself to communicating the intensity of a debate while the genre of the royal inscriptions cited above is rhetorically more reserved since it is constrained by the typical pattern and formulaic language of royal inscriptions. Therefore, the narrative genre may be more responsible than the theocratic ideology of 1 Samuel 8 for making Samuel's denunciation of kingship in Israel appear as a uniquely strong protest against the institution of kingship in the ancient Near East.

The reluctance to entitle as "king" the ruler in Israel is not totally unique to Israel. Although there is no known evidence of reserving the title of king to the protector deity in the nations neighboring Israel in the eleventh century BC, such a practice is in evidence in a few Mesopotamian cities at the beginning of the second millennium BC. It cannot be said then that the theocratic ideal defended by Samuel is a unique creation of Israel. Rather such an ideal functions in 1 Samuel 8 either to preserve the judgeship or to provide grounds for criticizing and limiting the kingship. In other words, Samuel's protest is either an extreme conservative reaction or a response to a long and difficult ordeal under a tyrant. At any rate, the view that adherence to a protector deity and the entitling of the earthly ruler as king are incompatible would simply be one side of the debate in a polity contemplating the inauguration of kingship.

CHAPTER 10

Water in the First Creation Account of Genesis 1 in the *Commentary on Genesis* of Ephrem the Syrian

EDWARD G. MATHEWS JR.

For a scholar who has spent a good deal of the recent part of his life investigating the imagery of natural phenomena in the Bible, it would seem that a fitting tribute might also involve a study of some natural phenomena or even of the elements themselves. Thus, I would like in this paper to consider one element in particular, that one which Pindar once called "the best"—water.[1] And I will not so much engage in a historical-critical, linguistic or philological investigation of the biblical text[2] as much as I will attempt to set out how the element of water underlies the interpretation of the first creation account by a certain fourth-century ecclesiastical author, Ephrem the Syrian, as found in his

[1] Pindar, *Olympian Ode* 1.1: *ariston men hydōr*.

[2] In addition to the standard commentaries, e. g., C. Westermann, *Genesis 1-11: A Commentary* (Minneapolis: Augsburg, 1984), U. Cassuto, *A Commentary on the Book of Genesis: From Adam to Noah* (Jerusalem: Magnes, 1961), this has already been done in D. T. Tsumura, *The Earth and the Waters in Genesis 1 and 2: A Linguistic Investigation* (JSOT Supplement Series 83; Sheffield: JSOT, 1989). For the importance of water in the Old Testament, from both a sociological and a theological point of view, see P. Reymond, *L'eau, sa vie, et sa signification dans l'ancien testament* (SVT 6; Leiden: Brill, 1958).

Commentary on Genesis.[3] Then, by attempting to identify his sources, I will thereby endeavor to set Ephrem in the context of his times and to uncover the currents of interpretation that seem to have influenced him.

Ephrem was born in or near the frontier city of Nisibis around 309, and served as deacon and possibly as "interpreter"[4] until 363, when Nisibis was finally taken by the Persians under Shapur II, and officially ceded to them by the newly crowned Roman Emperor Jovian. Thus exiled from his native city, Ephrem eventually made his way to the much more cosmopolitan city of Edessa where he spent the last few years of his life. It is here during less than a decade spent in Edessa that Ephrem seems to have generated the greater part of his literary output. During this short period he most certainly became engaged in impassioned polemics against numerous opponents of Nicene orthodoxy, but particularly against the heresies of Bardaisan, Marcion and Mani, whose teachings plagued Syrian Christian communities during Ephrem's lifetime and even much later.

Ephrem was widely renowned in his day for his writings and particularly for his commentaries. His *Commentary on Genesis* stands at the head of a long history of Syriac literature that finds its source in the first book of the Bible.[5] The book of Genesis was clearly a book to

---

[3] *Sancti Ephraem Syri in Genesim et in Exodum commentarii* (CSCO 152-153; ed. R. Tonneau; Louvain: Peeters, 1955) 3-121. While there are differing traditions of a *Commentary on Genesis* attributed to Ephrem, all references in this paper will be to this edition of the Syriac text. The English translation used in this paper is mine as found in E. G. Mathews, Jr. and J. P. Amar, *Selected Prose Works of Ephrem the Syrian* (FC 91; Washington: Catholic University, 1994) [hereafter, Mathews, *Ephrem the Syrian*]. See the introduction to the *Commentary on Genesis* in this volume for a brief discussion of the other Genesis commentaries claiming Ephremic authorship.

[4] I.e., teacher in the school system; Syr., *měpaššěqānâ* . The precise date of Ephrem's birth is unknown; I therefore follow scholarly consensus. For a more detailed description of Ephrem's life, see the general introduction in Mathews, *Ephrem the Syrian*, and the sources cited there.

[5] From such figures as Narsai, Jacob of Sarug, Jacob of Edessa, Moshe bar Kepha, Ishodad of Merv, Dionysius bar Salibi, Theodore Bar Koni and the great Monophysite polymath Bar Hebraeus, this literature comprises narrative commentaries, several treatises in question and answer format, numerous poetic treatments, as well as an important Syriac Hexaemeral tradition. For a concise overview, see E. Ten Napel, "Some Remarks on the Hexaemeral Literature in Syriac," *OCA* 229 (Rome: Pontificium Institutum Orientale, 1987) 57-69.

which Ephrem returned over and over throughout his writings, not just in his Commentary, but throughout his hymns.[6] In the preface to his *Commentary on Genesis,* Ephrem claims that he "had not wanted to write a commentary on the first book of Creation, lest we should now repeat what we had set down in the metrical homilies and hymns. Nevertheless, compelled by the love of friends, we have written briefly of those things of which we wrote at length in the metrical homilies and in the hymns."[7] From this prologue then, we can postulate that the *Commentary on Genesis* must also be included among those works that Ephrem composed during that short period at the end of his life while he was dwelling in Edessa.

In independent studies. T. Jansma and A. Guillaumont have shown that Ephrem's entire account of the six days of creation, on the surface a very literal commentary, is a polemic aimed primarily against the teachings of Bardaisan.[8] Against Bardaisan's theories of eternal elements from which the world was made, Ephrem's polemic is centered on his position that God is (a) the only self-subsistent being and (b) the creator of everything else that exists. To take any other position would be, in Ephrem's view, to make God an "arranger" and not "the Creator." According to Ephrem, Bardaisan composed 150 hymns as did David,[9] in which he taught that there were five eternal principles (in Syriac, *ʾityê*)[10] each in its own region: light in the East, wind in the West, fire in the South, water in the North, while darkness inhabited the lower regions. The Lord of All (another *ʾityâ*) occupied the region above. As a result of some sort of mingling of these eternal elements chaos ensued, and from the resultant mixture of the elements the Lord

---

[6] See T. Kronholm, *Motifs from Genesis 1-11 in the Genuine Hymns of Ephrem the Syrian* (ConBOT 11; Uppsala: CWK Gleerup, 1978).

[7] *Sancti Ephraem Syri in Genesim,* 3; Mathews, *Ephrem the Syrian,* 67.

[8] See T. Jansma, "Ephraems Beschreibung des ersten Tages der Schöpfung," *OCP* 37 (1971) 300-305; and A. Guillaumont, "Genèse 1,1-2 selon les commentateurs syriaques," in *IN PRINCIPIO: Interpretations des premiers versets de la Genèse* (EA 152; Paris: Études augustiniennes, 1973) 115-32.

[9] *Des Heiligen Ephraem des Syrers Hymnen contra Haereses* (CSCO 169-170; ed. E. Beck; Louvain: Peeters, 1957) 53.6.

[10] Syriac has a number of words deriving from the word *ʾit,* cognate to Hebrew *yš,* which denote existence. For Ephrem, these words can be applied only to God. See Mathews, *Ephrem the Syrian,* 75, n. 26, for discussion of this term with further bibliography.

of All made the world and set it into order.[11] While there is now little doubt that in his *Commentary on Genesis* Ephrem is polemicizing against the false teachings of Bardaisan, scholars now concur that this polemic extends also to the teachings of Marcion and Mani, who held similar opinions on the origins of the world.

With regard to Ephrem's background and influence, Sebastian Brock has noted, on more than one occasion, that in addition to his native Syrian traditions, Ephrem was the recipient of a triple heritage: Mesopotamian traditions, Jewish traditions and, towards the end of his life, certain Hellenistic traditions.[12] Ephrem derived the dialogue poem, at least indirectly, from Mesopotamian models, as well as the expression *samm hayyê*, his favorite term for the Eucharist. It also seems likely that Ephrem's notion that the spring of Paradise in Gen 2:6 travelled through some sort of water-pipe in order to spout forth into four rivers and to water the earth can be traced back, at least in part, to Babylonian traditions such as that found in the Creation of the World according to Marduk.[13] From contemporary Hellenistic thought Ephrem no doubt became conversant with some philosophical and theological concepts, but to date it is the Jewish background to Ephrem's thought that has most preoccupied scholars. Nisibis seems to have been a stronghold of Jewish culture at this time and there is little

[11] See *Des Heiligen Ephraem des Syrers Hymnen contra Haereses*, 3.4, 41.7, and *S. Ephraim's Prose Refutations of Mani, Marcion and Bardaisan I* (ed. C. W. Mitchell; London: Text and Translation Society, 1912), II (ed. E. A. Bevan and F. C. Burkitt; London: Text and Translation Society, 1921) passim. For Bardaisan's myth, see H. J. W. Drijvers, *Bardaisan of Edessa* (SSN 6; Assen: Royal Van Gorcum, 1966) 96-126, and for Ephrem's treatment of Bardaisan, 133-43. See also E. Beck, "Bardaisan und Seine Schule bei Ephräm," *LM* 91 (1978) 271-333, especially 271-88; B. Ehlers, "Bardesanes—ein Syrische Gnostiker," *ZKG* 81 (1970) 334-51; studies XI-XIII in H. J. W. Drijvers, *East of Antioch: Studies in Early Syriac Christianity* (CS 198; London: Variorum Reprints, 1984); H. Kruse, "Die 'mythologischen Irrtümer' Bar-Daiṣāns," *OC* 71 (1987) 24-52; and most recently, J. Teixidor, *Bardesane d'Edesse: La première philosophie syriaque* (Patrimones Christianisme 7; Paris: Cerf, 1992).

[12] See S. P. Brock, "Jewish Traditions in Syriac Sources," *JJS* 30 (1979) 212, and more recently, S. P. Brock, *The Luminous Eye: The Spiritual World Vision of St. Ephrem* (Placid Lectures 6; Rome, CIIS, 1985) 6-9 [2d ed., CSS 124; Kalamazoo: Cistercian, 1992]).

[13] *Sancti Ephraem Syri in Genesim*, 29; Mathews, *Ephrem the Syrian*, 101. See "The Creation of the World by Marduk," 11, in A. Heidel, *The Babylonian Genesis* (Chicago: University of Chicago, 1963) 62.

doubt that of the three traditions enumerated by Brock, it is to the Jewish milieu, despite his bitter theological polemics against the Jews, that Ephrem is most in debt.[14]

Before plunging directly into our investigation, it might be helpful here to summarize, ever so briefly, Ephrem's exegetical method. In sharp, and deliberate, contrast to certain prevailing trends of interpretation at that time, Ephrem is very careful to keep to a very literal reading of the text. In his own comments on Gen 1:1, Ephrem himself provides for the reader a clear and straightforward representation of his *modus operandi*:

> Let no one think that there is anything allegorical in the works of the six days.[15] No one can rightly say that the things that pertain to these days were symbolic, nor can one say that they were meaningless names or that other things were symbolized for us by their names. Rather, let us know in just what manner heaven and earth were created in the beginning. They were truly heaven and earth.

---

[14] For general studies of the Jewish background of Ephrem's method of exegesis, see D. Gerson, "Die Commentarien des Ephraem Syrus im Verhältnis zur jüdischen Exegese: Ein Beitrag zur Geschichte der Exegese," *MGWJ* 17 (1868) 15-33, 64-72, 98-109, 141-149; T. J. Lamy, "L'exégèse en orient au IVe siècle ou les commentaires de Saint Ephrem," *RB* 2 (1893), 5-25, 161-81, 465-86; Brock, "Jewish Traditions in Syriac Sources," 212-232; Kronholm, *Motifs,* where many rabbinic parallels are enumerated; and P. Féghali, "Influence des Targums sur la pensée exégètique d'Ephrem?" *OCA* 229 (Rome: Pontificium Institutum Orientale, 1984) 71-82. Further material can also be found in R. Tonneau, "Moïse dans la tradition Syrienne," in *Moïse, l'homme de l'Alliance* (Paris: Desclée, 1955) 242-54; A. Guillaumont, "Un midrash d'Exode 4, 24-26 dans Aphraate et Ephrem de Nisibe," in *A Tribute to Arthur Vööbus,* ed. R. Fischer (Chicago: Lutheran School of Theology, 1977) 109-31. A concise summary of the difficulties in trying to detect Ephrem's sources, albeit written with respect to his hymns, can be found in N. Sed, "Les hymnes sur le paradis de saint Ephrem," *LM* 81 (1968) 456: "En général, les attaches judaïques des symboles d'Ephrem sont évidentes. La présence d'un ensemble de faits convergents constitue ici un indice probant. Cependant, nous ne trouvons jamais d'emprunts matérials, copies serviles de formules ou de sentences rabbiniques."

[15] On Ephrem and allegory, see N. El-Khoury, *Die Interpretation der Welt bei Ephräm dem Syrer: Beitrag zur Geistesgeschichte* (Tübinger Theologische Studien 6; Mainz: Matthias-Grünewald, 1976) 49-62, and Kronholm, *Motifs,* 41-43. For precisely what Ephrem means by this and similar terms, see the study of T. Bou Mansour, *La pensée symbolique de Saint Ephrem le Syrien* (Bibliothèque de l'Université Saint-Esprit 16; Kaslik: l'Université Saint-Esprit, 1988).

There was no other thing signified by the names "heaven" and "earth." The rest of the works and things made that followed were not meaningless significations either, for the substances of their natures correspond to what their names signify.[16]

Ephrem here takes a strong stand against the allegorizing of the Alexandrians, of whom he may or may not have known directly, but especially and deliberately against the mythical interpretations as proferred by those above-named heretics against whom Ephrem expended so much energy in his polemics. Ephrem has generally been placed in the Antiochian school of exegesis, with its emphasis on the typological interpretation of scripture.[17] Despite his literalness, however, Ephrem has adopted certain interpretations from his culture that influenced his understanding of the biblical text. It is these influences that lie behind his interpretation of the water in Genesis 1, that we will attempt to set out here. I should like to concentrate my remarks on three particular aspects of water that underlie Ephrem's account of the six days of creation.[18] In the course of Ephrem's *Commentary on Genesis*, these particular aspects are not of tremendous importance in terms of the overall theology of the work, but they are important in so far as they help the reader to discern Ephrem's sources and they also provide a glimpse, however brief, of certain controversies that existed in his day.

Genesis 1:20—Water, the Source of Everything

The first aspect of water is one that should not detain us long. Underlying Ephrem's entire account of the creation in Genesis 1 is the fact

---

[16] In the thought of Ephrem, for something to have a name is to have a *qnômâ*, or substance, and that name designates just what that substance is. See *Des Heiligen Ephraem des Syrers Hymnen de Fide* (CSCO 154-155; ed. E. Beck; Louvain: Peeters, 1955) 16.2: "in the names are the substances"; *Des Heiligen Ephraem des Syrers Hymnen contra Haereses*, 48.2: "the name Creator testifies to God who created everything"; and *Des Heiligen Ephraem des Syrers Sermones de Fide* (CSCO 212-213; ed. E. Beck; Louvain: Peeters, 1961) 2. See also the discussion in El-Khoury, *Die Interpretation der Welt bei Ephraem*, 45.

[17] See, for example, Kronholm, *Motifs*, 25-28.

[18] Other aspects, such as the pericope of the rivers in Gen 2:10-14, are also of interest, as Ephrem is the first in the Syrian tradition to posit that the Pishon is to be equated with the Danube. See *Sancti Ephraem Syri in Genesim*, 29; Mathews, *Ephrem the Syrian*, 100, with n. 125. See also our remarks on the water-pipe above.

that water is an essential element in the creation of all things. While the biblical text only explicitly states that the "swarms of living creatures" had come directly out of the water, Ephrem nevertheless, finds the water component at least implied in the rest of creation as well. As for the sprouting of the vegetation in verse II, Ephrem, not surprisingly, presumes that the moisture left in the earth after the departure of the waters into the seas was as empirically demonstrable then as it is now.[19] Moreover, Ephrem states in his *Commentary on Genesis* I.10, that "through light and water the earth brought forth everything."[20] Further down at I.26, Ephrem explicitly states that the waters "brought forth swarming things and fish from within them; the serpents were created in the abysses and the birds soared in flocks out of the waves into the air."[21] In his *Commentary on Genesis* II.3, speaking of the spring of Gen 2:6, Ephrem further qualifies these remarks by saying that "it was not that God was unable to bring forth everything from the earth in another way. Rather, it was His will that [the earth] should bring forth by means of water. [God] did it this way right from the beginning so that this procedure would be perpetuated until the end of time."[22]

In this matter of the creation from water, Ephrem seems to be in harmony with all of his contemporaries, both Jewish and Christian. Basil of Caesarea, presumably following Origen, takes it already as tradition that Gen 1:20 is to be interpreted in this manner, but does so in slightly more nuanced fashion. He explains that the birds, as well as the fish, were brought out from the waters "because the flying creatures share a certain relationship, as it were, with those that swim. For, just as fish tread the water, going forward with the motion of their fins . . . so also birds can be seen moving through the air with their wings in similar fashion."[23] Such diverse commentators as Augustine, Ambrose and Cyril of Alexandria also follow this interpretation.

---

[19] *Sancti Ephraem Syri in Genesim*, 20; Mathews, *Ephrem the Syrian*, 89. That all life originated in the seas is still, of course, the fundamental principle in most modern theories of evolution.

[20] *Sancti Ephraem Syri in Genesim*, 13; Mathews, *Ephrem the Syrian*, 82.

[21] *Sancti Ephraem Syri in Genesim*, 22; Mathews, *Ephrem the Syrian*, 92.

[22] *Sancti Ephraem Syri in Genesim*, 27; Mathews, *Ephrem the Syrian*, 98. Ephrem no doubt has his baptismal theology in mind here; for this, see E. Beck, "Le Baptême chez St. Ephrem," *OS* I (1956) III-36.

[23] Basil, *Hom. in Hex.*, 8.2. See also his *Ep.*, 188.15. See Origen, *Hom. in Gen.* 1.8. Origen's source is likely Philo, *De Opif. Mundi*, 63.

Among Jewish sources, *Gen. Rab.* 7 presumes the same tradition and also offers a defense of God's having brought forth even birds and other non-aquatic creatures from the water: In ordinary circumstances a mortal king draws a picture on dry ground. But the Holy One, blessed be He, draws pictures on water, as it is said, "And God said, 'Let the waters produce pictures.'"[24] *PRE* 9 and 11, and Philo, *De Opif. Mundi* 63, also presume that all creatures came forth from the water,[25] while *Tg. Ps.-J.* at 1:20 reads *rqq*—"alluvial mud" in the place of the *mym*—"water" of the Hebrew text, the same rendering as found in *b. Hul.* 27b and *b. Erub.* 28a.[26]

One must also note here that it was a common notion in the ancient Near East that water was the basis of creation. It can be found in Egyptian mythology: Nu(n), the god of the primeval waters, was considered to be the source of everything.[27] S. Kramer has already noted that "Sumerian thinkers assumed that before the universe came into being there existed nothing but water, that is, they postulated the existence of a primeval sea."[28] In the *Enuma Elish,* even the gods were born of the mingling of the primeval waters, Apsu and Mummu-

---

[24] Translation from J. Neusner, *Genesis Rabbah: The Judaic Commentary to the Book of Genesis. A New American Translation* (Brown Judaic Studies 104; Atlanta: Scholars, 1985) I.67, where in VIII.I.1.C, it is explained that "the root for the [Hebrew] word for 'draw a picture' occurs in the root for the word 'swarm.'"

[25] For a general overview, see L. Ginzberg, *The Legends of the Jews* (Philadelphia: Jewish Publication Society, 1909) I. 28, and M. Alexandre, *Le Commencement du Livre Genèse I-V. La version grecque de la Septante et sa réception* (CA 3; Paris: Beauchesne, 1988) 148-149. In addition to the sources that Alexandre mentions, see also *Pesiq. Rab. Kah.,* 4.35a, *Konen,* 26, *Koh. Rab.,* 7.23, *Tan. B.,* 4.112, *Tan. Huk.,* 6, and *Bar.,* 19.3. I am making no claims here about the dating of these Jewish sources; I am only pointing to their parallel witness to this particular exegesis concerning the water.

[26] Interestingly, Augustine, *De Gen. add litt.* 6.2, 13, says that Adam was made from limus—"slime." It is not clear, however, if the same word found in Origen, *Hom. in Gen.,* I.13, translates the corresponding Greek word employed by Origen or is rather due to the Latin translator Rufinus of Aquileia.

[27] See the discussion of the various forms of this myth in S. G. F. Brandon, *Creation Legends of the Ancient Near East* (London: Hodder and Stoughton, 1963) 14-65, and the remarks in J. K. Hoffmeier, "Some Thoughts on Genesis 1 & 2 and Egyptian Cosmology," *JANES* 15 (1983) 39-49.

[28] S. N. Kramer, *The Sumerians: Their History, Culture, and Character* (Chicago: University of Chicago, 1963) 113.

Tiamat.[29] Similar parallels can also be found in other ancient NE cultures.[30] For Homer, Okeanos is the source, Gk. *genesis*, of the gods, while for Thales and Anaximander, as well as for Pindar, cited above, water is the principal element.[31] While it seems, therefore, that on this matter Ephrem is just following a "pan-Mediterranean" tradition, his position is most likely mediated by the Judeo-Christian tradition. It is perhaps not without import that only Ephrem and *Gen. Rab.* feel compelled to proffer an apology for God's method of creating land creatures by means of the waters.

Genesis 1:6—The Constitution of the Firmament

Of this "all-creative" water, Ephrem also makes two other explicit claims that bear some consideration.[32] The first is his claim that the firmament in Gen 1:6-8 was made from the congealed waters: "The firmament between the waters was pressed together from the waters."[33] While the translations *stereōma* found in the LXX and other Greek versions and *firmamentum* found in the Vulgate both may or may not suggest some third solid element, there is no doubt that the Homeric epithets *chalkeos* and *sidēreos* clearly do. On this matter, however, the great Christian exegetes are on the whole relatively silent.

---

[29] I am following here B. W. Anderson, *Creation Versus Chaos* (Philadelphia: Fortress, 1987) 18.

[30] See, for example, Brandon, *Creation Legends of the Ancient Near East*, s.v. "water" in index; W. G. Lambert, "A New Look at the Babylonian Background of Genesis," *JTS* 16 (1965) 287-300; and W. G. Lambert, "Old Testament Mythology in its Ancient Near Eastern Context," *Congress Volume: Jerusalem 1986* (SVT 40; Leiden: Brill, 1988) 124-143.

[31] *Il.*, 14.201, 246, 302, 18.489; Thales, *Frags.*, 84-85, in G. S. Kirk, J. E. Raven and M. Schofield, *The Presocratic Philosophers* (2d ed.; Cambridge: Cambridge University, 1983) 88-89.

[32] I am aware that the following presupposes rather the fruits of research than the full arguments, but exigencies of space have precluded the inclusion here of all the details of the arguments.

[33] *Sancti Ephraem Syri in Genesim*, 17; Mathews, *Ephrem the Syrian*, 87. Ephrem may here have in mind such biblical texts as Job 38:30 or Ps 104:3. This interpretation of Ephrem was also preserved in the later Nestorian Syriac tradition, no doubt on the authority of Ephrem; see T. Jansma, "Investigations into the Early Syrian Fathers on Genesis," *OTS* 12 (1958) 114-16.

Ambrose, Augustine, Origen, and Theodoret of Cyr of the surviving commentaries say nothing at all about the constitution of the firmament. Basil of Caesarea maintains that the firmament is of some unnamed solid and unbending substance, but he was aware that there were those who maintained that the firmament was made of water as he sharply rebuked as "childish and of simple intellect" those who held that the firmament could have been made out of water.[34] John Chrysostom also knew of such an interpretation, not improbably from Basil. He, however, does not discount the possibility that the firmament was composed of water as did Basil but, nevertheless, he refused to adopt any particular interpretation and chose to leave the question open. Who were those against whom Basil spoke? To my knowledge only Hippolytus of Rome[35] and Severian of Gabala,[36] among Greek Christian exegetes, make this claim. While Hippolytus' training and sources are yet to be recovered, it is generally presumed that he is from somewhere in the East. His works display a knowledge of Greek philosophy such that he is generally considered to be a product of the school of Alexandria, where he could have been aware of non-Christian traditions.[37] As for Severian of Gabala, it has already been demonstrated that in several instances, including the identification of the Pishon in Gen 2:11 with the Danube, he manifests not a few correspondences with Syriac exegesis and in particular with those found in the

---

[34] Basil, *Hom. in Hex.*, 3.4. Among the later commentators, Procopius of Gaza, *Comm. in Genesin* (PG 87) 68C-D, and John Philoponus, *De Opif. Mundi Libri VII* (ed. G. Reichardt; Leipzig: Teubner, 1897) 3.16, both argued, perhaps echoing Basil, against those who considered the firmament to be made out of water.

[35] Hippolytus, *In Gen.* (PG 10) 585B. Hippolytus argues that God divided the waters into three parts: one, the waters above; two, the firmament; three, the waters below: *Tote to triton meros tōn hydatōn pēgnysin en mesō. To triton de eis to anō exōrisen analambanōn tē heautou dynamei hama tō stereōmati. To de triton eis to katō katelipe pros xrēsin kai apolausin tois anthrōpois.*

[36] Severian of Gabala, *In mundi creationem Or.* (PG 56) 442, 452: *ton ouranon touton . . . ex hydatōn epoiēsen ho theos, pēxas hōs krystallon.* Cited, with apparent approbation, in Cosmas Indicopleustès, *Topographie Chrétienne* (SC 197; ed. W. Wolska-Conus; Paris: Cerf, 1973) X. 25; see also III. 31.

[37] See J. Quasten, *Patrology* (Utrecht-Antwerp: Spectrum, 1975) II. 163-65, and M. Richard, "Hippolyte de Rome (saint)," *DS* 7 (1969) 531-71.

exegetical works of Ephrem.[38] Other than in the writings of these two figures, I find nothing else similar among the Christian exegetes.

When we turn to Jewish sources, however, we find the situation somewhat different. In *Gen. Rab.* IV.2, the firmament was clearly made from the solidified water, and in IV.5, there is recorded the argument over the precise width of this watery firmament: "thick as a metal plate;" or "thick as two or three fingers," which latter position is also echoed in *Tg. Ps.-J.*, at 1:6. Jos., *Ant.*, I.30 simply states that the firmament was made from congealed ice, Gr. *krystallos*.[39] The Alexandrian Philo says nothing on this matter in his extant works, as unfortunately nothing has survived of the material on Genesis 1, from his *Questions on Genesis*.

It would seem then that in the matter of the composition of the firmament Ephrem, along with Severian of Gabala though whether directly or indirectly is unknown, is following a tradition much closer to the prevailing Jewish exegesis of that time and is thus in that very camp against whom Basil so ardently polemicized. While Ephrem's interpretation remained standard in later Syrian exegesis,[40] it was no doubt due to the authority of Basil that this interpretation never really entered into the realm of Western Christian tradition.

Genesis 1:9—The Nature of the Waters Above and Below the Firmament

The third and last proposition to consider here is that when God made the firmament to divide the upper waters from the lower waters and later called the lower waters to gather themselves into seas, Ephrem

[38] See J. Zellinger, *Die Genesishomilien des Bischofs Severian von Gabala* (ATAbh 7.1; Munster: Aschendorffschen Buchhandlung, 1916) *passim;* see pp. 102-3, for the identification of the Pishon.

[39] See also *Yal. Gen.* 5. The great medieval exegete Rashi, in his *Commentary on Genesis*, at 1:6, follows Rab in *Gen. Rab.*, 4.2, who maintained that the heavens were created on the first day in liquid form and then solidified on the second day.

[40] See A. Levene, *The Early Syrian Fathers on Genesis, from a Syriac MS. on the Pentateuch in the Mingana Collection* (London: Taylor's Foreign, 1951) 73, 134-35. See also T. Jansma, "Investigations into the Early Syrian Fathers on Genesis," in *Studies on the Book of Genesis* (B. Gemser, et al. ed.; Oudtestamentische Studien 12; Leiden: Brill, 1958) 114-16.

goes on at some length to demonstrate that the upper waters were sweet, while the lower waters, particularly those in the seas, were salty. The passage in question, *Commentary on Genesis* I.10-13, deserves to be cited here *in toto*:

> The waters that the earth drank on the first day were not salty. Even if these waters were like the deep on the surface of the earth, they were not yet seas. For it was in the seas that these waters, which were not salty before being gathered together, became salty. When they were sent throughout the entire earth for the earth to drink they were sweet, but when they were gathered into seas on the third day, they became salty, lest they become stagnant due to their being gathered together, and so that they might receive the rivers that enter into them without increasing. For the quantity that a sea requires for nourishment is the measure of the rivers that flow down into it. Rivers flow down into seas lest the heat of the sun dry them up. The saltiness [of the seas] then swallows up [the rivers] lest they increase, rise up, and cover the earth. Thus the rivers turn into nothing, as it were, because the saltiness of the sea swallows them up.[41]
>
> The seas had been created when the waters were created and were hidden in those waters, and although the seas became bitter, the waters above them were not bitter. Just as there were seas in the flood, but they were covered over [by those waters], they were not able to change into their bitter nature the sweet waters of the flood which came from above. If these waters had been bitter, how would the olives and all the plants have been preserved in them? How did those of the house of Noah and those with them drink from them?
>
> Although Noah had commanded that all sorts of food be brought for himself and those with him because there would be no food anywhere, he did not allow water to be brought because those who had entered the ark would be able to take from the water outside of the ark to drink. Therefore, just as the waters of the flood were not salty while the seas were hidden within them, neither were the waters that were gathered on the third day bitter even though the seas below them were bitter.
>
> Just as the gathering of the waters did not precede that word which said, *"Let the waters be gathered and let the dry land appear,"*[42] neither did the seas exist until that moment when *God*

---

[41] Cf. Eccl 1:7.
[42] Gen 1:9.

called the gathering of water "seas."[43] When they received their name they were changed. In their [new] place the [waters] attained that saltiness that had not been theirs [even] outside of their [old] place. For [their place] became deep at that very moment when [God] said, *"Let the waters be gathered into one place."* Then either the land [under] the sea was brought down below the [level of the] earth to receive within it its own waters along with the waters that were above the entire earth, or the waters swallowed each other so that the place might be sufficient for them, or the place of the sea shook and it became a great depth and the waters quickly hastened into that basin. Although the will of God had gathered these waters when the earth was created, a gate was opened for them to be gathered into one place. Just as in the gathering of the first and second waters there was found no gathering place because there was no place from which they might go out, so now do these waters come down with all the rains and showers and are gathered into seas along paths and roads which had been prepared for them on the first day.

The upper waters, because they had been separated on the second day from the lower waters by the firmament set between them, were also sweet like the lower waters. (The upper waters are not those that became salty in the seas on the third day, but are those that were separated from them on the second day.) They were not salty, therefore, because they would not have become stagnant, for they had not been left on the land to become stagnant. The air there does not serve to cause [things] to be born or to swarm, nor do rivers flow into them to keep them from evaporating for there is no sun there to generate heat that would cause them to evaporate. They remain there for the dew of blessing and are kept there for the floodgates of wrath.[44]

Clearly, this is not an unimportant issue for Ephrem. Such a lengthy comment suggests a defense, if not a mild polemic, on the part of Ephrem. Here the sources are sparse, but suggestive nonetheless. In short, I find nothing at all in any Christian source, Syriac Greek or Latin. It seems that the very question itself that some waters were sweet or fresh while others were salty was never an issue or even a consideration. One's first impulse, therefore, is to suggest that Ephrem has taken this stance against a counter position held by Bardaisan, Mar-

---

[43] Gen 1:10.
[44] *Sancti Ephraem Syri in Genesim*, 14-15; Mathews, *Ephrem the Syrian*, 82-84.

cion or Mani. While it may have been the case, nothing has survived in the extant sources to allow for such a conclusion. It is not clear here just who Ephrem's opponent here might have been.

We do, on the other hand, find traces of a similar tradition in Jewish sources. In *Gen. Rab.* 4.5, 5.8, and 13.10, and *PRE* 9, one finds hints that such a tradition still merited discussion. One also finds that Philo, *De Opif. Mundi* 38 shows a similar concern to that of Ephrem in insisting that the sweet waters be distinguished from the salty:

> God ordained that all the water which was salty and destined to be a cause of barrenness to seeds and trees should be gathered together, flowing forth out from all the holes throughout the entire earth; and he commanded the dry land to appear, that the liquid which had any sweetness in it be left on [the dry land] to secure its durability. For this sweet liquid, in due proportions, is as a sort of glue for the different substances, preventing the earth from being utterly dried up. . . . [45]

It thus seems more than likely, as no other parallel can be found, that here too Ephrem was passing on traditions that he found current in the thought of his contemporary Jewish exegetes.

Conclusion

That the creation account found in the book of Genesis was of paramount importance to both Jewish and Christian exegetes needs no defense. Genesis was clearly the basis for Jewish and Christian battles over cosmology against many of the varied groups and trends of thought that flourished in Late Antiquity, both pagan and those who claimed to have some connection with either the Jewish or the Christian way of thought. The book of Genesis, part of the revealed word of God in both Jewish and Christian traditions, was unique in its insistence on the one God being the sole creator of everything in the heavens and on the earth. And both Jews and Christians steadfastly maintained this position in the face of all opposition, whether originating from within or without their respective camps.

---

[45] Translation, with minor adaptations from C. D. Yonge, tr., *The Works of Philo* (rev. ed.; Peabody, Mass.: Hendrickson, 1993) 6.

Nevertheless, while Jews and Christians shared the Genesis creation account, along with many other books and traditions, there was still no congeniality between them. The enmity between Jews and Christians in the early centuries of the Christian era is too well known to be rehearsed here. In fact, on one issue at least, the book of Genesis itself served as the very ground on which Jews and Christians fought, particularly as the Jews tried to reassert themselves in the face of the new imperial favor enjoyed by the Christians in the post-Constantinian, or as is much more probable in the post-Julianic, era.[46] Ephrem himself, in contrast to his contemporary Aphrahat, was one of the, if not the most, bitter opponents of Judaism.[47] While Ephrem did indeed exhibit a bitter hostility toward Judaism, he has nonetheless, as has often been demonstrated, preserved many Jewish traditions in his hymns. These traditions that have heretofore been uncovered are all of an exegetical nature.[48] These same exegetical traditions are readily to be found throughout his *Commentary on Genesis*.[49] As mentioned above, Ephrem has not adopted these traditions in any literal or slavish fashion; he has adopted and molded them into his own unique Christian theology.

[46] See the arguments in J. Neusner, *Genesis and Judaism: The Perspectives of Genesis Rabbah* (Atlanta: Scholars, 1985); and more fully in J. Neusner, *Judaism and Christianity in the Age of Constantine: History, Messiah, Israel, and the Initial Confrontation* (Chicago: University of Chicago, 1987). From a different perspective, see P. S. Alexander, "Pre-Emptive Exegesis: *Genesis Rabba*'s Reading of the Story of the Creation," *JJS* 43 (1992) 230-245. From the Christian side, see G. T. Armstrong, *Die Genesis in der Alten Kirche* (BGBH 4; Tubingen: J. C. B. Mohr, 1962).

[47] See, for example, *Des Heiligen Ephraem des Syrers Paschahymnen* (CSCO 247-248; ed. E. Beck; Louvain: Peeters, 1964). R. Murray, *Symbols of Church and Kingdom: A Study in Early Syriac Tradition* (Cambridge: Cambridge University, 1975) 41-68; on p. 19, Murray points out that "the Christians in Mesopotamia lived at the door of the Jews like poor relations not on speaking terms. Ephrem's bitterness is less surprising than Aphrahat's courtesy." On this issue, see also K. McVey, "The Anti-Judaic Polemic of Ephrem Syrus' Hymns on the Nativity," in *Of Scribes and Scrolls: Studies in the Hebrew Bible, Intertestamental Judaism, and Christian Origins* (ed. H. W. Attridge, J. J. Collins, and T. H. Tobin; Lanham: University Press of America, 1990) 229-40; and A. P. Hayman, "The Image of the Jew in the Syriac Anti-Jewish Polemical Literature," in *To See Ourselves as Others See Us:" Christians, Jews, "Others" in Late Antiquity* (ed. J. Neusner and E. S. Frerichs; Atlanta: Scholars, 1985) 423-41.

[48] See n. 14, above.

[49] A very preliminary investigation into these traditions can be found in the notes to my translation of Ephrem's *Commentary on Genesis* in Mathews, *Ephrem the Syrian*.

While the evidence presented here hardly does justice to the topic,[50] I have attempted to demonstrate that not only did Ephrem adopt a significant number of exegetical traditions, he has inherited and retained certain elements of Jewish cosmology as well. While a complete examination would be impossible here, it is hoped that the evidence that has been set out here will suffice to demonstrate that while some of the cosmological presuppositions of Ephrem might already be found among Mediterranean peoples, Ephrem is following, even where the idea can be labelled "pan-Mediterranean," the particular manifestation of the idea as it is found in the Jewish thought of his time. As with the Jewish exegetical traditions found in his hymns, however, nothing of literary dependency can be clearly demonstrated. It is finally to be hoped that this initial investigation, as Br. Aloysius' own researches into meteorological imagery have done for Biblical studies, will serve to show not only the importance of non-exegetical traditions, but also to incite further research into the importance of cosmological presumptions in Jewish and Christian traditions in Late Antiquity.

[50] In addition to the cursory nature of this study, I have been unable to consult the encyclopedic work of M. M. Kasher, *Torah Shelemah*, vol. I (Jerusalem: Bet Torah Shelemah, 1927).

CHAPTER 11

The Verb Syntax of the Idol Passage of Isaiah 44:9–20

DEIRDRE DEMPSEY

The idol parody passage of Isa 44:9-20 has presented translators and exegetes with numerous problems. See, for example, the proliferation of notes following the translation of Isa 44:9-20 in Elliger's commentary on Deutero-Isaiah.[1] The text of Isa 44:9-20 in a few places shows signs of being in disorder. Though what the text is ultimately about is absolutely clear (the absurdity of idol worship), the argument does not seem well-ordered; not, at least, by modern standards. In not a few places it has all the appearances of being poetry with clearly balanced cola forming lines and with a similar balance between the lines. This is the view of the *JPSV* and the *NEB* as opposed to the *NAB* and the *NRSV*; and of *BHS* as opposed to *BHK*. In my translation I have attempted to arrange Isa 44:9-20 as poetry. Admittedly it is difficult to work out a completely satisfactory stichometry. This may well indicate that the text is in serious disorder and that the strange concatenation of tenses it contains is to be explained as the result of faulty text transmission. *BHS* attempts to resolve the problem of the tenses in the piece by suggesting a full nine occurrences where *wayyiqtol* in the text should be emended to *weyiqtol*. This *weyiqtol* would then function as

---

[1] Karl Elliger, *Deuterojesaja* (BKAT 11/1; Neukirchen: Neukirchener, 1978).

a *yiqtol* as a timeless present of general experience,[2] with a simple
waw; this *yiqtol* as a timeless present is the basic verb form of not only
the idol passage of Isa 44, but also the idol passages of Isa 40:19-20 and
Isa 41:6-7. This solution leaves unanswered the question of what the
Masoretes thought they were doing with their pointing of the passage.
In this article, I offer an explanation of the Masoretic pointing of the
text. My solution hinges on the use of *wayyiqtol* as a past relative to
timeless presents of truths of experience.

BHS text of Isa 44:9-20:

9 יֹצְרֵי־פֶסֶל כֻּלָּם תֹּהוּ וַחֲמוּדֵיהֶם בַּל־יוֹעִילוּ
וְעֵדֵיהֶם הֵמָּה בַּל־יִרְאוּ וּבַל־יֵדְעוּ לְמַעַן יֵבֹשׁוּ:

10 מִי־יָצַר אֵל וּפֶסֶל נָסָךְ לְבִלְתִּי הוֹעִיל:

11 הֵן כָּל־חֲבֵרָיו יֵבֹשׁוּ וְחָרָשִׁים הֵמָּה מֵאָדָם
יִתְקַבְּצוּ כֻלָּם יַעֲמֹדוּ יִפְחֲדוּ יֵבֹשׁוּ יָחַד:

12 חָרַשׁ בַּרְזֶל מַעֲצָד וּפָעַל בַּפֶּחָם
וּבַמַּקָּבוֹת יִצְּרֵהוּ וַיִּפְעָלֵהוּ בִּזְרוֹעַ כֹּחוֹ
גַּם־רָעֵב וְאֵין כֹּחַ לֹא־שָׁתָה מַיִם וַיִּיעָף:

13 חָרַשׁ עֵצִים נָטָה קָו יְתָאֲרֵהוּ בַשֶּׂרֶד
יַעֲשֵׂהוּ בַּמַּקְצֻעוֹת וּבַמְּחוּגָה יְתָאֳרֵהוּ
וַיַּעֲשֵׂהוּ כְּתַבְנִית אִישׁ כְּתִפְאֶרֶת אָדָם לָשֶׁבֶת בָּיִת:

14 לִכְרָת־לוֹ אֲרָזִים וַיִּקַּח תִּרְזָה וְאַלּוֹן
וַיְאַמֶּץ־לוֹ בַּעֲצֵי־יָעַר נָטַע אֹרֶן וְגֶשֶׁם יְגַדֵּל:

15 וְהָיָה לְאָדָם לְבָעֵר וַיִּקַּח מֵהֶם וַיָּחָם אַף־יַשִּׂיק וְאָפָה לָחֶם
אַף־יִפְעַל־אֵל וַיִּשְׁתָּחוּ עָשָׂהוּ פֶסֶל וַיִּסְגָּד־לָמוֹ:

---

[2] This is the form identified by Waltke-O'Connor as "habitual non-perfective"
(Waltke, B., and M. O'Connor, *An Introduction to Biblical Hebrew Syntax.* p. 506, 31.3e
Winona Lake: Eisenbrauns, 1990). The form is discussed in GKC, §107; P. Joüon, *Gram-*
maire de l'hebreu biblique (Rome: PBI, 1923), §113c.

16 חֶצְיוֹ שָׂרַף בְּמוֹ־אֵשׁ עַל־חֶצְיוֹ בָּשָׂר יֹאכֵל יִצְלֶה צָלִי וְיִשְׂבָּע
אַף־יָחֹם וְיֹאמַר הֶאָח חַמּוֹתִי רָאִיתִי אוּר:

17 וּשְׁאֵרִיתוֹ לְאֵל עָשָׂה לְפִסְלוֹ יִסְגָּד־לוֹ וְיִשְׁתַּחוּ
וְיִתְפַּלֵּל אֵלָיו וְיֹאמַר הַצִּילֵנִי כִּי אֵלִי אָתָּה:

18 לֹא יָדְעוּ וְלֹא יָבִינוּ כִּי טַח מֵרְאוֹת עֵינֵיהֶם מֵהַשְׂכִּיל לִבֹּתָם:

19 וְלֹא־יָשִׁיב אֶל־לִבּוֹ וְלֹא דַעַת וְלֹא־תְבוּנָה לֵאמֹר
חֶצְיוֹ שָׂרַפְתִּי בְמוֹ־אֵשׁ וְאַף אָפִיתִי עַל־גֶּחָלָיו לֶחֶם אֶצְלֶה בָשָׂר וְאֹכֵל
וְיִתְרוֹ לְתוֹעֵבָה אֶעֱשֶׂה לְבוּל עֵץ אֶסְגּוֹד:

20 רֹעֶה אֵפֶר לֵב הוּתַל הִטָּהוּ וְלֹא־יַצִּיל אֶת־נַפְשׁוֹ
וְלֹא יֹאמַר הֲלוֹא שֶׁקֶר בִּימִינִי:

Translation

9 Those who manufacture idols, all of them are of no account;
  the things in which they delight bring no profit.
 They are their own witnesses;
  they cannot see,
 They cannot understand,
  deafer are they than men;[3]
  consequently they come to shame.

10 Whoever has manufactured a god or cast an idol
  profits nothing.

11 All his friends come to shame.[4]
  When all of them assemble and stand forth to argue in court,
 all become afraid and ashamed.

12 The ironworker fashions an image;[5]

---

[3] Insert וְחָרָשִׁים חֵמָּה מֵאָדָם, misplaced and partially misvocalized in v. 11, after וּבַל־יֵדְעוּ in v. 9. See *NAB Textual Notes*, 414-15.

[4] Transpose וחרשים המה מאדם to v. 9. See preceding note.

[5] מַעֲצָד seems impossible here. The word occurs here and in Jer 10:3, which is also concerned with idol-making. It is connected with Arabic *mi‘did*, a cutting tool (‘*adada* = to cut), and that is the sense of the word in Jer 10:3, where it is a carving tool for shaping a *wooden* idol. The similar vocabulary there, מַעֲשֵׂה יְדֵי־חָרָשׁ בַּמַּעֲצָד, in a similar context may have triggered the introduction of the word in the present context. With an eye on Jer 44:19 (לְהַעֲצִבָה = לְהַעֲצִבָה [*HALAT* 818] = "making images in her likeness"), *The NAB Textual Notes* suggests מַעֲצֵב = "to make an image."

he works it over the coals;
he shapes it with hammers.
After he has worked it with his mighty arm,
he is hungry and without strength.
Since he did not drink water, he is exhausted.

13 Once the carpenter has stretched out his line,
he traces out the idol with a stylus.
He shapes it with scrapers,
he measures it with a compass.
He shapes it[6] in the image of a man;
like a comely man, that it might dwell in a shrine.

14 After he has cut down cedars,
after he has laid hold of a holm and an oak,
After he has taken hold of other trees of the forest,
which the Lord[7] had planted,
Which the rain over the years had made to grow,

15 and had been intended to become available to man for
burning,
After he has taken some of the wood and has warmed himself,
then he starts a fire and bakes bread.
After he has labored for days at making a god and
bowed down to it,
after he has fashioned the wood into an idol and worshipped
it,

16 After he has set on fire the other half of it,
on that half he roasts meat,[8]
he eats what he has roasted and becomes satisfied.
He warms himself and says: Good!
I am warm, I feel the fire.

17 When he has made out of the rest of it a god, his idol,
he prostrates himself before it and bows down.
He prays to it, saying:
Save me, for you are my god!

18 The idols know nothing, they can understand nothing.

---

[6] וַיַּעֲשֵׂהוּ should be read as יַעֲשֵׂהוּ (present form is a result of dittography), or as וְיַעֲשֵׂהוּ.

[7] אֹרֶן should be read as אָדֹן, "the Lord," with LXX, or perhaps better, since absolute אָדֹן is used elsewhere of the Lord only in Ps 114:7, אֲדֹנָי (loss of י before the graphically similar ו, haplography). The text has a little ו—see the margin—probably to indicate that the Masoretes had questions about the text.

[8] Transpose יֹאכַל יִצְלֶה, on the basis of LXX and v. 19.

> Their eyes are coated over so that they cannot see;
> their hearts too, so that they understand nothing.
> 19 Still no one takes this to heart;
> no one[9] has the sense or perception so as to say:
> I have burned half of the wood in the fire,
> I have baked bread on the coals.
> I am roasting meat and eating it.
> Should I now make the rest of it into an abomination,
> should I bow down before a block of wood?
> 20 The idol-maker shepherds dust.
> When the flame consumes it,[10]
> it cannot save itself.
> Yet he cannot say:
> Isn't this thing in my right hand a sham?

The first step toward understanding the use of *wayyiqtol* as a past relative to timeless presents of truths of experience is to examine the use of the *qatal* as a past relative to timeless truths of experience. Isa 40:19 is the first occurrence in Second Isaiah of this phenomenon, which is not adequately treated in the standard Biblical Hebrew grammars.

BHS text of Isa 40:18-20:

18 אֶל־מִי תְּדַמְּיוּן אֵל וּמַה־דְּמוּת תַּעַרְכוּ לוֹ:

19 הַפֶּסֶל נָסַךְ חָרָשׁ וְצֹרֵף בַּזָּהָב יְרַקְּעֶנּוּ
וּרְתֻקוֹת כֶּסֶף צוֹרֵף: 20 הַמְסֻכָּן תְּרוּמָה עֵץ לֹא־יִרְקַב יִבְחָר
חָרָשׁ חָכָם יְבַקֶּשׁ־לוֹ לְהָכִין פֶּסֶל לֹא יִמּוֹט:

Translation[11]
> 18 With whom can you compare God;
> and what likeness can you offer for him?
> 19 The image, which after the (metal) worker has cast it,

---

[9] Read וְלֹא דַעַת לוֹ וְלֹא־תְבוּנָה, the homophone was lost before וְלֹא.

[10] The MT, לֵב הוּתַל הִטָּהוּ, "a heart which is deceived has led him astray," makes sense. But a modest redivision of the consonantal text produces an even stronger argument. Read, with the *NAB*, לבה תלהטהו.

[11] My treatment of Isa 40:19-20 and 41:6-7 is based on A. Fitzgerald, F.S.C., "The Technology of Isa 40:19-20 + 41:6-7," *CBQ* 51 (1989) 426-46.

the worker in fine metals plates with gold,
and inlays[12] with silver wire?
20 X-wood as a platform,
wood that does not rot, he selects for it.
A skilled (wood) worker he searches out for it, to set the image
on its base so it won't topple over.

In this instance, Isa 40:19, the *qatal* נָסַךְ ("which after the [metal]
worker has cast it") is past as regards the following *yiqtol* יְרַקְּעֶנּוּ ("the
worker in fine metals plates with gold"). Joüon discusses the *qatal* as
pluperfect, past action anterior to another past action (Joüon §112c, an
example is Gen 31:34, ". . . and he entered [*wayyiqtol* = past] the tent of
Rachel. Now Rachel had taken [*qatal* = action anterior to the preceding *wayyiqtol*]) the idols . . .") and as future perfect, action anterior to
another action in the future (Joüon §112i, an example is Jer 8:3, "death
will be preferred [*weqataltí* = *yiqtol* = future] to life by all the remaining remnant of this wicked race who remain in any of the places to
which I shall have banished them [*qatal* = action anterior to the preceding *weqataltí*], oracle of the Lord of hosts").

Bergsträsser[13] discusses the *qatal* as pluperfect (B II 6d), but puts off
the discussion of future perfect for his section on syntax, which was
never completed: "Die Verwendung des Perf. in besonderen Satzarten
(Fragesätzen, bestimmten Arten der Nebensätze) ist der Syntax
zuzuweisen" (B II 6k). While neither Joüon nor Bergstrásser discusses
the situation where the relative past is past as regards a timeless present, analogy suggests this analysis of נָסַךְ. If *qatal* can be used for
action anterior to past action and for action anterior to a future action,
it seems to me perfectly natural to accept *qatal* used for action anterior
to a timeless present.

I identify this use of *qatal* as past relative to a timeless present of
truths of experience in two other Isaiah passages: Isa 44:10, 12, 13, 15, 16,
17; and Isa 55:10.

---

[12] The participle צוֹרֵף is regarded as a metathesized form of רֹצֵף. The *NAB* emendation to יְצָרֵף is possible but not necessary, since the participle substituting for the
yiqtol functions as a timeless present of truths of experience. Isa 41:7 provides another
example within these texts of a predicate participle functioning as a timeless present of
truths of experience.

[13] W. Gesenius—G. Bergsträsser, *Hebräische Grammatik* (2 vols.; Leipzig: Hinrichs,
1918–29).

BHS Text of Isa 55:10:

כִּי כַּאֲשֶׁר יֵרֵד הַגֶּשֶׁם וְהַשֶּׁלֶג מִן־הַשָּׁמַיִם

וְשָׁמָּה לֹא יָשׁוּב כִּי אִם־הִרְוָה אֶת־הָאָרֶץ

וְהוֹלִידָהּ וְהִצְמִיחָהּ וְנָתַן זֶרַע לַזֹּרֵעַ וְלֶחֶם לָאֹכֵל:

As the rain and the snow descend (יֵרֵד, *yiqtol* as timeless present) from the heavens, and do not return (יָשׁוּב, *yiqtol* as timeless present) there until they have watered (הִרְוָה, *qatal* as past relative to timeless present) the earth, and caused it to bear and sprout (וְהוֹלִידָהּ וְהִצְמִיחָהּ, non-converting *weqatal* as past relative to timeless present), giving seed to the sower and food to the one who eats.

For examples outside of Second Isaiah I cite proverbs where the typical tense is the *yiqtol* of experience (Joüon 113c), as well as examples from Job and Psalms:

Prov 11:15:

רַע־יֵרוֹעַ כִּי־עָרַב זָר

One suffers injury (יֵרוֹעַ, *yiqtol* as timeless present of truths of experience) if one has become a pledge for a stranger (עָרַב, *qatal* as relative past as regards a timeless present).

Prov 14:6:

בִּקֶּשׁ־לֵץ חָכְמָה וָאָיִן

The senseless man has sought (בִּקֶּשׁ, *qatal* as relative past) wisdom, but there isn't any (nominal sentence = timeless present of truths of experience).

Prov 19:24:

טָמַן עָצֵל יָדוֹ בַּצַּלָּחַת גַּם־אֶל־פִּיהוּ לֹא יְשִׁיבֶנָּה:

After the sluggard has buried (טָמַן, *qatal* as relative past) his hand in the dish, he doesn't even lift it (יְשִׁיבֶנָּה, *yiqtol* as timeless present) to his mouth.

Prov 22:3:

עָרוּם רָאָה רָעָה וְיִסְתָּר וּפְתָיִים עָבְרוּ וְנֶעֱנָשׁוּ:

When the wise man has seen (רָאָה, *qatal* as relative past) evil he hides (*yiqtol* as timeless present, possible with both the *ketib*, וְיִסָּתֵר, and the *qere*, וְנִסְתָּר) while simpletons have continued along (עָבְרוּ, *qatal* as relative past) and are punished (וְנֶעֱנָשׁוּ, *yiqtol* as timeless present).

Prov 22:9:

טוֹב־עַיִן הוּא יְבֹרָךְ כִּי־נָתַן מִלַּחְמוֹ לַדָּל:

The kindly man receives blessings (יְבֹרָךְ, *yiqtol* as timeless present), for he has shared (נָתַן, *qatal* as relative past) his food with the poor.

Isa 24:13:

כִּי כֹה יִהְיֶה בְּקֶרֶב הָאָרֶץ בְּתוֹךְ הָעַמִּים

כְּנֹקֶף זַיִת כְּעוֹלֵלֹת אִם־כָּלָה בָצִיר:

For thus it shall be on the earth and in the midst of nations, as when an olive tree is beaten (כְּנֹקֶף, participle as timeless present), as at the gleaning (כְּעוֹלֵלֹת, participle as timeless present) when the harvest has ended (אִם־כָּלָה, *qatal* as relative past).

Isa 1:12:

כִּי תָבֹאוּ לֵרָאוֹת פָּנָי

מִי־בִקֵּשׁ זֹאת מִיֶּדְכֶם רְמֹס חֲצֵרָי:

When you come (תָבֹאוּ, *yiqtol* as timeless present) to appear before me, who sought (בִקֵּשׁ, *qatal* as relative past) this from you, trampling my courts?

Job 14:12:

וְאִישׁ שָׁכַב וְלֹא־יָקוּם עַד־בִּלְתִּי שָׁמַיִם לֹא יָקִיצוּ וְלֹא־יֵעֹרוּ מִשְּׁנָתָם:

After a man has lain down (שָׁכַב, *qatal* as relative past) he doesn't rise again (לֹא־יָקוּם, *yiqtol* as timeless present), until the heavens are no more they do not wake (לֹא יָקִיצוּ, *yiqtol* as timeless present), and are not stirred (לֹא־יֵעֹרוּ, *yiqtol* as timeless present) from their sleep.

Ps 103:16:

כִּי רוּחַ עָבְרָה־בּוֹ וְאֵינֶנּוּ וְלֹא־יַכִּירֶנּוּ עוֹד מְקוֹמוֹ:

When the wind has passed (עָבְרָה, *qatal* as relative past) over it, it is no more (וְאֵינֶנּוּ, nominal sentence as timeless present) and its place no longer recognizes it (וְלֹא־יַכִּירֶנּוּ, *yiqtol* as timeless present).

In the idol parody passage of Isa 41:6-7, we encounter the use of the *wayyiqtol* = *qatal* = relative past as regards the following timeless present.

BHS text of Isa 41:6-7:

6 אִישׁ אֶת־רֵעֵהוּ יַעְזֹרוּ וּלְאָחִיו יֹאמַר חֲזָק:

7 וַיְחַזֵּק חָרָשׁ אֶת־צֹרֵף מַחֲלִיק פַּטִּישׁ אֶת־הוֹלֶם פָּעַם

אֹמֵר לַדֶּבֶק טוֹב הוּא וַיְחַזְּקֵהוּ בְמַסְמְרִים לֹא יִמּוֹט:

6 [14]Each one assists his co-worker;
   to his companion he says: Do good work!
7 Once the (metal) worker has urged on the worker in
      fine metals;
   the one who planishes with a hammer, the one
      who hammers the footing,
He says about the fit: That's fine!
Then after he has jammed it tightly into place with the
      tenons, it does not topple over.

Here in Isa 41:7 we encounter two *wayyiqtol* forms, וַיְחַזְּקֵהוּ and וַיְחַזֵּק. Both forms are difficult. The basic tense of both Isa 40:19-20 and Isa 41:6-7 is the timeless present of truths of experience, represented eight times by *yiqtol* (Joüon §113c) and two times by the predicate participle (Joüon §121d). Both *wayyiqtol* verbs here in Isa 41:7 could simply be revocalized as *weyiqtol* = a timeless present of truths of experience with simply coordinating ן. This option, however, was also available to the Masoretes, and the question arises why they interpreted the forms as *wayyiqtol*.

---

[14] Insert Isa 41:6-7 after Isa 40:20, on the basis of vocabulary and the former's incompatability in its position in Isaiah 41.

My solution to the problem is that the Masora saw a relation between these *wayyiqtol* forms and the timeless presents that follow them analogous to the relation between נָסַךְ and יְרַקְעֶנּוּ in Isa 40:18; i.e., both *wayyiqtol* forms were interpreted as relative pasts as regards the following timeless present. The sequence of tenses is very similar in each case, save for the fact that וְנָסַ begins its sequence.

Isa 40:19: נָסַךְ, once the metal worker has cast (relative past) יְרַקְעֶנּוּ, the goldsmith plates (timeless present).

Isa 41:6-7: יֹאמַר, he says (timeless present)

      וַיְחַזֵּק, once the metal worker has urged on (relative past)

      אֹמֵר, (participle), he says (timeless present)

      וַיְחַזְּקֵהוּ, then once he has jammed (relative past)

      לֹא יִמּוֹט, it does not topple over (timeless present)

The sequence of tenses here is, of course, unusual, and not directly noted by the standard grammars; but it is not completely without parallels:

Job 7:17-18:

17 מָה־אֱנוֹשׁ כִּי תְגַדְּלֶנּוּ וְכִי־תָשִׁית אֵלָיו לִבֶּךָ׃

18 וַתִּפְקְדֶנּוּ לִבְקָרִים לִרְגָעִים תִּבְחָנֶנּוּ׃

What is man, that you make so much (תְגַדְּלֶנּוּ, *yiqtol* as timeless present) of him, that you pay such heed (תָשִׁית, *yiqtol* as timeless present) to him; after you have inspected him (וַתִּפְקְדֶנּוּ, *wayyiqtol* as relative past) every morning, you test him (תִּבְחָנֶנּוּ, *yiqtol* as timeless present) at every moment.

Job 14:10:

10 וְגֶבֶר יָמוּת וַיֶּחֱלָשׁ וַיִּגְוַע אָדָם וְאַיּוֹ׃

Man dies (יָמוּת, *yiqtol* as timeless present) and is prostrate (וַיֶּחֱלָשׁ, stative *wayyiqtol* as timeless present), once he has perished (וַיִּגְוַע, *wayyiqtol* as relative past), where is he (nominal sentence as timeless present)?

It should be noted too that the idea of temporal succession expected in the *wayyiqtol* is clearly evidenced in וַיְחַזֵּק in Isa 41:7: "he says . . . then once he has jammed." The other examples listed above of *wayyiqtol* as a relative past as regards the following timeless present do not seem to involve the idea of temporal succession as regards the preceding verb. They are rather explanatory *wayyiqtol* (Joüon §118j).

That the Masora has vocalized these forms correctly as *wayyiqtol*, relative pasts as regards the following timeless present, is impossible to prove. We may be dealing here with Masoretic rather than genuine Biblical Hebrew grammar. But it does not seem to me that there is anything here that violates the nature of the *wayyiqtol* form in Biblical Hebrew.

I have identified seven more examples of *wayyiqtol* in Second Isaiah as further instances of *wayyiqtol* as relative past as regards a following timeless present. Each of these examples could be revocalized as *weyiqtol* = timeless present. These examples occur in the Isaian idol passage translated at the beginning of this article (Isa 44:9-20). Again the text contains instances of *qatal* = relative past as regards a following timeless present. For example:

Isa 44:12 Since he did not drink (לֹא שָׁתָה, *qatal* as relative past), he is tired (וַיִּיעָף, stative *wayyiqtol* as timeless present).

Isa 44:13 Once the carpenter has stretched (נָטָה, *qatal* as relative past), he traces it (יְתָאֲרֵהוּ, *yiqtol* as timeless present).

I list here these further instances of *wayyiqtol* as a relative past as regards a following timeless present because it will be helpful to the reader to see the instances of this unusual sequence of tenses together.

Isa 44:12 He shapes it (יִצְּרֵהוּ, *yiqtol* as timeless present) with hammers. Then after he has worked it (וַיִּפְעָלֵהוּ, *wayyiqtol* as relative past) with his mighty arm, he is hungry (רָעֵב, *qatal* stative as timeless present) and without strength

There does not seem to be any idea of succession in the relative past *wayyiqtol*.

Isa 44:14-15 After he has cut down (לִכְרָת) cedars (or: he cuts down cedars), after he has laid hold (וַיִּקַּח) of a holm and an oak, after he has taken hold (וַיְאַמֶּץ) of other trees of the forest, which the Lord had planted, which the rain over the years had made to grow, and had been intended to become available to man for burning, after he has taken (וַיִּקַּח) some of the wood and warmed himself (וַיָּחָם), then he starts a fire (יַשִּׂיק) and bakes (וְאָפָה) bread.

The predicate *liqtol* that starts the sequence is ambiguous. If it takes its tense from the following *wayyiqtol,* it too is a relative past tense as regards יָשִׂיק, the timeless present in the final colon. If the nominal sentence with *liqtol* as predicate is a present, the usual value of nominal sentences where the present or future character of the sentence is not marked by הָיָה (past) or יִהְיֶה (future) (Joüon §154m), then the sequence is the same as in the preceding examples:

לִכְרֹת, he cuts (*liqtol* as timeless present)

וַיִּחַם, וַיִּקַּח, וַיֹּאמֶץ, וַיִּקַּח, after he has laid hold, taken hold, has taken and has warmed (*wayyiqtol* as relative past)

יַשִׂיק, he starts a fire (*yiqtol* as timeless present)

In each one of these *wayyiqtol*s the idea of succession is present.

The final two examples from Isaiah 44 are contained in an even more unusual concatenation of tenses. Again the examples could both be pointed *weyiqtol* = timeless present, but note how in these examples *wayyiqtol* alternates with *qatal*, both used as relative pasts as regards the following timeless present. In both cases the *wayyiqtol* forms contain a clear notion of temporal succession.

Isa 44:15-16 After he has labored for days at making (יִפְעַל, past durative as a relative past) a god, after he has bowed down (וַיִּשְׁתַּחוּ), after he has made (עָשָׂהוּ) the wood into an idol, after he has worshipped it (וַיִּסְגָּד), after he has set on fire (שָׂרַף) the other half of it, on that half he roasts (יִצְלֶה) meat.

The combination of verb forms involved here is, of course, as strange as any to be found in the Hebrew Bible. At the same time the alternation of *qatal* as a relative past with *wayyiqtol* as a relative past is strongly suggestive of the explanation why the Masora vocalized both וישתחו and ויסגד as *wayyiqtol*. The Masora interprets them as relative past as regards the string of *yiqtol*s and *weyiqtol*s that follows, וַיֹּאמֶר, יָחֹם, וְיִשְׂבָּע, יֹאכֵל, יִצְלֶה: he roasts, eats, becomes satisfied, warms himself, says (all timeless presents).

The verb forms just discussed are not easy, and this use of *wayyiqtol* is not common. I feel rather sure I have explained what the Masora does with the text. The option to revocalize them all as *weyiqtol* = timeless present is in each case open. At the same time I see nothing inherent in *wayyiqtol* as a form that renders the Masora's interpretation unreasonable. The analogy of the future perfect and the pluperfect suggests its legitimacy.

CHAPTER 12

The New Exodus in
Jeremiah 50:33–38

ALICE OGDEN BELLIS

The structural analysis of Jeremiah 50–51 is a difficult task and commentators who attempt to divide the material into individual poems are not in agreement. While commentators in the first half of the twentieth century tended to dismiss the material as poorly organized and lacking thematic development, some scholars have in recent years been more optimistic about the possibility of discerning structure and theme in these chapters.[1]

In line with this trend, it is the contention of this paper that Jer 50:33-38 is a poem[2] that is unified by theme and imagery and that may be distinguished from what precedes and follows. Jer 50:33-38 has two parts. The first section, 50:33-34, states the problem, the Babylonians' oppression of the Israelites, and the fact that Yahweh will champion their cause. The second section, 50:35-38, presents the solution, the destruc-

[1] See R. P. Carroll, *Jeremiah: A Commentary* (Old Testament Library, London: SCM, 1986) 814-15. Although Carroll does not himself try to divide the material, he provides a brief history of scholarly attitudes. In addition W. Holladay, (*Jeremiah 2: A Commentary of the Prophet Jeremiah, Chapters 26-52* [Minneapolis: Fortress, 1989] 411-14) divides these chapters into ten poems.

[2] Holladay (*Jeremiah 2*, 413) agrees that 50:33-38 is a poem. K. T. Aitken ("The Oracles Against the Babylon in Jeremiah 50-51: Structures and Perspectives," *TynBul* 35 [1984] 25-63) identifies 50:33 as the beginning of what he calls a movement which, however, he does not see ending until the end of the scriptural additions (50:46).

tion of the Babylonian inhabitants and Babylon's most precious resource—water. The first section takes the form of an adapted legal complaint. The second section is the punishment pronounced on the guilty party.

In addition, the poet uses language reminiscent of the exodus. The complaint states that the Babylonians have oppressed Israel and Judah, refusing to let them go, just as Pharaoh refused to let the Hebrews go (Exod 4:23; 7:26-27; 9:1-2; 10:3-4). The punishment is a series of swords (*ḥereb*) upon Babylon's inhabitants. The series concludes with a dry heat (*ḥōreb*) upon Babylon's waters which results in their being dried up. In the context of the exodus language in 50:33 this dry heat is probably the same east wind with which Yahweh dried up the Reed Sea (Exod 14:21), allowing the Hebrews to go free.

The Poem

The first section can be divided into four lines and the second, into five lines. Parentheses enclose sections that are missing in OG. Brackets are placed around sections that may be additions, though they appear in OG.

I   33   Thus says Yahweh (of Armies):
          The Israelites are oppressed
          and the Judahites too.
          All their captors hold them fast,
          refusing to let them go.
    34   Their kinsman is strong.
          Yahweh of Armies is his name.
          He indeed champions[a] their cause,
          in order to give the world rest[b]
          and unrest to the inhabitants of Babylon.

II   35   A sword upon the Chaldeans — (oracle of Yahweh)[c] —
          and upon the inhabitants of Babylon
          [and upon her princes and wise men].[d]
    36   (A sword upon the soothsayers,[e] that they may become fools.)[f]
          A sword upon her soldiers, that they may be dismayed.
    37   A sword [upon his horses and chariotry and][g] upon (all) the
             company in her midst, that they may become women.
          A sword upon her storehouses, that they may be plundered;

38 (A dry heat)[h] upon her waters, that they may be dried up.
    Indeed, it is a land of idols
    that glories in its shocking gods.[i]

[a] The infinitive construct *ryb* is substituted for the infinitive absolute *rwb*, for reasons of assonance. See Joüon §81e.

[b] *ḥrgyʿ* and *ḥrgyz* are probably to be understood as abnormal infinitives with i vowels. See GKC §531, Joüon §54c.

[c] Missing in OG. MT frequently adds these prophetic clichés. See J. G. Janzen, *Studies in the Text of Jeremiah* (HSM 6: Cambridge: Harvard, 1973), 82-84.

[d] This third colon is perhaps secondary from 51:57. It breaks up the semantic parallelism of v 35abα. Since the poem involves allusions to the exodus (see discussion below), this colon may have been added under the influence of the exodus traditions.

[e] W. Holladay (*Jeremiah 2: A Commentary of the Prophet Jeremiah, Chapters 26-52* [Minneapolis: Fortress, 1989] 420) states that *bdym* in the sense of "soothsayers" also occurs in Isa 44:25, but that the meaning of "bragging" or "braggart" is attested in Jer 48:30. He notes that *HALAT* includes an Amorite word *baddum* for a functionary, so he suggests the possibility of a pun in 50:36 on liars.

[f] This colon is missing in OG. The semantic parallelism of vv 36b-37a is clear. The lack of a suffix on *bdym* in v 36a further suggests the secondary nature of this colon. The only problem with vv 36b-37a being a line of two parallel cola is that v 37a is long. It is possible that *ʾšr btwkh* was added very early, although there is no textual evidence for this conjecture.

Since the poem involves allusions to the exodus (see the discussion below), v 36a may have been added under the influence of the exodus traditions.

[g] Although the bracketed section is present in OG, it may still be a secondary addition. Note the masculine suffixes where the feminine is the norm. In addition, the result clause at the end, "that they may become women," is hardly appropriate with "horses and chariotry" as subject. Since the poem involves allusions to the exodus (see discussion below), this phrase may have been added under the influence of Exodus 14-15 (see discussion on pp. 166-67). It could also have been influenced by *sws wrkbw* (the horse and its rider) and *rkb wrkbw* (the chariot and its driver) in 51:21. This is an indication that the process of expansion of chaps. 50-51, so evident from the comparison of MT and OG, was already at work at the stage of the text represented by the *Vorlage* of the OG. See J. G. Janzen, *Studies in the Text of Jeremiah*, 131-35.

[h] This word is missing in the OG. The translators probably interpreted *ḥrb* as sword and let the final *ḥereb* in v 37 do double duty.

Most read *ḥereb* here for MT *ḥōreb*. The sword would be used on the Babylonians, who could no longer keep the dikes of the canals in order. The Masoretes, obviously influenced by *wybšw*, thought of dry heat, and that can possibly be defended. The change in voweling resulting in a different word is one form of paronomasia. I. Casanowicz (*Paronomasia in the Old Testament* [Boston: Norwood, 1894] 35) includes this passage in his list of examples of paronomasia. It is also included in J. Sasson's article on wordplay in the *Supplementary Volume of the IDB* (Nashville: Abingdon, 1976) 969. The different word with the same consonants closes out the list in vv 35-38a.

The practice of varying the last item in a series to indicate the end of the series is a fairly common practice in the OT. For example, in the creation story in Genesis 1, the refrain throughout the stages of creation is *wyr* *'lhym* (. . .) *ky ṭwb* (vv 4, 10, 12, 18, 21, 25). The close of the history of creation is marked in v 31 by *wyr* *'lhym . . . whnh ṭwb m'd*. The use of *whnh ṭwb m'd* as a variant on *ky ṭwb* marks the end of the series. See Qoh 3:2-8 (list of *'t* + *liqtol/qĕtol* concluded with *'t mlḥmh* and *'t šlwm*); Isa 44:24-28 (list of adjectival participles with a few relative clauses with *yiqtol*'s concluded with predicate *liqtol*).

ⁱ W. Rudolph (*Jeremia* [HAT 12; 3d ed.; Tübingen: Mohr, 1968] 304) has suggested that this line is an addition, because the stated reason for Babylon's destruction is her oppression of the Hebrews (v 33), not her idols. He may be right, even though the line does appear in the OG. There was clearly a tendency toward additions dealing with specifically religious concerns. Cf. *hbyšw 'ṣbyh* and *ḥtw glwlyh* in 50:2; *ky lYhwh ḥṭ'h* in 50:14; and *nqmt kyklw* in 50:28. None of these additions is in OG. However, it is possible that the line is original.

Following the MT vocalization of the verb *yithōlālû*, there are two ways of understanding the line, based on two different interpretations of the word *'ymym*. The first assumes that *'ymym* stands for the terrors that Yahweh will inflict upon the Babylonians. Because Babylon is a land of idols, its gods can do nothing when disaster comes. The resultant translation reads:

> Indeed, it is a land of idols,
> and they will go crazy over the terrors.

The second interpretation understands *'ymym* to refer contemptuously to the Babylonian idols. The Babylonians go crazy because of their shocking idols. I interpret *'ymym* this way, but with the OG (*katekauchōnto*) revocalize the verb *yithallālû*, "they glory." That produces a better parallelism and is matched by Ps 97:7 *hammithalĕlîm bā'ĕlîlîm*, "those who glory in false gods." The question of whether the idols fit into the thought pattern of the poem will be addressed in the discussion of the poem that follows.

The Legal Language in the Poem

By form vv 33-38 are a literary imitation of the language of the process of law in ancient Israel. Adaptations have been made because Yahweh takes part in the proceedings. Thus there is, for example, no jury or judge or witnesses. Yahweh performs all their functions.[3] In form the poem of Jer 50:33-38 bears remarkable resemblance to Yahweh's *rîb* in Hos 4:1-3.[4]

---

[3] See K. Nielsen, *Yahweh as Prosecutor and Judge: An Investigation of the Prophetic Lawsuit (Rîb-Pattern)* (JSOTSup 9: Sheffield: JSOT, 1978).

[4] See H. J. Boecker, *Redeformen des Rechtslebens im Alten Testament* (WMANT 14; Neukirchen-Vluyn: Neukirchener Verlag, 1964) 152-53.

1 Hear the word of Yahweh,
  O Israelites!
  Yahweh has a *rîb*
  with the inhabitants of the land.
  There is no fidelity, no mercy,
  no knowledge of God in the land.
2 There is only false swearing lying murder,
  stealing, and adultery.
  In their wantonness
  one deed of blood has followed another.
3 Therefore, the whole land will wither;
  its inhabitants will languish.
  The beasts of the field, the birds of the heavens
  and even the fish of the sea will perish.

In Hos 4:3 the penalty for the crimes is announced. That parallels Jer 50:35-38. Hos 4:1abα identifies the parties to the conflict, Yahweh and the inhabitants of the land. Vv 1bβ-2 list the complaint. That parallels Jer 50:33. The complaint in Jer 50:33, as will be seen below, is Babylon's refusal to manumit enslaved Israel-Judah. The one whose rights have been violated is Israel-Judah, but Israel-Judah is in too weak a position adequately to claim his rights. In this particular case Yahweh intervenes as Israel-Judah's *gōᵓēl* to see that his rights are vindicated and that guilty Babylon is punished.

The words and phrases used in vv 33-34 that are obviously derived from the practice of law are *ryb yryb ᵓt rybm*[5] and *gᵓl* in v 34. Yahweh will plead the cause of Israel-Judah on the basis of the *gōᵓēl* relation

---

[5] M. de Roche's contention in "Yahweh's *rîb* Against Israel: A Reassessment of the So-called 'Prophetic Lawsuit' in the Preexilic Prophets" (*JBL* 102 [1983] 563-74) that the *rîb* oracles do not reflect judicial processes is not convincing. In the case of Hos 4:1-3 (see de Roche, 570) Yahweh's decision to destroy the land in v 3 is like that of a sovereign whose power is supreme under the law, and whose punitive actions with respect to his subjects are a result of his judicial authority. There is a clear appeal to the law, by which every king in the ancient Near East (Yahweh included), as well as his subjects, was bound. See the story of Naboth in 1 Kgs 21:1-29. The picture is certainly not of two equal parties who have become embroiled in a dispute, in which the stronger of the two holds sway, simply because of his greater strength. Implicit is the concept that Yahweh's action is just and in accord with the law. It is just, because Yahweh is the divine judge, all of whose judgments are just. As Lord of history Yahweh has the power to enforce judgments.

that exists between them. In secular usage the term *gōʾēl* refers to a person's nearest relative, a brother, uncle, cousin, or some other relative who is responsible for standing up for them or maintaining their rights. The reason for this was the strong feeling of tribal solidarity. The members of each clan, along with their possessions, formed an organic unity, every disruption of which was regarded as intolerable, requiring restoration or reparation.[6]

How much of the secular usage is to be heard in the metaphor in v 34 is not clear, but it is related to the imagery of Yahweh as the father of his people (Deut 32:6) or Israel as the son of Yahweh (Exod 4:22). It is impossible, however, to be certain that a reference to kinship is to be heard in this derived use. Jer 50:34 may be similar to Prov 23:10-11, where it is possible that the defenselessness of the orphan is the sole basis of the *gōʾēl* relationship of Yahweh.

> Don't move the ancient boundary;
>   don't enter the field of orphans.
> Their *gōʾēl* is strong;
>   he will champion their cause against you.

The language here is obviously close to Jer 50:34 (*gʾlm ḥzq . . . ryb yryb ʾt rybm*, Jer 50:34 = *gʾlm ḥzq . . . yryb ʾt rybm*, Prov 23:11).

The legal language in v 33 is not so immediately obvious. In certain contexts *ʿšq* appears to have a nuance close to "to deprive of human rights" and its use in laws show that it is a legal term. In 1 Sam 12:3 Samuel asks:

> Whose ox did I take? Whose ass did I take? Whom did I deprive of their rights (*ʿšq*)? Whom did I oppress? From whom did I take a bribe?

Deut 24:14 commands:

> You must not deprive of his rights (*ʿšq*); the poor and needy hireling from among your brothers or aliens.

Lev 19:13 commands:

> You must not deprive your neighbor of his rights (*ʿšq*); you must not rob him; the pay of your hired hand you must not withhold overnight.

---

[6] H. Ringgren, "*gāʾal . . .*," *TDOT*, 2. 351.

What the particular right was of which Israel-Judah had been deprived is made clear by the verb *šlḥ* in the Piel. The verb is used of the manumission of slaves.[7] The Israelite laws concerning slavery are contained in The Book of the Covenant (Exod 21:2-11, 26-27), The Holiness Code (Lev 19:20-22; 25:39-55), and Deut 15:12-18. The vocabulary of Jer 50:33 bears the closest resemblance to that of the Deuteronomy text, which uses Piel *šlḥ* + *ḥpšy* (Deut 15:12, 13, 18) and the shortened form of the phrase, Piel *šlḥ* (Deut 15:13), in the sense "to manumit." Exod 21:2-11 uses the Qal of *yṣʾ* + *lḥpšy/ḥpšy* or the shortened form of the phrase, the Qal of *yṣʾ*, in the sense "to be manumitted." Lev 19:20-22 uses the noun *ḥupšâ*, "manumission" and the Pual of *ḥpš* in the sense of "to be manumitted." Thus, it is only Deuteronomy (15:13) that reflects the usage, Piel *šlḥ* without *lḥpšy/ḥpšy*, in the sense "to manumit." This is the sense in which Piel *šlḥ* is used in Jer 50:33.

The poems in Jeremiah 50-51 were probably written during the exilic period.[8] That the law of Deut 15:12-18 influenced legal thought in the period is made probable by the way it is cited in the story of the manumission of Hebrew male and female slaves in Jerusalem during Nebuchadrezzar's siege of Jerusalem and their consequent re-enslavement during a temporary lifting of the siege at the beginning of the year 587 (Jer 34:8-22).[9] As in Deuteronomy, the Jeremiah text uses both Piel *šlḥ* + *ḥpšy* and plain Piel *šlḥ* in the sense "to manumit."

It is impossible on the basis of the use of Piel *šlḥ* in the sense "to manumit" in both Jer 50:33-38 and Deut 15:12-18, to claim that Jer 50:33-38 contains an allusion to Deuteronomy 15 like those in Jer 34:8-22. The situations presumed in Jer 50:33-38 and Deut 15:12-18 are completely different. The slave laws of Deuteronomy, like all Israelite slave laws, are

---

[7] D. Daube, *The Exodus Pattern in the Bible* (London: Faber and Faber, 1963) 29-30.

[8] W. Rudolph (*Jeremia* [HAT 12; 3d ed.; Tübingen: Mohr, 1968] 299) dates Jer 50:2—51:58 between 550-538. J. Bright (*Jeremiah* [AB 21; Garden City: Doubleday, 1965] 360) dates the material before 539 and probably before 550 when Cyrus overthrew the Medean king Astyages. Carroll (*Jeremiah*, 817) believes this material was written in the period after 587. Only Holladay (*Jeremiah* 2, 414) dates it earlier, to 594, though some passages he concedes must have been later.

[9] See N. Sarna, "Zedekiah's Emancipation of Slaves and the Sabbatical Year," *AOAT* 22 (1973) 143-49; I. Cardellini, *Die biblischen "Sklaven"-Gesetze im Lichte des keilschriftlichen Sklavenrechts: Ein Beitrag zur Tradition, Überlieferung und Redaktion der alttestamentlichen Rechtstexte* (Bonn: Hanstein, 1981) 317; Bright, *Jeremiah*, 223-24; Rudolph, *Jeremia*, 189.

laws meant to be applied in Israel. There are no laws regulating the circumstances of Israelite slaves held by foreigners abroad. As quixotic as some Israelite slave law may have been (e.g., Lev 25:39-55), no Israelite law-giver attempted to write slave laws meant to be applicable on the international scene.

At the same time, Deut 15:15 does offer a motive for the proper treatment of slaves, which may be the key to the correct reading of Jer 50:33-38:

> For remember that you too were once a slave in the land of Egypt, and Yahweh, your God, ransomed you.

This same motive for freeing slaves is mentioned in Jer 34:13-14 and appears in the slavery legislation of The Holiness Code (Lev 25:42). This suggests that Yahweh's freeing the Israelite slaves in Egypt is the ultimate model for his freeing the Israelite slaves in Babylon and that the implied return of the exiles is conceived of as a new exodus.[10] That could in part have been mined out of Deut 15:15 as well as out of the exodus traditions.

The Exodus Imagery

D. Daube in his illuminating study of the exodus traditions[11] has demonstrated that they are filled with legal language and ideas derived from Israelite slave law. Throughout Exodus 4-14 the Piel of *šlḥ* is used over and over again with the denotation "to manumit" in describing what Pharaoh is expected to do to the enslaved Israelites.[12] Several texts are particularly close to Jer 50:33.

Exod 4:23   I said to you: "Manumit (Piel *šl*) my son, that he might serve me!" But you have refused (Piel *mʾn*) to manumit (Piel *šlḥ*) him.

---

[10] The exodus connection is noticed by Holladay (*Jeremiah 2*, 420) who says of 50:33: "The verb 'refuse' (*mʾn* piʿel) is common in Jrm, but with 'to let go' (*šlḥ* piʿel) the phrase specifically recollects the exodus tradition. . . . Babylon thus takes on the role of Pharaoh of old.

[11] D. Daube, *The Exodus Pattern in the Bible*.

[12] In addition to the texts cited below, see also Exod 5:1, 2, 6:1, 11; 7:2, 14, 16; 8:4, 24, 25, 28; 9:7, 13, 17, 28, 35; 10:7, 10, 20, 27; 11:1, 10; 12:33; 13:15, 17; 14:5.

Exod 7:26-27	Manumit (Piel *šlḥ*) my people, that they may serve me, and if you refuse (Piel; *m'n*) to manumit (Piel *šlḥ*) . . .
Exod 8:16-17	Manumit (Piel *šlḥ*) my people, that they may serve me, for if you do not manumit (Piel *šlḥ*) my people . . .
Exod 9:1-2	Manumit (Piel *šlḥ*) my people, that they may serve me. If you refuse (Piel *m'n*) to manumit (Piel *šlḥ*) them and if you continue to keep them enslaved (Hiphil *ḥzq*) . . .
Exod 10:3-4	How long will you refuse (Piel *m'n*) to humble yourself before me? Manumit (Piel *šlḥ*) my people, that they may serve me, for if you refuse (Piel *m'n*) to manumit (piel *šlḥ*) my people . . .
Jer 50:33	All their captors keep them enslaved (Hiphil *ḥzq*); they refuse (Piel *m'n*) to manumit (Piel *šlḥ*) them.

To be noted are the repetition of "refuse to manumit" in each text except Exod 8:16-17, where *'ynk* substitutes for *m'n*, and the use of Hiphil *ḥzq* in the denotation "to keep enslaved" in Jer 50:33 and Exod 9:1. Read in the light of Exod 4:23, 7:26-27; 8:16-17; 9:1-2; 10:3-4 and, perhaps, Deut 15:15, it is clear that the basis for the *rîb* of Israel-Judah and Yahweh with Babylon is the continued enslavement of the exiles and that the implied return of the exiles is viewed as a new exodus.

On the basis of what has been said to this point, it is fairly probable that the exodus traditions about Yahweh's bringing Israel out of Egypt, the "house of bondage" (Exod 20:2), are the basis of the argument in Jer 50:33-38. The blatant allusions to these traditions have already been treated. But once the connection to these exodus traditions has been made, other less obvious allusions to those traditions become clear or at least probable.

The structure of vv 35-38 is noteworthy. The verses contain a series of nominal optative sentences, which follow the pattern *rb 'l/'l* + object.[13] This series of sentences is, perhaps, meant to echo the series of plagues (Exod 7:14-12:30) that ultimately led Pharaoh to let Yahweh's people go (Exod 12:31-32). The description of the exiles in Babylon as *'šwqym* (Jer 50:33) could ultimately reflect Yahweh's seeing the *ʿŏnî* of the Israelites (Exod 4:31) or hearing their *nĕ'āqâ* (Exod 6:5). The presentation of Yahweh as the *gō'ēl* of Israel (Jer 50:34) could be influenced by Yahweh's redeeming his people (Qal *g'l*) in Exod 6:6; 15:13.

---

[13] See Ruth 2:4: *Yhwh 'mkm.* "May Yahweh be with you." See also Joüon §163b.

Jer 50:36b-37a identifies the soldiers (*gbwrym*) and mercenaries (*ʿrb*) as among those doomed to be slain by the sword. The Egyptian army is destroyed in the Reed Sea (Exod 14:23-15:21). The plundering of the treasure houses of Babylon (Jer 50:37b) may reflect Israel's despoliation of the Egyptians (Exod 11:1-3, 12:35-36).

Jer 50:35bβ-36a specifies Babylon's princes (*śrym*), wise men (*ḥkmym*), and soothsayers (*bdym*) as included in the list of those to be killed. 50:35bβ and 50:36a may be additions, as indicated above. They could have been added under the influence of the exodus traditions. The princes (v 35bβ) may reflect the killing of all firstborn males, including Pharaoh's own son (Exod 12:29). The wise men (v 35bβ) and soothsayers (v 36a) may reflect the wise men (*ḥkmym*, Exod 7:11), sorcerers (*mkšpym*, Exod 7:11), magicians (*ḥrṭmym*, Exod 7:11, 22; 8:3, 14, 15; 9:11), and advisors of Pharaoh (*ʿbdy prʿh*, Exod 10:7; 12:30; 14:5). These Babylonian officials will prove as equally ineffective in resisting Yahweh's will as Pharaoh's were.

In Jer 50:37, the MT opens with: *ḥrb ʾl swsyw wʾl rkbw wʾl kl hʿrb ʾšr btwkh*, "A sword [upon his horses and upon his chariotry and] upon all the company in her midst." The bracketed words are present in the OG, but for reasons indicated above (n. g) are probably secondary. They can be regarded as a plus out of Jer 51:21 (*sws wrkbw* and *rkb wrkbw*). That may be so, but it is also probable that the prominence of Pharaoh's horses and chariots in Egypt's defeat at the Reed Sea helped bring this plus into the text (Exod 14:6, 7, 9, 17, 18, 23, 26, 28; 15:1, 4, 19, 21).

The list of nominal sentences that open *ḥereb ʾl/ʿl* in Jer 50:35-37 concludes with a similarly constructed sentence (v 38) that opens *ḥōreb ʾel*. This *ḥōreb* is frequently revocalized *ḥereb*, to conform to the sentences that precede. The corrected text is usually explained as a reference to the attackers of Babylon destroying her canals, which no longer continue to bring water for irrigation. The Masora is obviously basing its interpretation on the word that follows: "A dry heat (*ḥōreb*) upon her waters, that they may be dried up (*wĕyābēšû*)." Read in the light of the exodus traditions, that makes perfect sense. In Exod 14:21 Yahweh sweeps the sea with a mighty east wind, the sirocco (*rwḥ qdym ʿzh*),[14] and turns the sea into dry land (*ḥārābâ*). Israel crosses the

---

[14] The term "sirocco" comes from *sharqiyyeh*, which means an east wind and is known in Egypt as *khamsin*. It refers to a set of phenomena including strong thermal inversions in which trapped stagnant air is compressed, heated, and dessicated and strong dust-carrying east winds. A sirocco storm may last from two or three days to

sea on dry land (*yabbāšâ*, Exod 14:16, 29; 15:19). Thus, Babylon is attacked not only by the sword (Jer 50:35-37), but also by the east wind (50:38), and it is thereby turned into a desert. In the Jeremiah text there is no need to cut a path through the sea for the Israelite escape. The east wind is thus used to turn Babylon into a desert.

Although an east wind could have been responsible for drying up a small body of water like the Reed Sea, it is unlikely that the poet expected an east wind actually to be part of Babylon's downfall. Rather, the east wind is an image drawn from the exodus tradition, which makes the expected return from exile typologically a new exodus. Just as Yahweh used all of the divine powers as the Lord of history and of nature to effect the exodus, so in this new situation Yahweh will use every means possible to free Israel-Judah from bondage.

Similarly, the drying up of the waters, which would result in Babylon's becoming a desert, should not be taken too literally. It, too, is imagery derived from the exodus traditions.

The Final Line of the Poem

The final line of the poem, "Indeed, it is a land of idols, that glories in its shocking gods," is often thought to be an addition as indicated in n. i. The poem is primarily focused on the Babylonian oppression of Israel-Judah and Yahweh's championing their cause. However, it is possible that the line is original. It draws a contrast between Yahweh, who is strong and effective (50:34) and the Babylonian gods who are little terrors. This possibility is strengthened by the inclusion of Babylon's soothsayers as objects of destruction by the sword (50:36), if this phrase is original. In the exodus story Moses and Aaron vie with Pharaoh's soothsayers and magicians, and Moses and Aaron, representing Yahweh, ultimately win the contest.

In the exodus story an important element of the tradition is that the Egyptians recognize that Yahweh is God (Exod 7:5, 17; 8:6, 15, 18; 9:14, 16, 20-21, 27, 29-30; 10:16-17; 14:18) and that the Israelites themselves

---

three weeks and temperatures may rise rapidly as much as 16-22 F. Relative humidity can drop as much as 40%. Biblical references to the sirocco are found in Isa 27:8; 40:6-8; Ezek 17:10; Hos 12:1; 13:15; Ps 103:16; Job 37:16-17; Luke 12:55; Jas 1:11. See Frank S. Frick, "Climate of Palestine" in *The Anchor Bible Dictionary*, vol. 5 (New York: Doubleday, 1992), 125-26, and the literature cited there.

understand this (Exod 10:2; 13:3, 8; 14:31; 15:1-21). Similarly, the destruction of Babylon is not just about the death of her inhabitants and the drying up of her waters. Above all it is about the vindication of Yahweh in the minds of the people over the Babylonian gods.

Understood this way the last line of the poem, "Indeed it is a land of idols, that glories in its shocking gods," is the ultimate response to the opening complaint, that the Hebrews have been oppressed (by the Babylonians), and contention, that Yahweh is their kinsman who will champion their cause (51:33). Not only will Yahweh subject Babylon to the sword the the east wind and bring about a new exodus for his people, Yahweh's actions will make it clear that the Babylonian gods are nothing but idols and its residents fools who glory in them.

The Beginning and End of the Poem

The end of this poem, whether or not the last line is included, is indicated by the fact that in 50:39-46 a series of adapted and rearranged scriptural passages (Isa 13:19-22; Jer 49:18-21; Jer 6:22-24) has been added by an editor. Although it is theoretically possible that the three sections in Jer 50:39-46 are original in Jeremiah 50 and borrowed in Isa 13:19-22, Jer 6:22-24, and Jer 49:18-21, it is very unlikely that the poets who wrote these poems would each have drawn a few lines from Jer 50:39-46. It is much more likely that an editor has appended these passages, with slight revisions, at the end of the poems in Jer 50:2-38.

The beginning of this poem is marked by *kh ᵓmr Yhwh ṣbᵓwt*. In addition the legal and exodus imagery of Jer 50:33-38 does not occur anywhere else in Jeremiah 50.

Finally, *r-b* alliteration ties the poem togther phonemically. Beginning with *rîb yārîb ᵓet rîbām* in 50:34 and concluding with the series of *ḥereb/ᶜereb* in 50:35-38, the *r-b* alliteration is also found in *rkbw* and *ḥᶜrb* in 50:37 and in reverse in *gbryh* in 50:36.[15]

Conclusion

Although many commentators believe that thematic development is minimal in Jeremiah 50-51, Jer 50:33-38 is evidence that there is much more to this ancient poetry than often meets the modern eye.

---

[15] I am indebted to Lawrence Boadt for these observations.

CHAPTER 13

Re-Examining a Preexilic Redaction of Isaiah 1–39

Lawrence Boadt

Shifting Contemporary Approaches to the Book of Isaiah

Scholars using historical-critical methods generally have agreed that the Book of Isaiah was a classic example of success in identifying the redactional development of a biblical bloc of tradition. Particularly since the work of Bernhard Duhm at the end of the last century, there has been a majority acceptance that Isaiah had three major sections (chaps. 1–39; 40–55; 56–66) basically written at different times and *added* together by one or two moments of editorial activity to create a single larger work.[1] This was achieved by coordinating three major analytic tools of historical criticism. First, scholars used form critical techniques to identify literary genres and their original settings in Israelite religion, thereby concluding that the three sections used quite different literary forms representing differing social and historical situations.[2]

---

[1] B. Duhm, *Das Buch Jesaia* (HKAT 3; Göttingen: Vandenhoek & Ruprecht, 1892). See O. Eissfeldt, *The Old Testament: An Introduction; The History of the Formation of the Old Testament* (New York: Harper & Row, 1965) 303–30. See also popular introductions such as B. Anderson, *Understanding the Old Testament* (3rd ed.; Englewood Cliffs, N.J.: Prentice-Hall, 1975) 300–302.

[2] See G. B. Gray, *A Critical and Exegetical Commentary on the Book of Isaiah I–XXXIX* (New York: Charles Scribner's Sons, 1912) 1:lvii–lix; lxviii–lxxx; E. Kissane,

Second, they studied the enormous amounts of comparative historical information from the Ancient Near East of the eighth to fifth centuries that has become available in this century. From this they worked
out a "history of Israelite religion" in the light of the shifting political
realities.[3] They then deduced how each section responded to a quite
specific challenge from a different political and religious source:
Assyria in chaps. 1–39; Babylon in chaps. 40–55; Persia in chaps. 56–66.

Third, they worked with complicated assumptions of how Israel's
theology developed historically, borrowing much from other biblical
materials such as the deuteronomistic history or from what they considered as authentic independent traditions found in the reworked history of Ezra-Nehemiah and Chronicles.[4]

As a result, stages of development could be traced through each of
the three sections for such concepts as royal messianism, Zion theology, the nature of the divine plan, and Israel as the servant of God.[5]

This was an enormous accomplishment. It opened up the Book of
Isaiah as the mirror to three centuries of an Israelite faith that especially in times of great trial proved itself adaptable, growing, and pro-
foundly sophisticated in its understanding of divine ways. Believers
could still read Isaiah as a book emphasizing promise and prediction

---

The Book of Isaiah Translated from a Critically Revised Hebrew Text with Commentary (Dublin: Browne and Nolan, 1943) 2:xvii–xix.

[3] See, e.g., W. J. Doorly, Isaiah of Jerusalem: An Introduction (Mahwah, NJ: Paulist,
1992).

[4] This is well illustrated by the efforts of John Bright and other American commentators interested in the historical reliability of the text to reconstruct the actual events
behind the siege of Jerusalem in 701. See his excursus evaluating the sources available in
his A History of Israel (3d ed.; Philadelphia: Westminster Press, 1981) 298–309. Hans
Wildberger, Jesaja (BKAT 10,3; Neukirchen-Vluyn, 1982) 1369–1495, makes extensive
efforts to establish the history in order to recover links between Isaiah and the
deuteronomistic school, esp. in chaps. 36–39. C. Brekelmans, "Deuteronomistic Influence in Isaiah 1–12," BETL LXXXI (1989) 167–76, on the other hand finds no DTR influence in the first part of Isaiah.

[5] See B. Childs, Introduction to the Old Testament as Scripture (Philadelphia:
Fortress, 1979) 325–36; or E. Kissane, The Book of Isaiah, 2:xvi–xix. For a recent tracing
of the shift in the Zion tradition, see B. Webb, "Zion in Transformation: A Literary
Approach to Isaiah," The Bible in Three Dimensions: Essays in Celebration of Forty
Years of Biblical Studies in the University of Sheffield (Sheffield: JSOT Press, 1990)
65–84. Also, J. J. M. Roberts, "Isaiah in Old Testament Theology," Interpreting the
Prophets, ed. J. L. Mays and P. Achtemeier (Philadelphia: Fortress, 1987) 62–75.

of a messianic future, but scholars had now established real historical connections between Israel's hope and the words or events of the supposed prophetic lifetimes. Christian readers had now to reckon with the book's integrity for its own long time period, and not merely see it as the promise of Jesus as the future messiah.

However, all of this presupposed that scholarship had proven that (1) the book as a whole was composed of three independent parts, (2) from three different historical moments, and (3) the parts were only subsequently joined together, so that Isaiah grew from chaps. 1–39 by the addition first of chaps. 40–55 and then of 56–66.[6]

Recent scholarship on Isaiah has moved away from this particular historical-critical approach, considering it inadequate to explain the overall unity of the book and its structural techniques and themes which recur throughout all three parts. Attention has turned to searching for a consistent perspective on the part of the final redactors, i.e. a literary unity based on a single overall viewpoint. This normally means seeing the book from a time of composition in the late 6th or early 5th centuries, and in light of the experience of exile as its focal concern.[7]

From the standpoint of the redaction, whatever one might say about the traditions and literary remains of the original Isaiah of the eighth century, they have been reworked and now are subsumed in a later literary author's theological world so that it is difficult if not impossible to know what the original Isaiah's message really was.[8] And since the earlier material has been organized in the service of an exilic and postexilic perspective, it serves no usable purpose to speculate at length what those who preserved the eighth-century Isian materials wanted to teach by them. Peter Miscall expresses this succinctly:

---

[6] A classical expression of this position is found in G.B. Gray, *op. cit.*, lv–lvii. Theories will differ. R. E. Clements, "The Unity of the Book of Isaiah," *Interpretation* 36 (1982) 117–29, sees 1–39 and 40–55 redacted as one together and 56–66 added much later, while Eissfeldt thinks both 40–55 and 56–66 were added significantly after 1–39 was redacted as a unit (*The Old Testament: An Introduction*, 302).

[7] See J. D. Watts, *Isaiah 1–33* (WBC 24; Waco: Word Publishing, 1985) xxix–xxxii, who proposes editor(s) about 435 BCE.

[8] See O. Kaiser, *Isaiah 1–12* (Old Testament Library, second edition; Philadelphia: Westminster Press, 1983) 24.

With Watts and Conrad I share the assumption of a unified work composed in the postexilic period, probably in the fifth century. However, I do not enter into further debate about date, authorship or the process of composition. I assume the postexilic author(s) used much existing material, written and oral, some perhaps deriving from the eighth century, but I am not attempting to isolate any of that material, particularly "original prophetic speeches."[9]

Shortly after this paragraph, he notes, "Isaiah 1–39 are a postexilic representation and interpretation of the pre-exilic period. . . . At the same time and on another level, Isaiah, the fifth-century prophet-poet-author, draws analogies between these past times and his fifth-century situation."[10]

Edgar Conrad joins Miscall in opting for a totally literary reading of Isaiah 1–66 as a whole in order to search for its overall viewpoint and message.[11] He brackets nearly all of the historical-critical concerns common in older commentaries without denying their contributive value to understanding many questions in the book.

But other commentators blend the older and newer methods more fully. Distinguished historical-critical scholars such as Ronald Clements, John Oswalt, John D. Watts, and Jacques Vermeylan concentrate their recent efforts on identifying the unity and purpose of the final redaction in the fifth century, while subordinating but not denying the existence of earlier stages of redaction.[12] In fact, they often draw conclusions on how the final shape of the book emerged based on the existence of former stages of redaction that were undertaken due to changes in Israel's political situation.[13]

---

[9] Peter Miscall, *Isaiah* (Sheffield: JSOT Press, 1993) 11.

[10] Miscall, *op. cit.*, 12.

[11] E. Conrad, *Reading Isaiah* (Overtures in Biblical Theology; Minneapolis: Fortress, 1991) 27–33 presents his overall reading of the text through the "implied audience" of the final whole book.

[12] R. Clements, *Isaiah 1–39*, (The New Century Bible Commentary; Grand Rapids: Eerdmans, 1980); J. Oswalt, *The Book of Isaiah: Chapters 1–39* (NICOT; Grand Rapids: Eerdmans, 1986); J. D. Watts, *op. cit.*; Jacques Vermeylen, *Du prophète Isaïe à l'apocalyptique* (Paris: Gabalda, 1978).

[13] This should be the natural import of Oswalt's analysis that each level of tradition (Isaiah 1–39 and 40–55) left unfinished questions about God's intentions and were answered by the further addition of the next level of redaction until completed by chaps. 56–66. However, as an evangelical, he tries to argue that all stem substantially from eighth-century Isaiah himself in stages. See *op. cit.* 23–28.

Reopening the Question of a Pre-Exilic Isaiah 1–39

The emphasis on the exilic or postexilic perspective of the book as a whole often leaves in doubt whether there was an original Isaian corpus in written form before the Exile. The crux of contemporary problems with the pre-exilic existence of such a "book" of the words of the eighth century Isaiah of Jerusalem is *coherence*, the question of internal consistency. Examination of the different literary units within chaps. 1–39 raises a great number of questions about attributing individual passages to the lifetime and ministry of Isaiah. These problem texts include such long-argued "additions" as the so-called "Isaian Apocalypse" of chaps. 24–27;[14] the oracles against Babylon in chaps. 13–14, 21:1-10, and 23:13-18;[15] the prose account of the Assyrian invasion in chaps. 36–37, which is also reported in 2 Kings 18–19;[16] and the parallel occurence of 2:1-4 in Micah 4:1-3.[17] When we consider also (a) the substantial doubts raised about the existence of Oracles against Foreign Nations in pre-exilic collections,[18] (b) the conviction that the special "Immanuel" passages reflect postexilic hopes for a return of

---

[14] W. R. Millar, *Isaiah 24–27 and the Origin of Apocalyptic* (HSM 11; Missoula, MT: Scholar's Press, 1976); G. W. Anderson, "Isaiah XXIV–XXVII Reconsidered," *Congress Volume: Bonn, 1962* (VTSup 9; Leiden: Brill, 1963) 118–26; J. H. Hayes and S. Irvine, *Isaiah the Eighth Century Prophet: His Times and Preaching* (Nashville: Abingdon, 1987) 294–320. These authors propose dates for Isaiah 24–27 that range from the second century B.C.E. to the eighth.

[15] S. Erlandsson, *The Burden of Babylon: A Study of Isaiah 13:2–14:23* (ConBOT 4; Lund: C. W. K. Gleerup, 1970) challenges the standing position that these oracles must date from the time of Isaiah 40–55.

[16] C. Seitz, *Zion's Final Destiny: The Development of the Book of Isaiah; A Reassessment of Isaiah 36–39* (Minneapolis: Fortress, 1991) re-examines the redactional question of these chapters and challenges the common assumption of the priority of 2 Kings over Isaiah. Older commentators, such as Eissfeldt, saw them as intentionally added "bridges" between a unified 1–35 and 40–66 (*The Old Testament: An Introduction*, 306; also Clements, "The Unity of the Book of Isaiah," 120–24.

[17] The battle over Isaian origins of 2:2-4 raged as early as Gray, *op. cit.* 42–44, who placed it in the Babylonian period, versus T. K. Cheyne, *The Prophecies of Isaiah: A New Translation with Commentary and Appendices* (New York: Thomas Whitaker, 1895) 1:14–16, who held that it was even older than Isaiah.

[18] See A. K. Jenkins, "The Development of the Isaiah Tradition in Isaiah 13–23," *The Book of Isaiah/Le Livre d'Isaïe: Les oracles et leur relectures. Unité et complexité de l'ouvrage* (BETL LXXXI; Leuven: University Press/Uitgeverig Peeters, 1989) 237–51 and Vermeylen, "L'organisation des grands recueils prophètique" (ibid.) 147–53.

monarchy,[19] and (c) the stylistic and thematic links between chaps. 34–35 and Second Isaiah,[20] there might seem very little substance left for a major collection of traditions and oracles from the ministry of the First Isaiah. These doubts are reinforced by claims that the suspect passages would seem to cohere with whatever genuine Isaian passages there are only if they were all read from the perspective of the postexilic community of the late sixth or even fifth century.[21] The judgment that so much is late material gives a clear signal to many scholars that the primary organization of these thirty-nine chapters is exilic or later.

But can such doubts about eighth-century authenticity and the assertion of late provenance for text after text stand as proven? Can chaps. 1–39 really be coherently understood if their Isaian traditions only have an integrity in conjunction to Second and Third Isaiah? Can we then show any indications that 1–39 possess a unity and purpose that would suggest these chapters were already structured in the years before the Babylonian conquests of Jerusalem in 598 and 587? Are there signs that such a "book" gathered the words and traditions of Isaiah during the Assyrian crisis of the late eighth century in order to speak, not to exiles, but to a Zion-centered Jerusalem theology of the later years of Hezekiah and those of his successors? Are the themes of such a collection able to be understood only in the light of the exile, or do the basic elements speak primarily to a nation still under its own kings?[22] Or to put it another way, can we at least detect that the per-

---

[19] So Duhm, *Das Buch Jesaja*; see the discussion of the doubts expressed by earlier commentators in F. Moriarty, "The Immanuel Prophecies," *CBQ* 19 (1957) 226–33. Clements, *Isaiah 1–39*, 103–5, argues for an Isaianic date.

[20] J. D. W. Watts, *Isaiah 34–66* (WBC 25; Waco: Word Publishing, 1987) 17–18, presupposes the exilic setting of chaps. 34–35; Oswalt, *op. cit.*, 606–9 takes them as eighth century.

[21] This is the basic thesis of J. Watts, *op. cit.*, throughout his commentary. He posits a perspective of the final redactor about 435 B.C.E., as do Miscall, Conrad and others.

[22] Thus B. Wiklander, *Prophecy as Literature: A Text— linguistic and Rhetorical Approach to Isaiah 2–44* (ConBOT 22; Lund: C. W. K. Gleerup, 1984) argues for a text generated in writing between 734 and 622. The basic proposition of Edgar Conrad, on the other hand is that Isaiah is governed by a vision of kingship in which the office is transformed from an individual to a royal people by the *Exilic* experience. See Conrad, *op. cit.*, 34–51; also his "The Royal Narratives and the Structure of Isaiah," *JSOT* 41 (1988) 67–81, esp. his statement that the book "is looking beyond the time of Davidic kingship to a time when the people will be king" (p. 77).

suasive rhetoric, unique language and distinctive imagery could speak in a coherent and unified way to an audience who lived under Assyrian control and not just to a people who already knew of the Babylonian destruction of Jerusalem and the exile?

The main question then is whether we might be able to identify a fundamental literary organization of 1–39 belonging to the Assyrian period prior to any exilic additions or redaction. Several scholars have argued such a case for the *Josian* era.[23] But I will argue that the structure itself may be still earlier, even from the later years of Hezekiah. In any case, an early redaction is an attractive position because indeed many of the conclusions of the earlier historical critics remain valid despite the newer observations. It is still impressive, e.g., how chaps. 1–39 and 40–55 remain completely separate in their *clear* references to time periods: 1–39 is set totally in the Assyrian period; 40–55 (56–66) entirely in the late Babylonian—early Persian era. Servant theology dominates 40–55, but is lacking in 1–39. Literary genres and vocabulary patterns remain strikingly distinct among all three sections. Moreover, historically identified personages, including the kings, royal officials, and Isaiah himself play key roles in 1–39, while historical figures other than Cyrus the Great remain completely absent from 40–66.

Can a single authorial vision allow such sharp differences to stand side by side unless a pre-existent text with its own style is being used as a source? The most likely scenario would be that the final author(s) commented in 40–66 on an earlier theological masterpiece which they wished to reorient and redirect for coreligionists who had lived through the exile and were strongly attracted to the portrait of the God of salvation in First Isaiah's message but were confounded by its anachronis-

---

[23] See the studies of H. Barth, *Die Jesaja-Worte in der Josiazeit: Israel und Assur als Thema einer produktiven Neuinterpretation der Jesajaüberlieferung* (WMANT 48; Neukirchen-Vluyn: Neukirchener Verlag, 1977) and Clements, *Isaiah 1–39*, both of whom maintain a redaction of chaps. 1–39 during the reign of Josiah and reflecting conditions connected to the collapse of Assyria. In general I support their arguments for an Assyrian hegemony as the milieu but see the possibility of an even earlier redaction by Hezekiah's court circles *after* the events of 701. Erlandsson, *The Burden of Babylon*, chapter 3, surveys the different proposals for an early unity of 1–39. K. Budde, "Über die Schranken, die Jesajas prophetischer Botschaft zu setzen sind," *ZAW* 41 (1923) 154–203, long ago saw 1–39 as a document reworked by later hands (p. 165).

tic royal Zionism and its conviction of a future monarchical renewal.[24] Building on a carefully presented lesson found in chaps. 2–38, chaps. 40–55 and 56–66 reflect a modified response of the post-monarchical community of Israel. The final redaction of all three parts together meant many modifications to chaps. 2–38, but the whole book is firmly rooted in a knowledge of the vision and words of First Isaiah.

If such a unified structure reflecting the eighth century cannot be shown, we must assume that the final authors and editors gathered a hodge-podge of useful traditions about the older prophet to create a fifth century vision using at least some eighth century fragments to give grounding and authority to their work.[25]

But this latter view is likely too minimalist, since already Isa 8:16-17 and 30:8 suggest that Isaiah's oracles had a written history among disciples in and after the lifetime of the prophet himself.[26] They at least suggest, if not presuppose, that some type of organized Isaianic tradition existed before the Exile. While proponents of a single compositional perspective for reading Isaiah do not deny the likelihood that there was an organized collection of Isaiah's words before the Exile, they are too negative on the presence of a coherent basic unity when they assert that we cannot recover it.[27]

The following reflections merely point to suggestive structural links that unite sections of chaps. 1–39 into a unified work. More detailed argumentation will have to await a longer study. In examining the pas-

[24] See, e.g., the efforts of A. Laato, *The Servant of YHWH and Cyrus: A Reinterpretation of the Exilic Messianic Programme in Isaiah 40–55* (ConBOT 35; Stockholm: Almqvist & Wiksell, 1992).

[25] Generally, scholars who posit an exilic or postexilic perspective do not deny the possibility of earlier organized and written collections of eighth century Isaiah's words, but posit an ongoing and building "body of tradition cultivated by disciples of his 'school'." Thus Watts, *op. cit.* xlii. The strongest proponent of a First Isaiah worked over by a band of disciples, in a *liturgical* setting, is J. Eaton, "The Isaiah Tradition," *Israel's Prophetic Tradition: Essays on Honour of Peter Ackroyd* (ed. R. Coggins, A. Phillips, and M. Knibb; Cambridge: Cambridge University Press, 1982) 58–76.

[26] For fuller reflections on this, see D. R. Jones, "The Traditio of the Oracles of Isaiah of Jerusalem," *ZAW* 67 (1955) 226–46. See also D. G. Meade, *Pseudonymity and Canon: An Investigation into the Relationship of Authorship and Authority in Jewish and Earliest Christian Tradition* (Grand Rapids, MI: Eerdmans, 1986) 42–43.

[27] Thus Miscall, *op. cit.*, 11: "We have too little independent information about pre- or postexilic Israel to reconstruct a history or process of writing except in the most general respects."

sages that make up Isaiah 1–39, it is not necessary that all present texts are part of the original work. The task is to see if there is *enough* to make a credible original document. There is no good reason to deny that when this original work was incorporated into 40–66, many editorial seams and even whole passages were inserted from a sixth century perspective to tie the first thirty-nine chapters into the rest of the finished book. Two caveats: (1) if later authors did the rewriting well, we may never be sure of all these editorial additions; and (2) in any case, we should not expect to find a literary unity typical of modern authors.

Major Themes and Patterns in Isaiah 1–39

Before we examine the proposed unified structure of chaps. 1–39, it is well to look at a few of the more important topical themes that stand out in these chapters, especially those that do not play a significant role in chaps. 40–66. In the following examples, the topic is connected to specific vocabulary which appears prominently in chaps. 1–39 but is largely lacking in later chapters. If these topics prove to play important parts in the structured message of 1–39, then it will serve to strengthen our conviction that the focus of "First Isaiah" is already in place with its own purposes prior to the exilic experience of 586.

(1) *ʿimmānûʾēl*. Although the word itself occurs only in 7:14 and 8:10, the language of the installation of the royal son as king (or at least his praise) not only is the topical center of chap. 7, but is echoed in the royal coronation language of 9:5-6 and 11:1-9. The same theme probably lies behind the "branch" (*ṣemaḥ yhwh*) in 4:2 and its poem (4:2-6), since both chaps. 4 and 11 follow the royal seed theme with the hope for salvation of Israel's remnant (variants of the root *šʾr* in 4:3; 11:11, 16). The loss of the northern kingdom in 722 lies behind these texts, since the mention of Hamath, Ethiopia, Elam in 11:11 fit the world of Assyrian politics and that of the Kushite 25th dynasty of Piankhi (747–716) and Shabaka (716–702), but not that of sixth century Babylon. These Immanuel passages are further elucidated by the long anti-Assyrian poems of 10:5-22, 23-27, 28-34. They in turn show a close relationship to the theme of chapter 8 in which the prophet's child will be a sign concerning Assyria's chastisement of the northern kingdom, but also a warning to Judah to avoid alliances with the Assyrians. One more section can be joined to these, the warning against the injustice of Israel

(and Judah) in chaps. 5:8-30 and 9:7–10:4 that presage the attack of Assyria and establish it as God's instrument. Finally, the Song of the Vineyard in 5:1-7 now serves as a preface to all of chaps. 5–12. The entire section is a dialogical interplay between national disaster for the North, a reminder to Judah that living faithfully to the promise to the royal house of David can deliver it from the same fate, and a conviction that there is hope of salvation in turn for the survivors. Nowhere in chaps. 40–66 can be found such a sustained response to the dangers of foreign imperialism that relies on the royal Davidic ideology of Jerusalem.

(2) A second major theme that appears only in Isaiah 1–39 is *har ṣiyyôn*, "the Mountain of Zion" (8:18; 10:12; 16:1; 18:7; 24:33; 29:8; 31:4; 37:32); and its significant parallels, e.g., *har bêt ṣiyyôn* in 10:32, *har yhwh*, "the mountain of the Lord" (4:5, 30:29), *har qodšî*, "my holy mountain"(10:32; with variant *běhar haqqōdeš*, 27:13), and *har bêt yhwh*, "the mountain of the Lord's house" (2:2,3). Clearly related to these is *bāhār hazzeh*, "on this mountain," in 25:6,7, 10, which although unnamed continues the description of the fortified city that God will restore. In the singular, *har* occurs only six other times in First Isaiah (13:2; 14:13; 22:5; 28:21; 30:17,25) always of mountains as high promontories. In Isaiah 40–55, it occurs only at 40:4,9 also as high places, which cannot be readily identified with Zion at all unless one posits that the voice of God speaks from Jerusalem rather than Babylon; and that it in fact does specify Zion, something to be assumed only if First Isaiah's frequent reference to Zion as the temple mount is already in place in the book. Moreover, despite the emphasis on Zion in the rest of Isaiah 40–55, never is the term *har*, so central to First Isaiah, employed to describe it.

It is only when we come to Third Isaiah that we find the recurrence of the phrase, *har qodšî* (56:7; 57:13; 65:11; 66:20) in key theological passages, suggesting that the authors of this section in fact bypassed Second Isaiah to return to a major theme of First Isaiah. If 40–55 was composed as a separate unit, then 56:1-8 should form the opening narrative of a new division of the book. But many scholars question the lack of a comparable opening passage that matches in some way the summons genre found in both 1:1-20 and 40:1-11.[28] Others point to links

---

[28] Thus, e.g. Watts, *Isaiah 34–66*, 240–51, treats Isa 54:17–56:8 as a unit, seeing no break at 56:1 in his schema of ten "acts."

with Isaiah 40–55 but fail to see any connection to 1–39.[29] Yet 56:1-8 can easily be read as a postexilic reflection on Isa 2:1-5 that further delineates who qualify as the *haggôyīm* and *ʿammîm rabbîm* of 2:2-3. Thus read, 2:1-5 and 56:1-8 are matching introductions to texts whose primary foci are about the proper conditions for dwelling *on* Mount Zion, participating in temple worship, and not, like 40–55, about returning *from* exile *to* Zion. Although much more can be spelled out in support of these parallels, it is sufficient here to indicate that the case for an independent Isaiah 1–39 is strengthened by tracing the theme of the *har haqqōdeš*.[30]

(3) A similar situation exists in the case of the pairing of *mišpāṭ* and *ṣĕdāqâ*. These matched concepts in 5:7 form the climactic theme of the poem of the vineyard, and occur at other key points of First Isaiah: 1:27; 5:16; 9:6; 28:17; 32:16; 33:5 (note also the related correlation of *mišpāṭ* and *ṣedeq* in 1:21; 16:5; 26:9; 32:1). This word pair does not occur in chaps. 40–55 (although the terms are found together in a common context at 50:8 and 54:17, but with a different semantic and grammatical relationship). The pair *mišpāṭ/ṣĕdāqâ* then reappears significantly in the opening passages of chaps. 56–66 at 56:1(!); 58:2; 59:9; 59:14; while the related *mišpāṭ/ṣedeq* occurs in 58:2.

(4) And these are not the only themes that seem to be important structurally in chaps. 1–39 but do not play correspondingly important roles in 40–55. For example, K. T. Aitken has shown that seeing/hearing and knowing/understanding make carefully interwoven but contrasting thematic pairs that structure the development of thought in chaps. 1–39.[31] Even when such presentations find an echo in chaps. 40–66, the

[29] C. Stuhlmueller, *NJBC* #21, "Deutero-Isaiah and Trito-Isaiah," 329–48, links 56:1-8 to Isaiah 40–55 on p 344 but gives no cross-references to Isaiah 1–39. See also J. A. Soggin, *Introduction to the Old Testament* (OTL; 3d ed.; Louisville, KY: Westminster/John Knox, 1989) 393–97.

[30] While Seitz, *Zion's Final Destiny*, and Webb, "Zion in Transformation: A Literary Approach to Isaiah," both maintain the key principle of organization of the book is around "Zion," neither pays much attention to the recurrent theme of "the holy mountain." R. Murray, *The Cosmic Covenant* (Heythrop Monographs; London: Sheed & Ward, 1992) 103–10 does develop the holy mountain theme in connection with 11:1-9.

[31] K. T. Aitken, "Hearing and Seeing: Metamorphoses of a Motif in Isaiah 1–39," *Among the Prophets,* (ed. P. Davies and D. J. A. Clines; JSOTSup 144; Sheffield: JSOT Press, 1993) 12–41.

simpler and more cogent explanation of the inter-relationship, at least from the above examples, is that the usage in 1–39 is both primary and prior. Many other themes that link 1–39 to 40–55 or to 56–66, or are found in all three sections of the book, play important roles for the message of 1–39 as a self-contained unity, but their use in these chapters do not necessarily reflect a perspective later than the Assyrian period.[32]

The Overall Structure of an Eighth Century Redaction

We can only sketch here an overview of the significant structural elements that seem to stand out in Isaiah 1–39, and which point towards a unified work presenting the words and work of Isaiah to an Israelite society before the exilic period. What emerges from the foregoing observations about major themes and patterns is that all of these are verbally played out against a backdrop that images the historical situation of the late eighth century. More specifically, chaps. 1–39 propose a prophetic message that was proclaimed by Isaiah through his public words and confrontations with kings Ahaz and Hezekiah over their political decisions in three crucial periods of danger in the last four decades of the eighth century. These three "moments" were (1) the involvement of Ahaz in the Syro-Ephraimite war of 734–732; (2) the efforts of Hezekiah to forge, or at least to join, anti-Assyrian alliances in the period from 715–705; and (3) Hezekiah's revolt against Assyria and its consequences in 705–701.

Since these three periods can also be coordinated with most of the oracular material of Isaiah, an investigation of possible structural keys to the organization of First Isaiah should search for indications that there might be three cycles of collected words and stories. Each of the cycles would no doubt center on the issues raised by one of the three historical periods of crisis. Each of the three stages in royal policy therefore reflects a concrete number of oracles and responses on the part of the prophet, as well as narratives about specific encounters or conflicts between the king and prophet during the crisis. If the col-

---

[32] Thus the "Holy One of Israel" as a title can be more readily understood as part of the royal Zion temple language of the Isaian monarchy period extended in use by Second Isaiah than vice-versa.

lected materials are time-conditioned, then it follows that the present collection will be relatively loose, with disparate but relevant materials from the Isaian tradition that pertain to the events of the years in question as well as added redactional material either reworked from genuine Isaian oracles or taken from narratives generated about the prophet in order to provide an interpretive framework within each stage.[33] Nor should we expect that these collections for each period will be of even length or exactly parallel in shape and structure. Because of the inherent differences in (1)the historical circumstances of each crisis, (2) the changing role played by the prophet in each period, and (3) the number of years involved for each period, there will be considerable variations in the size of each of the three cycles of collections.

Given these preliminary considerations, it seems to me that the current sequence of materials in chaps. 1–39 do indicate just such a threefold pattern. Three cycles of oracles, reflecting somewhat parallel dynamics and organizational keys, can be coordinated with the three periods of Isaiah's ministry. Thus, stage one, which deals with the early ministry of the prophet and the Syro-Ephraimite war, takes up chaps. 1–12. Stage two, however, includes all of chaps. 13 to 33, mainly because the intrigues of the period from 730 to 705, leading up to and including the decision to revolt against Sennacherib, were complicated and occurred over a long span of time. During this period, Hezekiah, chafing under Assyrian overlordship, faced a number of crucial options to revolt at different critical junctures, almost certainly all after the fall of northern Israel in 723–22, and probably all of them after Hezekiah's sole rise to power in 715. The oracles are thus more diffuse because they are not concentrated at a single moment of crisis such as we find in the first or third stages. Stage three comprises chaps. 34–38 and centers on the invasion of Sennacherib in 701. It is shorter, both because it is more highly focused, and because it involves a *positive* response on the part of the king, thereby obviating the need for extensive oracles of warning and judgment characteristic of the other two sections (and of prophetic collections in general!)

This can be briefly diagrammed as follows:

---

[33] In my view, D. Carr, "Reaching for Unity in Isaiah" *JSOT* 57 (1993) 61–80 expresses this very effectively and accurately.

I.	II.	III.
Isaiah 2–12	Isaiah 13–33	Isaiah 34–38
(734–732 BCE)	(715–701 BCE)	(701 BCE)
A.	A.	A.
Isa 2:6—4:6	Isa 13:1—14:27	Isa 34:1—35:10
B.	B.	B.
Isa 5:1—9:7	Isa 15:1—32:20	Isa 36:1—37:38
C.	C.	C.
Isa 9:8–12:6	Isa 33:1-24	Isa 38:1-22

Examining the Threefold Structure

A. *Chaps. 2–12.* There is widespread scholarly consensus that chaps. 2–12 are a cohesive unit, and that they contain by and large oracles and events from the crisis of 734–732.[34] There is less agreement whether chap. 1 was originally part of this bloc or has been constructed as a (later) prologue to either 1–39 or 1–55 or 1–66.[35] Instead, we begin with a separate prologue in 2:1-5, which contains an initial label of its own and employs a hymn which stands apart in its uniqueness, possibly derived from the cult rather than Isaiah himself.[36] Isaiah's clear message opens with a thematic vision of the Day of the Lord in 2:6-22. This is followed by a series of oracles that move from condemnation of evil to both a "day" of purification or punishment and hymnic visions of a better "day" (*bayyôm hāhû'*: 18 times in 2–12). The text can be divided into the following blocs:

[34] A recent attempt to show the very tight structural and philological unity of chaps. 2–12 has been forcefully made by A. Bartelt, *The Book around Immanuel: Style and Structure in Isaiah 2–12* (Winona Lake, IN: Eisenbrauns, 1996).

[35] H. Wildberger, *Isaiah 1–12: A Commentary* (Continental Commentaries; Minneapolis: Fortress, 1991) 1–80, treats chap. 1 as Isaian; Clements, *Isaiah 1–39*, 28–29, acknowledges its Isaian origin but views the chapter as an exilic collection.

[36] The fact that 2:1-4 recurs in Micah 4:1-3 may suggest this. Arguments may be found for possible origins in Wildberger, *Isaiah 1–12*, 83–87.

2:6-22 Vision of the Day of the Lord

3:1–4:1 condemnation

5:1-30 condemnation

4:2-6 A purified Zion

8:23–9:7 A purified king

(6:1–8:22 example of Ahaz)

9:8–10:4 punishment

11:1-16 A renewed people

(10:5-37 example of Assyria)

12:1-6 Praise of God's victory

There is general consensus also that the bloc of prose in 6:1 to 8:22 is the centerpiece of the text; i.e., the actions of Ahaz in refusing to heed the word of the prophet are the leading illustration of why Judah is being severely punished by Assyrian hegemony. The people are deaf, blind and rebellious, but their king is the prime representative. One cycle of condemnation and hope precedes the center (3:1–4:1); one follows it (9:8–11:16); and one encircles it (5:1-30; 8:23–9:7). The last cycle includes a second application of disobedience: not Ahaz, but the Assyrians themselves (10:5-37). This claim to universal divine justice with special concern for Zion provides the basis for the promise of hope that not only closes the whole section solemnly (12:1-6), but is envisioned in the conclusion of each smaller cycle (4:2-6; 8:23–9:7; and 11:1-16).

B. *Chaps. 13–33.* These chapters are much more heterogeneous than 1–12. They include the blocs of specific oracles against foreign nations (chaps. 13–23), the conflict between Zion as rebellious and Zion as faithful in chaps. 24–27; and the lesson of northern Israel's fate for Jerusalem and Judah in 28–33. Without arguing the point, it seems to me that most of the oracles in this lengthy collection are to be connected with the original book as Isaiah's words (either authentically or in reported accounts) largely directed against Hezekiah's dallying with Babylon (and other small nation states) to arrange military coalitions to win independence from Assyrian control. We have insufficient concrete information available in these oracles to know the actual occasion on which they were delivered. Even a brief glance at commentaries reveals the inability of scholars to develop a coherent situation in the struggle against Babylon in the Exile that would fit the language, alliances, and imagery easily. And yet, political events involving Assyria in the late eighth century and early seventh century do generally fit. Four times the Babylonian native leader, Merodach Baladan, attempted to forge anti-Assyrian coalitions during Hezekiah's reign, and the young king was no doubt involved (cf. the authentic memory in chap. 39).[37] Isaiah's opposition to any Egyptian or Tyrian alliance in that struggle also reflects the historical reality. Assyrian records mention it, and a famous stele of Esarhaddon brags how he subdued both Tyre and Egypt together.[38]

This second cycle is similar to the first. It opens in 13:1-15 with a vision of the devastating Day of the Lord. It then combines a number of different ad hoc oracles against nations in chaps. 13–23, which begin with Babylon and end with Egypt and Tyre, and include such small states as Philistia, Moab, Damascus and the Arab tribes, all of whom at one time or another joined in the anti-Assyrian coalitions. Interspersed among these Oracles against Foreign Nations are specific words of warning and promise to Israel, and especially Jerusalem (14:1-2; 14:24-27; 14:32; 16:1-5; 17:7-8; 18:7-8: 20:1-6; 22:8b-25). Moreover, the fate of Israel is also interwoven into several remaining passages (e.g., 17:3-6; 19:16-25). Thus the condemnation and warnings against foreign alliances becomes the central message of the body of these oracles as a whole. This is followed by a new bloc in chaps. 24–27 that both belongs with and parallels chaps. 13–23, opening with a vision of the Day of the Lord in which Zion is destroyed because of its disobedience, and then restored in God's plan, and finally at peace while its enemy Assyria and its treacherous ally Egypt are themselves destroyed. Even given the ragtag collection of oracles here, and the possibility that many of the Babylonian references show significant expansion in the Exilic redaction, the arrangement of 13–27 to be parallel to 2–12 is evident.

---

[37] G. Ahlström, *The History of Ancient Palestine from the Paleolithic Period to Alexander's Conquest* (ed. Diana Edelman; JSOTSup 146; Sheffield: JSOT Press, 1993) 691–96.

[38] See ANEP 447 and the Stele of Esarhaddon holding both king Baꞌlu of Tyre and Tirharqa of Egypt by ropes; also the *Prism* A and B of Esarhaddon in *ANET* 290–91, and his *Annals, ANET* 292, for detailed descriptions of his conquest of Egypt and defeat of Tyre.

Chaps. 28–33 show a mini-cycle in the same pattern, a round three, so to speak. Chap. 28 opens with a day of destruction from Yahweh against the northern kingdom. It continues with a series of oracles directed to Jerusalem not to follow in their path of disobedience and bring down Assyrian destruction on themselves (28:1–29:24); then comes special warning against opposing Yahweh's will by military alliance with Egypt (30:1–31:5); it closes with the destruction of Assyria (31:6-9; 33:1-12 passim) and peace for Zion under God's rule (32:1-20; 33:13-24).

C. *Chaps. 34–38.* If this is to be seen as a unit, it is necessary to overcome much of modern critical opinion. Chaps. 34–35 have long been disputed, and a majority of commentators usually identify them as part of the thought world of Second Isaiah that have been attached to an original chaps. 1–33 as a bridge to reinforce the message of hope that will be continued by 40–55.[39] Chaps. 36–38 are most often assumed to have been added as an appendix taken from 2 Kings 18–19 to further illustrate the message of hope.[40] However, the literary structure parallels once again the major movements in the previous two large sections. Chapter 34 opens with a vision of the Day of the Lord, which is followed by restoration in chap. 35. Like chaps. 6–8 and 20, chaps. 36–37 then insert a prose narrative section with a lesson: to summon Israel to hear, see and heed Isaiah's call to trust that God alone can save. Finally, chapter 38 reinforces the contrast between Ahaz and Hezekiah by offering a second instance of his trust in Yahweh's word of deliverance. This finale echoes the prologue in 2:1-5, thus ending the whole of 2–38 where it began, at the House of the Lord (*bêt yhwh*, 2:2 and 38:22).

The unit of 34–38 is both shorter and moves to a different conclusion than do 2–12 and 13–33, mainly because unlike Ahaz's response to the prophet's word, or Hezekiah's long resistance to it in his earlier years, during the final crisis of 701 Hezekiah did change and heed the prophet's call to trust not in arms and foreign allies but in God's

---

[39] C. C. Torrey, *The Second Isaiah* (New York: Scribner's, 1928) sees chaps. 34–35 as the original introduction to 40–55; Clements, *Isaiah 1–39*, 271–72 also sets them in an exilic viewpoint foreign to the eighth century Isaiah.

[40] Seitz, *Zion's Final Destiny*, 47–72, rehearses the various arguments for and against the priority of Isaiah 36–37 over the account of 2 Kings 18–19.

promise to stand by Zion and its king. Thus condemnation and warning against disobedience has dissolved in favor of an emphasis on the obedience of Hezekiah, his conversion through prayer, and the assured fulfillment of the word spoken by Isaiah.

The Schematic Pattern of the First Edition of Chapters 1–39

A simplified way to understand the movement of the original collection of Isaian materials is to see it proposed as a lesson plan for Hezekiah's successors to learn to imitate his fidelity to the true Zion tradition which insisted upon the king maintaining the justice of God (*mišpāṭ/ṣĕdāqâ*; see Psalm 72) and spurning foreign alignments which would bring obligations to pagan national policies and therefore to their gods.

Stage One from the early years of Isaiah's ministry is found in chaps. 2–12, which describe the reign of Ahaz as a time of both severe injustice and refusal to trust in Yahweh alone. There are three blocs: (a) The Day of the Lord will be against Israel itself for its evil ways in order to prepare for a better Zion (chaps. 2–5); (b) Ahaz then refuses Isaiah's word of deliverance against his enemies in Damascus and northern Israel and instead chooses an Assyrian alliance, which elicits the sign of Immanuel as a promise beyond the present (chaps. 6–8); (c) but God's will and plan shall find vindication despite the king's attitude: Judah's sins shall be purified; the promise of a better king will be fulfilled; Assyria will be punished; and God will reign with blessing on all creation (chaps. 9–12). Because of Ahaz's failure to follow Isaiah's word, however, this is a failed step, and the divine vindication remains a future vision.[41]

Stage Two encompasses the long years of Hezekiah's own attempts at engaging in foreign alliances, this time to free himself from the very oppression of Assyria that Isaiah had warned against. The opening oracle of the Day of the Lord is directed against the nations, but soon

---

[41] This is the theological viewpoint of the text. P. Ackroyd, "Isaiah I–XII, Presentation of a Prophet," *Congress Volume: Göttingen 1977* (VTSup 29; Leiden: Brill, 1978) 16–48, describes Ahaz as a practical king who succeeded in his strategy despite Isaiah's position, while the book now presents Isaiah in idealistic terms and Ahaz in negative ones.

focuses on the Babylon of Merodach Baladan. As with the first cycle, the Day of the Lord is not tied to a particular battle or specific expectation but shares in the cosmic mythology of the royal ideology of Zion, applied loosely to the current enemy.[42] In this mythopoetic consciousness the sequence of oracles against various nations moves easily between historical specifics and cosmic vision.[43]

Thus 13–33 can be broken into three movements in rough parallel to those in 2-12: (a) chaps. 13–27 in which the vision of the Day of the Lord leads into oracles against both the foreign nations and Judah alike, with the question of reliance on Egypt at the center (chaps. 19–22) and yet mixed with visionary elements of Zion's future; (b) chaps. 28–31, which specifically focus on the example of how royal intrigue to secure Egypt's help against Assyria stands in opposition to God's plan;[44] (c) chaps. 32–33, in which Assyria shall be defeated by God without foreign help, the king will be faithful, and Zion will be restored.

Stage Three covers the final invasion of Sennacherib in 701 in the same threefold schema: (a) a vision of the Day of the Lord against all enemies in chap. 34 leads to a vision of God's victory and restoration of Zion in chap. 35; (b) this is proven true by the example of Hezekiah's faith and his response to Isaiah's word during Sennacherib's siege in chaps. 36–37; (c) chap. 38 further describes Hezekiah as the faithful king who is healed of his illness. This parallels the vision in the final bloc of the second stage which foresees a Zion in which no one will be sick (33:24). And unlike Ahaz in the first stage, the king does seek God's will by asking for a sign. However, it soon becomes a question of two signs. Isaiah offers one sign of the sundial moving backwards to

---

[42] See studies on the centrality of the Zion mythology for Isaiah in, e.g., R. J. Clifford, "The Unity of the Book of Isaiah and its Cosmogonic Language," *CBQ* 55 (1993) 1–17.

[43] Recognizing this trait of prophetic thinking goes a long way to understanding the juxtaposition of the cosmic vision of chaps. 24–27 next to the more concrete historical references frequent in 13–23. See also Jeremiah's description of the "foe from the North" in the context of concrete accusations of Judah, or Ezekiel's language in chaps. 38–39 after the historical promises of chaps. 33–37. Cf. L. Boadt, "Mythological Themes and the Unity of Ezekiel," *Literary Structure and Rhetorical Strategies in the Hebrew Bible* (ed. L. de Regt, J. de Waard, and J. P. Fokkelman; Assen: Van Gorcum/ Winona Lake: Eisenbrauns, 1996) 211–31.

[44] Note the close parallels between 6–8 and 28–31, esp. 7:4-5 and 30:15; 8:11-20 and 30:8-9.

accompany God's promise to heal the king, but in the final verse of his psalm in 38:9-20, the king longs for the house of the Lord and soon seeks another sign for when he shall be able to go to the temple. Yet his request is left unanswered. This is undoubtedly intentional. It both recalls and completes the vision of 2:1-5, but at the same time leaves the future open for the hearer, thus providing both a lesson and a warning from the experience of 701.

The Basic Movement of Isaiah 1–39 Restated

(Chapter 1)

2:1-5 Introductory Vision

Stage One: Chapters 2–12 (734–732 BCE)

(a) *The Day of the Lord* and its consequences (2:6–4:6):
   judgment, purification and future promise to Zion.
(b) Rebelliousness and its royal example (5:1–9:7):
   condemnation of the people, the prophetic call, example of Ahaz,
   and a promise of a better king.
(c) Sin, judgment and restoration of Zion (9:8–12:6):
   condemnation of the people, judgment on Assyria, the hope for a
   better king and restored Zion.

Stage Two: Chapters 13–33 (715–701 BCE)

(a) *The Day of the Lord* and its consequences (13:1–27:13):
   Judgment against Israel's neighbors, especially Isaiah's opposition
   to Egypt; Zion under siege and delivered.
(b) The example of sinful alliances (28:1–31:9):
   Ephraim's sin with Assyria; Judah's trust in Egypt both bring disaster, but God will stand by Zion.
(c) Assyria punished but Zion and its ruler restored (32:1–33:24):
   judgment on sinful Zion, Assyria destroyed in turn, and divine salvation for Zion and a better king.

Stage Three: Chapters 34–38 (701 BCE)

(a) *The Day of the Lord* and its consequences (34:1–35:10):
   Judgment on the nations and a restoration of Zion.
(b) The example of Hezekiah's trust in God (36:1–37:38):
   Assyrian hubris and its defeat; Hezekiah's faithfulness to the royal
   ideal of loyalty to God; Zion's salvation.

(c) The Conversion of Hezekiah and his trust in God (38:1-22):
The final climax in which Hezekiah changes and turns fully to
God in trust, is heard and will lead the nation in fidelity to God in
the temple on Zion.

Each (a) section of the parallel blocs emphasizes the imagery and
language of the Day of the Lord. Each b) parallel focuses on the behav-
ior of the Israelite king, or high officials, or foreign rulers, all judged
on whether they fulfill God's plan as made known by the word of the
prophet Isaiah. Chaps. 6–8 and 36–37 form two focal points for the
entire corpus, standing in stark contrast to one another: Ahaz who will
not heed; Hezekiah who does. The (b) section of Stage Two (chaps.
28–31) contains no narrative of the king as example, since it reflects the
vague period of intrigue, but is more pointed on the key issue: failure
to heed the divine "purpose" (ʿēṣâ; found in some form in all three sections: 5:19; 7:5; 8:10; 28:29; 29:15; 30:1; 36:5; 37:26). The final (c) sections of
each stage articulate the hope for a king who will embody the royal
Zion ideology of justice and blessing for the people.

Limitations and Caveats on the Use of Models

I consider these parallels to be the basic outline of an early redaction
accenting the lessons of Isaiah's preaching that salvation comes only in
quiet and trust in God and avoidance of all foreign intrigue (as clearly
stated by the two commands to write down the prophet's words in 8:1-
8 and 30:8-18). Yet it remains only a loose schema because the editors
were concerned to preserve the words of Isaiah spoken on particular
occasions and addressed to quite diverse audiences and situations, and
they did not indulge the modern passion for rationality nor feel constrained to tinker severely with the oracles in order to be logical.

Repetitio mater studiorum. Knowing the basic three stages of the
prophet's ministry, and having his words in some form, constructing a
threefold rhetorically patterned "book" was a natural way of emphasis to an ancient.[45] Since the arrangement is suggestive and not rigid,
the editors fitted in what they could, and often used such devices as the

---

[45] See W. G. E. Watson, *Classical Hebrew Poetry: A Guide to its Techniques*
(JSOTSup 26; Sheffield JSOT Press, 1984) 180, 256, 380, *passim.*

echo of key words or traditional pairings or allusions to contemporary customs, many of which we simply don't know, to connect individual oracles to one another. But this structure also makes room for various later insertions that would not disturb the basic order, but could serve to link 1–38 with 40–66. Whether any given text is original to this plan or later must be argued on its merits. I have left aside chaps. 1 and 39, for example, from this basic structure. The first chapter contains many Isaian themes found throughout 2–38, and may well have been composed to head chaps. 2–38 as a general summary of Isaiah's call to conversion; but it functions more clearly at this stage as an introduction to all of 1–66, and is best bracketed for now. Chap. 39 serves as a definite editorial bridge to chaps. 40–66, but it may have originally been one further example of Hezekiah's righteousness before God in contrast to his father Ahaz. If original, it enhances the proposed structure; if later, then it serves its own purpose.[46]

---

[46] Since chap. 39 is found also in 2 Kings 20:12-19, and a reduced version is reflected in 2 Chronicles 31 with a different theological emphasis, it is reasonable to conclude that it is not an exilic editorial addition. C. Seitz, *Isaiah 1–39*, 254–66, has argued convincingly for the priority of the narratives in Isaiah 36–39 over the parallel versions in 2 Kings 18–20. A good case can be made that the DTR historians smoothed out what they considered inconsistencies in the Isaian account.

A List of the Writings of Aloysius Fitzgerald, F.S.C.

Dissertation

"The Lord of the East Wind." A book-length study of weather imagery in Hebrew poetry [1984], to be published in CBQMS.

Journal Articles

1967. "Hebrew *yd* = 'Love' and 'Beloved,'" *Catholic Biblical Quarterly* 29 (1967) 368-374.

1972. "The Mythological Background for the Presentation of Jerusalem as a Queen and False Worship as Adultery in the OT," *Catholic Biblical Quarterly* 34 (1972) 403-16.

1972. "A Note on G-Stem יִנָּצֵר Forms in the Old Testament," *Zeitschrift für die alttestamentliche Wissenschaft* 84 (1972) 90-92.

1974. "A Note on Psalm 29," *Bulletin of the American Schools of Oriental Research* 214 (1974) 61-63.

1974. "*MTNDBYM* in 1QS," *Catholic Biblical Quarterly* 36 (1974) 494-402.

1974. "*BTWLT* and *BT* as Titles for Capital Cities," *Catholic Biblical Quarterly* 37 (1974) 167-83.

1978. "The Interchange of L, N, and R in Biblical Hebrew," *Journal of Biblical Literature* 97 (1978) 481-88.

1989. "The Technology of Isaiah 40:19-20 + 41:6-7," *Catholic Biblical Quarterly* 41 (1989) 426-46.

Contributions to Reference Works

1967. "Poetry of the Old Testament," *New Catholic Encyclopedia* v. 11 (New York: McGraw-Hill, 1967) 461-64.

1968. "Baruch," in Raymond E. Brown, Joseph A. Fitzmyer, Roland E. Murphy (eds.), *The Jerome Biblical Commentary* (Englewood Cliffs, N.J.: Prentice-Hall, 1968) 614-19.

1968. "Hebrew Poetry," in *The Jerome Biblical Commentary* 238-44. Translated into Spanish: R. E. Brown, Joseph A. Fitzmyer, R. E. Murphy (eds.), A. de la Fuente Adanez y J. Valente Malla (tr.), *Commentario Biblico: San Jeronimo* (Madrid: Ediciones Cristiandad, 1971), "Baruc," pp. 707-20 & "Poesia hebrea," pp. 639-43.

1990. "Baruch," in Raymond E. Brown, Joseph A. Fitzmyer, Roland E. Murphy (eds.), *The New Jerome Biblical Commentary* (Englewood Cliffs, N.J.: Prentice Hall, 1990) 463-67.

1990. "Hebrew Poetry," in Raymond E. Brown, Joseph A. Fitzmyer, Roland E. Murphy (eds.), *The New Jerome Biblical Commentary* (Englewood Cliffs, N.J.: Prentice Hall, 1990) 201-8.

Editorial Participation

1991. *The Revised Psalms of the New American Bible; Authorized by the Board of Trustees of the Confraternity of Christian Doctrine and Approved by the Administrative Committee/Board of the National Conference of Catholic Bishops and the United States Catholic Conference* (New York: Catholic Book Publishing Co., 1991).

Book Reviews

1971. E. Lipiński, *Le poeme royal du Psaume LXXXIX, 104,* 20-38 (Cahiers de la Revue biblique 6; Paris: Gabalda, 1967) in *Catholic Biblical Quarterly* 33 (1971) 442-44.

1976. Jean-Baptiste Frey, *Corpus Inscriptionum Judaicarum: Jewish Inscriptions from the Third Century B.C. to the Seventh Century A.D.* (vol. 1; New York: Ktav, 1974), in *Catholic Biblical Quarterly* 38 (1976) 448-49.

1976. William R. Watters, *Formula Criticism and the Poetry of the Old Testament* (Beiheft zur Zeitschrift für die alttestamentliche Wissenschaft 138; Berlin & New York: Walter de Gruyter, 1976), in *Catholic Biblical Quarterly* 38 (1976) 604-7.

1978. Jesus Luis Cunchillos, *Cuando los angeles eran dioses* (Bibliotheca Salmanticensis 14, Study 12; Salamanca: Universidad Pontificia, 1976), in *Catholic Biblical Quarterly* 40 (1978) 236-37.

1979. Michael David Coogan, *West Semitic Personal Names in the Murašu Documents* (Harvard Semitic Monographs 7; Missoula, MT: Scholars Press, 1976), in *Catholic Biblical Quarterly* 41 (1979) 627-28.

1980. Bruno Chiesa, *L'Antico Testamento Ebraico secondo la tradizione Palistinese* (Bottega d'Erasmo, 1978), in *Journal of Biblical Literature* 99 (1980) 488-89.

1981. Erik Hornung & Othmar Keel (eds.), *Studien zu altägyptischen Lebenslehren* (Orbis biblicus et orientalis 28; Freiburg: Universitätsverlag; Göttingen: Vandenhoeck & Ruprecht, 1979), in *Catholic Biblical Quarterly* 43 (1981) 142-43.

1982. Andre Gunnel, *Determining the Destiny: PQD in the Old Testament* (ConBOT 16; Lund: Gleerup, 1980), in *Catholic Biblical Quarterly* 44 (1982) 472-73.

1982. Pierre Casetti et. al. (eds.), *Mélanges Dominique Barthelemy: Études bibliques offertes à l'occasion de son 60e anniversaire* (Orbis biblicus et orientalis 38; Fribourg: Editions universitaires; Göttingen: Vandenhoeck & Ruprecht, 1981), in *Catholic Biblical Quarterly* 44 (1982) 698-99.

1982. Karl Helmut Singer, *Die Metalle Gold, Silber, Bronze, Kupfer und Eisen im Alten Testament und ihre Symbolik* (Forschung zur Bibel 43; Würzburg: Echter Verlag, 1980), in *Catholic Biblical Quarterly* 44 (1982) 133-34.

1984. Michael Zohary, *Plants of the Bible: A Complete Handbook to all the Plants with 200 Full-Color Plates Taken in the Natural Habitat* (Cambridge; London, New York: Cambridge University, 1982), in *Catholic Biblical Quarterly* 46 (1984) 339-40.

1984. Innocenzo Cardellini, *Die biblischen "Sklaven"—Gesetze im Lichte des keilschriftlichen Sklavenrechts: Ein Beitrag zur Tradition, Überlieferung und Redaktion der alttestamentlichen Rechtstexte* (Bonner biblische Beiträge 44; Bonn: Hanstein, 1981), in *Catholic Biblical Quarterly* 47 (1984) 413-14.

1984. Ran Zadok, *The Jews in Babylonia during the Chaldean and Achaemenian Periods according to the Babylonian Sources* (Studies in the History of the Jewish People and the Land of Israel Monograph Series 3; Haifa: University of Haifa, 1979), in *Catholic Biblical Quarterly* 47 (1984) 444-46.

1988. Samuel N. Kramer, *In the World of Sumer: An Autobiography* (Wayne State Univ. Press, 1986), in *Catholic Biblical Quarterly* 40 (1988) 688-89.

1989. Kirsten Nielsen, *Incense in Ancient Israel* (Leiden: Brill, 1986), in *Catholic Biblical Quarterly* 41 (1989) 344-47.

1990. William L. Moran; tr. by Dominique Collon and Henri Cazelles, *Les Lettres d'El-Amarna: Correspondance diplomatique du pharaon* (Paris: Cerf, 1987), in *Catholic Biblical Quarterly* 42 (1990) 327-28.

OTA Abstracts

1986. *OTA* 9 (1986)

#432: Laurence Kutler, "A 'Strong' Case for Hebrew MAR," *UF* 16 (1984) 111-18.

#438: J. De Savignac, "Le sens du terme *Ṣâphôn*," *UF* 16 (1984) 273-78.

1987. *OTA* 10 (1987)

#90: Y. Avishur, "The 'Duties of the Son' in the 'Story of Aqhat' and Ezekiel's Prophecy on Idolatry (Ch. 8)," *UF* 17 (1986) 49-60.

#100: N. Wyatt, "Killing and Cosmogony in Canaanite and Biblical Thought," *UF* 17 (1986) 374-81.

#101: Ran Zadok, "Die nichthebräischen Namen der Israeliten vor dem hellenistischen Zeitalter," *UF* 17 (1986) 387-98.

#106: Jesse L. Boyd III, "The Etymological Relationship between *NDR* and *NZR* Reconsidered," *UF* 17 (1986) 61-74.

#111: M. Dietrich—O. Loretz, "Akkadisch *siparru* 'Bronze,' Ugaritisch *spr*, *ǵprt* and Hebräisch *spr*, *ʿprt*" *UF* 17 (1986) 401.

#112: M. Dietrich—O. Loretz, "Die akkadischen Tierbezeichnungen *immeru*, *puḫādu*, and *puḫālu* im Ugaritischen und Hebräischen," *UF* 17 (1986) 99-103.

#113: M. Dietrich—O. Loretz, "ʿ*DB* and ʿ*ḎB* im Ugaritischen," *UF* 17 (1986) 104-16.

#131: Herbert Niehr, "Zur Etymologie und Bedeutung von *ʾšr* I," *UF* 17 (1986) 231-34.

#136: Wolfram von Soden, "Hebräisch *nāṭār* I and II," *UF* 17 (1986) 412-14.

#169: Joaquin Sanmartin Ascaso, "Geschichte und Erzählung im Alten Orient (1): die Landnahme Israels," *UF* 17 (1986) 243-82.

#212: O. Loretz, "Die Ugaritistik in der Psalmeninterpretation (II)," *UF* 17 (1986) 213-17.

#219: Oswald Loretz, "Ugaritisches und Jüdisches, Weisheit und Tod in Psalm 49," *UF* 17 (1986) 189-212.

#222: Oswald Loretz, "Zur Parallelität zwischen KTU 1.6 II 28-30 und Ps 131, 2B," *UF* 17 (1986) 183-87.

#321: D. A. Carson, "The Limits of Dynamic Equivalence in Bible Translation," *ERT* 9 (1984) 200-13.

#380: E. M. Yamauchi, "The Proofs, Problems and Promises of Biblical Archaeology," *ERT* 9 (1984) 117-38.

#440: I. B. Gottlieb, "Light and Darkness in Perpetual Round: Genesis 18 and 19," *On the Path of Knowledge: Essays on Jewish Culture* (mostly Heb.; Festschrift Aharon Mirsky; ed. Zvi Malachi; Lod, Israel: Habermann Institute, 1986) 181-98.

#437: C. Conroy, "Jeremiah and Sainthood," *Saints in World Religions* (Studia Missionalia 34; ed. M. Dhavamony; Rome: Pontificia Università Gregoriana, 1986) 1-40.

#493: P. L. Schreiber, "Liberation Theology and the Old Testament: An Exegetical Critique," *CJ* 13 (1987) 27-46.

#601: H. W. Wolff, "Use of the Bible in Theology: A Case Study," *ERT* 11 (1987) 37-42.

OTA 11 (1988)

#21: Marjo C. A. Korpel and Johannes C. de Moor, "Fundamentals of Ugaritic and Hebrew Poetry," *UF* 18 (1986) 173-212.

#28: Stanislav Segert, "Preliminary Notes on the Structure of the Aramaic Poems in the Papyrus Amherst 63," *UF* 18 (1986) 271-99.

#30: Mark S. Smith, "Interpreting the Baal Cycle," *UF* 18 (1986) 313-39.

#42: David Toshio Tsumura, "Literary Insertion, AXB Pattern, in Hebrew and Ugaritic," *UF* 18 (1986) 341-61.

#47: N. Wyatt, "The Hollow Crown: Ambivalent Elements in West Semitic Royal Ideology," *UF* 18 (1986) 421-36.

#84: Thomas Podella, "Ein mediterraner Trauerritus," *UF* 18 (1986) 263-69.

#101: Bob Becking, "A Remark on a Post-exilic Seal," *UF* 18 (1986) 444-46.

#124: M. Dietrich and O. Loretz, "Die bipolare Position von ʿL im Ugaritischen und Hebräischen," *UF* 18 (1986) 449-40.

#133: Mayer I. Gruber, "Hebrew *QĔDĒŠĀH* and her Canaanite and Akkadian Cognates," *UF* 18 (1986) 133-48.

#139: Wolfram von Soden, "Hebräische Problemworter," *UF* 18 (1986) 341-44.

#143: Paolo Xella, "'Le Grand Froid': Le dieu *Baradu madu* à Ebla," *UF* 18 (1986) 437-44.

#219: Oswald Loretz, "Ugaritologische und kolometrische Anmerkungen zu Ps 19A," *UF* 18 (1986) 223-29.

#236: Ingo Kottsieper, "Die Bedeutung der Wz. ʿṣb and *skn* in Koh 10, 9," *UF* 18 (1986) 213-22.

#1063: Kjeld Nielsen, *Incense in Ancient Israel* (VTSup 38; Leiden: Brill, 1986).

#1073: Alejandro Diez Macho (with the collaboration of Angeles Navarro Peiro), *Biblia Babilonica: Fragmentos de Salmos, Job y Proverbios (Ms. 408 A del Seminario Teologico Judio de Nueva York)* (Textos y Estudios "Cardenal Cisneros" de la Biblia Poliglota Matritense 42; Madrid: Instituto de Filologia, C.S.I.C., Departamento de Filologia Biblica y de Oriente Antiguo, 1987).

#1074: Luiz Diez Merino, *Targum de Qohelet: Edicion Principe del ms. Villa-Amil n. 4 de Alfonso de Zamora* (Bibliotheca Hispana Biblica 13; Madrid: C.S.I.C., 1987).

#1074-1077: Frederico Perez Castro, et. al. (eds.), *El codice de profetas de El Cairo* vols. 4-6 (Textos y Estudios "Cardenal Cisneros" de la Biblia Poliglota Matritense 44; Madrid: Instituto de Filologia, C.S.I.C., Departamento de Filologia Biblica y de Oriente Antiguo, 1986-1988).

#1079: Amparo Alba Cecilia, *Biblia Babilonica: Jeremias* (Textos y Estudios "Cardenal Cisneros" de la Biblia Poliglota Matritense 41; Madrid: Instituto de Filologia, C.S.I.C., Departamento de Filologia Biblica y de Oriente Antiguo, 1987).

#1080: Maria Josefa de Azcarraga Servert, *Minhat Say de Y.S. de Norzi: Profetas Menores (Traduccion y anotacion critica)* (Textos y estudios "Cardenal Cisneros" de la Biblia Poliglota Matritense 40; Madrid: Instituto de Filologia, C.S.I.C., Departamento de Filologia Biblica y de Oriente Antiguo, 1987).

OTA 12 (1989)

#26: Laurence B. Kutler, "Features of the Battle Challenge in Biblical Hebrew, Akkadian and Ugaritic," *UF* 19 (1987) 94-99.

#42: Marvin H. Pope, "The Status of El at Ugarit," *UF* 19 (1987) 219-30.

#63: N. Wyatt, "Sea and Desert: Symbolic Geography in West Semitic Religious Thought," *UF* 19 (1987) 374-89.

#96: Thomas Schneider, "Die semitischen und ägyptischen Namen der syrischen Sklaven des Papyrus Brooklyn 34.1446 verso," *UF* 19 (1987) 244-82.

#103: M. Dietrich and O. Loretz, "Ugaritisch $\underline{T}^c/\underline{T}^cY$ und hebräisch $\check{S}W^c$," *UF* 19 (1987) 33-36.

#106: Ernst Axel Knauf and Sultan Maáni, "On the Phonemes of Fringe Canaanite: The Cases of Zerah-U$\underline{d}$ruḥ and 'Kamâš$\underline{h}$ltâ,'" *UF* 19 (1987) 91-94.

#112: H. Rouillard and J. Tropper, "Vom kanaanäischen Ahnenkult zur Zauberei: Eine Auslegungsgeschichte zu den hebräischen Begriffen ^{c}*wb* und *yd^{c}ny*," *UF* 19 (1987) 234-44.

#114: Josep Tropper, "*Tmym ^{c}m Yhwh* 'vollkommen vor dem Herrn,'" *UF* 19 (1987) 294-300.

#114: David Toshio Tsumura, "*Nabalkutu, tu-a-bi-[û]* and *tōhû wābōhû*," *UF* 19 (1987) 309-14.

#116: Marc Vervenne. "Hebrew *šālîš*—Ugaritic *tlt*," *UF* 19 (1987) 344-73.

#141: Eckart Otto, "Rechtssystematik im altbabylonischen 'Codex Ešnunna' und im altisraelitischen 'Bundesbuch'. Eine redaktionsgeschichtliche und rechtsvergleichende Analyse von CE 17; 18; 22-28 und Ex 21, 18-32; 22, 6-14; 23, 1-3, 6-8," *UF* 19 (1987) 174-97.

#193: N. Wyatt, "Echoes of the King and his *Ka*: An Ideological Motif in the Story of Solomon's Birth," *UF* 19 (1987) 399-404.

#266: Oswald Loretz, "Der ugaritische Topos b'l rkb und die 'Sprache Kanaans' in Jes 19, 1-24," *UF* 19 (1987) 101-12.

#273: Saul M. Olyan, "Some Observations Concerning the Identity of the Queen of Heaven," *UF* 19 (1987) 161-74.

#278: Mark Smith, "Death in Jeremiah, IX, 20," *UF* 19 (1987) 289-93.

#343: Graham A. Patrick, *F. J. A. Hort, Eminent Victorian* (Sheffield: Almond, 1988).

#387: William G. Dever, et. al., *Gezer IV: The 1969-71 Seasons in Field VI, the "Acropolis"* (Annual of the Nelson Glueck School of Biblical Archaeology; 2 parts; Jerusalem: Keter, 1986).

#388: Raphael Giveon, *Scarabs from Recent Excavation in Israel* (OBO 83; Freiburg, Switzerland: Universitätsverlag/Göttingen: Vandenhoeck & Ruprecht, 1988).

#390: James M. Robinson, gen. ed., *The Nag Hammadi Library in English* (3d rev. ed.; San Francisco: Harper & Row, 1988).

#701: Willem van der Meer and Johannes C. de Moor, eds., *The Structural Analysis of Biblical and Canaanite Poetry* (JSOTSup 74; Sheffield: JSOT, 1988).

#722: Milward Doublas Nelson, *The Syriac Version of the Wisdom of Ben Sira Compared to the Greek and Hebrew Materials* (SBLDS 107; Atlanta: Scholars Press, 1988).

#734: William L. Moran, tr., *Les Lettres d'El-Amarna: Correspondance diplomatique du pharaon* (tr. Dominique Collon and Henri Cazelles; Litteratures Anciennes du Proche-Orient 13; Paris: Cerf, 1987).

OTA 13 (1990)

#17: K. Koch, "Aschera als Himmelskönigin in Jerusalem," *UF* 20 (1988) 97-120.

#93: Johannes C. de Moor, "Narrative Poetry in Canaan," *UF* 20 (1988) 149-71.

#160: Ingo Kottsieper, "*mgg*—'Krieg Führen, Kämpfen,' eine bisher übersehene nordwestsemitische Wurzel," *UF* 20 (1988) 124-33.

#107: W. G. Lambert, "A Further Note on *tōhû wābōhû*," *UF* 20 (1988) 134.

#110: Johannes C. de Moor and Herman F. de Vries, "Hebrew *hēdād* 'Thunder-Storm,'" *UF* 20 (1988) 173-77.

#112: M. Pope, "Vestiges of Vocative *Lamedh* in the Bible," *UF* 20 (1988) 201-7.

#118: Wolfram von Soden, "Hurritisch *uatnannu* > Mittelassyrisch *utnannu* und > Ugaritisch *itnn* > Hebräisch *ʾatnan* 'ein Geschenk, Dirnenlohn,' *UF* 20 (1988) 309-11.

#179: D. T. Tsumura, "'The Deluge' (*mabbûl*) in Psalm 29:10," *UF* 20 (1988) 341-44.

#187: William T. Koopmans, "Psalm 78, Canto D - A Response," *UF* 20 (1988) 121-23.

#202: Antoon Schoors, "The Use of Vowel Letters in Qoheleth," *UF* 20 (1988) 277-86.

#464: Robert D. Hoberman, "Initial Consonant Clusters in Hebrew and Aramaic," *JNES* 48 (1989) 24-29.

#416: A. Hilhorst, "Ex 4, 10: Una variante textual ignorada en Origenes?" *EstBib* 44 (1987) 493-96.

Contributors

JOSEPH JENSEN, O.S.B., is Associate Professor at The Catholic University of America and Executive Secretary of The Catholic Biblical Association of America.

LESLIE J. HOPPE, O.F.M., is Professor of Old Testament Studies, Catholic Theological Union at Chicago.

MARK S. SMITH is Skirball Professor of Bible and Ancient Near Eastern Studies at New York University.

SUSAN F. MATHEWS is Professor of Theology at University of Scranton in Scranton, PA.

ABBOT GREGORY J. POLAN, O.S.B., is Professor of Old Testament at Conception Seminary College in Conception, MO.

MARIBETH HOWELL, O.P., is Professor of Scripture at St. Mary's Seminary and Graduate School of Theology in Wickliffe, OH.

MARK D. FUTATO is Professor of Old Testament at Reformed Theological Seminary in Orlando, FL.

JOHN J. FERRIE, JR., is an independent scholar.

IRENE NOWELL, O.S.B., is Adjunct Professor at St. John's University in Collegeville, MN.

Dale Launderville, O.S.B., is Associate Professor of Theology at St. John's University in Collegeville, MN.

EDWARD G. MATHEWS, JR., is an independent scholar.

REV. DR. ALICE OGDEN BELLIS is Associate Professor of Old Testament Language and Literature, Howard University School of Divinity, in Washington, DC.

DEIRDRE DEMPSEY is Associate Professor at Marquette University in Milwaukee, WI.

LAWRENCE BOADT, C.S.P., is Professor Emeritus of Sacred Scripture, Washington Theological Union, and President and Publisher of Paulist Press.

MONICA J. BLANCHARD is Semitics Librarian, The Catholic University of America.

Index of Ancient Sources

Index of Authors

214

Index of Subjects

The Catholic Biblical Quarterly
Monograph Series (CBQMS)

1. Patrick W. Skehan, *Studies in Israelite Poetry and Wisdom* (CBQMS 1) $9.00 ($7.20 for CBA members) ISBN 0-915170-00-0 (LC 77-153511)
2. Aloysius M. Ambrozic, *The Hidden Kingdom: A Redactional-Critical Study of the References to the Kingdom of God in Mark's Gospel* (CBQMS 2) $9.00 ($7.20 for CBA members) ISBN 0-915170-01-9 (LC 72-89100)
3. Joseph Jensen, O.S.B., *The Use of tôrâ by Isaiah: His Debate with the Wisdom Tradition* (CBQMS 3) $3.00 ($2.40 for CBA members) ISBN 0-915170-02-7 (LC 73-83134)
4. George W. Coats, *From Canaan to Egypt: Structural and Theological Context for the Joseph Story* (CBQMS 4) $4.00 ($3.20 for CBA members) ISBN 0-915170-03-5 (LC 75-11382)
5. O. Lamar Cope, *Matthew: A Scribe Trained for the Kingdom of Heaven* (CBQMS 5) $4.50 ($3.60 for CBA members) ISBN 0-915170-04-3 (LC 75-36778)
6. Madeleine Boucher, *The Mysterious Parable: A Literary Study* (CBQMS 6) $2.50 ($2.00 for CBA members) ISBN 0-915170-05-1 (LC 76-51260)
7. Jay Braverman, Jerome's Commentary on Daniel: A Study of Comparative Jewish and Christian Interpretations of the Hebrew Bible (CBQMS 7) $4.00 ($3.20 for CBA members) ISBN 0-915170-06-X (LC 78-55726)
8. Maurya P. Horgan, *Pesharim: Qumran Interpretations of Biblical Books* (CBQMS 8) $6.00 ($4.80 for CBA members) ISBN 0-915170-07-8 (LC 78-12910)
9. Harold W. Attridge and Robert A. Oden, Jr., *Philo of Byblos, The Phoenician History* (CBQMS 9) $3.50 ($2.80 for CBA members) ISBN 0-915170-08-6 (LC 80-25781)
10. Paul J. Kobelski, *Melchizedek and Melchireša͑* (CBQMS 10) $4.50 ($3.60 for CBA members) ISBN 0-915170-09-4 (LC 80-28379)
11. Homer Heater, *A Septuagint Translation Technique in the Book of Job* (CBQMS 11) $4.00 ($3.20 for CBA members) ISBN 0-915170-10-8 (LC 81-10085)
12. Robert Doran, *Temple Propaganda: The Purpose and Character of 2 Maccabees* (CBQMS 12) $4.50 ($3.60 for CBA members) ISBN 0-915170-11-6 (LC 81-10084)
13. James Thompson, *The Beginnings of Christian Philosophy: The Epistle to the Hebrews* (CBQMS 13) $5.50 ($4.50 for CBA members) ISBN 0-915170-12-4 (LC 81-12295)

14. Thomas H. Tobin, S.J., *The Creation of Man: Philo and the History of Interpretation* (CBQMS 14) $6.00 ($4.80 for CBA members) ISBN 0-915170-13-2 (LC 82-19891)

15. Carolyn Osiek, *Rich and Poor in the Shepherd of Hermes* (CBQMS 15) $6.00 ($4.80 for CBA members) ISBN 0-915170--14-0 (LC 83-7385)

16. James C. VanderKam, *Enoch and the Growth of an Apocalyptic Tradition* (CBQMS 16) $6.50 ($5.20 for CBA members) ISBN 0-915170-15-9 (LC 83-10134)

17. Antony F. Campbell, S.J., *Of Prophets and Kings: A Late Ninth-Century Document (1 Samuel 1-2 Kings 10)* (CBQMS 17) $7.50 ($6.00 for CBA members) ISBN 0-915170-16-7 (LC 85-12791)

18. John C. Endres, S.J., *Biblical Interpretation in the Book of Jubilees* (CBQMS 18) $8.50 ($6.80 for CBA members) ISBN 0-915170-17-5 (LC 86-6845)

19. Sharon Pace Jeansonne, *The Old Greek Translation of Daniel 7-12* (CBQMS 19) $5.00 ($4.00 for CBA members) ISBN 0-915170-18-3 (LC 87-15865)

20. Lloyd M. Barré, *The Rhetoric of Political Persuasion: The Narrative Artistry and Political Intentions of 2 Kings 9 -11* (CBQMS 20) $5.00 ($4.00 for CBA members) ISBN 0-915170-19-1 (LC 87-15878)

21. John J. Clabeaux, *A Lost Edition of the Letters of Paul: A Reassessment of the Text of the Pauline Corpus Attested by Marcion* (CBQMS 21) $8.50 ($6.80 for CBA members) ISBN 0-915170-20-5 (LC 88-28511)

22. Craig Koester, *The Dwelling of God: The Tabernacle in the Old Testament, Intertestamental Jewish Literature, and the New Testament* (CBQMS 22) $9.00 ($7.20 for CBA members) ISBN 0-915170-21-3 (LC 89-9853)

23. William Michael Soll, *Psalm 119: Matrix, Form, and Setting* (CBQMS 23) $9.00 ($7.20 for CBA members) ISBN 0-915170-22-1 (LC 90-27610)

24. Richard J. Clifford and John J. Collins (eds.), *Creation in the Biblical Traditions* (CBQMS 24) $7.00 ($5.60 for CBA members) ISBN 0-915170-23-X (LC 92-20268)

25. John E. Course, *Speech and Response: A Rhetorical Analysis of the Introductions to the Speeches of the Book of Job, Chaps. 4 - 24* (CBQMS 25) $8.50 ($6.80 for CBA members) ISBN 0-915170-24-8 (LC 94-26566)

26. Richard J. Clifford, *Creation Accounts in the Ancient Near East and in the Bible* (CBQMS 26) $9.00 ($7.20 for CBA members) ISBN 0-915170-25-6 (LC 94-26565)

27. John Paul Heil, *Blood and Water: The Death and Resurrection of Jesus in John 18 – 21* (CBQMS 27) $9.00 ($7.20 for CBA members) ISBN 0-915170-26-4 (LC 95-10479)

28. John Kaltner, *The Use of Arabic in Biblical Hebrew Lexicography* (CBQMS 28) $7.50 ($6.00 for CBA members) ISBN 0-915170-27-2 (LC 95-45182)

29. Michael L. Barré, S.S., *Wisdom, You Are My Sister: Studies in Honor of Roland E. Murphy, O.Carm., on the Occasion of His Eightieth Birthday* (CBQMS 29) $13.00 ($10.40 for CBA members) ISBN 0-915170-28-0 (LC 97-16060)

30. Warren Carter and John Paul Heil, *Matthew's Parables: Audience-Oriented Perspectives* (CBQMS 30) $10.00 ($8.00 for CBA members) ISBN 0-915170-29-9 (LC 97-44677)

31. David S. Williams, *The Structure of 1 Maccabees* (CBQMS 31) $7.00 ($5.60 for CBA members) ISBN 0-915170-30-2

32. Lawrence Boadt and Mark S. Smith (eds.), *Imagery and Imagination in Biblical Literature: Essays in Honor of Aloysius Fitzgerald, F.S.C.* (CBQMS 32) ISBN 0-915170-31-0 (LC 2001003305)

Order from:

The Catholic Biblical Association of America
The Catholic University of America
Washington, D.C. 20064